Contents

The Vision of Grid International Inc.

Grid is a world authority on human behavior
in organizations.

We are the leader in developing outstanding
relationships that drive exceptional performance.

Grid delivers the Power to Change.

The Power
to Change.

Rachel K. McKee & Bruce Carlson

Illustrated by
Karen McCormick, Grid International Inc.
Catherine Rawls, TRIVUE

The Power to Change.
by Rachel Kelly McKee and Bruce Carlson
Copyright © 1999 by Grid International, Inc.

ISBN: 0-9679981-0-7

Printed in the United States of America.

Grid International Inc.
2100 Kramer Lane
Austin, Texas 78758
Phone: (512) 794-3900
Fax: (512) 794-1177
Toll Free: 1-800-288-4743
www.grid-intl.com

Editors:
Cheryl Harder
Karen McCormick

Graphics Design:
Karen McCormick
Product Development Specialist
Grid International Inc.

Catherine Rawls
TRIVUE
8400 N. Mopac, Suite 100
Austin, TX 78759

Cover Design:
Corporate Vision
73 Laird Drive, Suite 205
Toronto, Ontario, M4G 3T4 Canada

Electronic Design and Production:
Karen McCormick
Product Development Specialist
Grid International Inc.

First Printing, January 2000
Second Printing, January 2001
Third Printing, January 2002

Preface

We undertook writing this book to put the power to change behavior in people's hands. If you have ever missed an opportunity because a "people" problem could not be resolved, then you know the frustration. If you have ever watched crucial resources lost because of "personality" problems, then you understand the feeling of waste. It's devastating to watch a person, team, or even an entire company, fumble resources because behaviors block crucial change. Not having the skills to confront and work through problems to resolve underlying causes is even more frustrating. Unresolved problems become a constant thread of tension that is never relieved. We become so accustomed to them that working around them becomes a way of life. We learn what *not* to say and what *not* to do to flare up a conflict, and become highly skilled at the dance of avoidance.

On the other hand, if you've ever confronted and resolved a problem, you know the sense of relief, confidence, and motivation that follows. When an individual gets to that point, a strong sense of pride and personal fulfillment develops. He or she owns the problem *and* the solution. When a team gets there, team members find new strength in mutual support and respect. Even if the end results are less than expected, people are not consumed with all the "what ifs" because they embraced the challenge and are ready to try again. When an entire company gets there, there is no limit to what it can accomplish.

The Grid® gives you the power to experience sound resolution by opening up a new door in communication. The Grid skills give you a way to have the crucial and sometimes difficult conversations that deal with sensitive issues of human behavior. These conversations are often difficult as they carry all the history, fears, intentions, and emotions that people share. All this baggage makes the discussions feel personal, even out of place. It's easier just to get back to work and leave it alone. These issues and moments, however, are *the* most critical discussions for motivating change in you and others. These discussions are where change really happens and so they need to be done "right." The problem is that "right" means ten different things to ten different people. Most people share no common standards or structure to establish an objective focus on behavior.

The Grid provides both a language and structure, making behavior objective, relevant, and focused on productivity. The skills show you how to describe the impact of personal behavior rather than evaluating people as "good" or "bad." This approach provides people with experience and practice in the use of candor, openness, and honesty—the most important skills of communication.

Problem solving results from taking action based on full awareness with a clear goal in mind. This is common sense in any setting, but behaviors are often not considered. Instead of addressing unsound behavior head-on, people often ignore obvious problems and move on, hoping they will go away. People rarely set out to block progress with their behaviors, but do so because they don't see how their behavior impacts the problem. The result may be a leader who exerts too much control, making people angry, or a manager who crumbles in the face of conflict, or an entire division consumed with indifference. Behaviors are deeply rooted and resistant to most change efforts. People stand back and watch these kinds of behaviors every day without realizing they have the power to bring about lasting change.

Grid doesn't make problems or fears go away, but it gives you the ability to address them with skill and confidence in the perspective or context of common goals. Teams learn how to integrate awareness and candor into every aspect of work. They learn to talk about reservations, doubts, and concerns in structured and measurable ways that promote progress. Something amazing happens when these discussions occur in teams previously constrained by fear. People start having fun! Awareness leads to understanding and a genuine desire to help rather than compete with each other. Team members start calling the controlling leader on his or her behavior so others don't get angry. Colleagues help the manager work through the conflict with confidence. People previously consumed with indifference begin to feel alive with commitment and enthusiasm.

Grid concepts and skills are common sense and can be put to immediate use in any relationship. They show you how to change from the inside out by going below surface behaviors to examine the values and attitudes that motivate behavior. No one can argue with mutual trust, respect, and candor as a sound strategy for teamwork. Where sound strategy and logic appeal to people at an intellectual level, the Grid appeals to people at a physical and emotional level. As co-founder Dr. Robert R. Blake puts it, "9,9 grabs people by the heart because it feels right." Embracing this ideal is the beginning of The Power to Change.

Rachel K. McKee, Bruce Carlson

Acknowledgements

This text continues the legacy that Drs. Robert Blake and Jane Mouton established with the Managerial Grid in 1964, and the worldwide network of dedicated consultants they developed. They were the first in the field to apply a scientific method to human dynamics by designing a measurable and lasting approach for personal and organization change. A devoted team, Drs. Blake and Mouton spanned the globe and demonstrated an endless commitment to developing and testing a learning methodology that is even more relevant today than it was in 1964. Together, they published more than 40 books and hundreds of articles in multiple languages around the world. Dr. Mouton passed away in 1987. In 1997, Dr. Blake retired, but maintains a consulting relationship with Grid International. We hope that in some small way we have been able to contribute to the rich legacy of this very creative and prolific relationship.

This edition results from six years of working directly with Dr. Robert Blake on Grid theory writing projects, and from the critique and feedback of experienced Grid practitioners around the globe. Although Dr. Blake has not been an author for this edition, his contribution as a consultant has been invaluable. His passion for the Grid continues today as strongly as it did while he was teaching at the National Training Laboratories in the 1950s, and working in organizations around the world with Dr. Mouton for the three decades that followed. He "lives and breathes Grid" and, at 82, he constantly looks for ways to improve the theory.

We would like to acknowledge several individuals who made a significant contribution to the writing. Cheryl Gerhardt demonstrated endless commitment as a content editor in helping us strengthen the theory presentation. She brought an invaluable objective opinion that constantly challenged us to step back and look at the book from the perspective of the reader. We also want to acknowledge the dedication of the worldwide Grid associate network in strengthening this edition. We especially want to thank the associates who spent a week in Austin during June of 1998 to design the new seminar that accompanies this book: Dr. Rudy Attems in Austria, Helen O'Sullivan in Australia, and Leslie D'Souza in India. We would also like to thank Karen McCormick for her contribution to enhancing the graphic images, editing for style and consistency, format redesign, electronic production, and for attention to many other "details" that can be so easily overlooked.

Rachel K. McKee, Bruce Carlson

Why Teamwork Is No Longer a Choice

1

Chapter

Few topics have generated more study, writing, and conversation in the business world than "Leadership." Historians, journalists, authors, and the general public engage in a continuous process of discussion and debate on the pros and cons of one leader's style versus another. There are still articles and presentations being made today about Alexander the Great (356–323 B.C.), Genghis Khan (A.D. 1162–1227), and Napoleon (1769–1821), to say nothing of Margaret Thatcher, John F. Kennedy, Bill Gates, and many thousands of others lesser known in the business, political, and academic communities. In fact, the practice of judging leadership begins very early in life when, as children, individuals start questioning their parents' use of power and authority on the rather weighty issues of fairness, integrity, and morality. There are few parents who have not been confronted by their children for not telling the truth on some occasion or for saying one thing and doing another.

Almost everyone has an opinion on the leadership of others, and given the right circumstances, almost everyone will quite passionately advocate what he or she thinks or feels. For all of mankind's centuries of inquiry and the preoccupation with the subject, there is still very little universal consensus on what works and what does not. What worked for one person in one set of circumstances doesn't work for someone else in another.

Over the past five decades many concepts of leadership have been advanced, often through clever marketing, which seem to inevitably fade from the scene a few years later. This "flavor of the month leadership" implies there is some magic formula, some prescription which, once discovered, will instantly create wonderfully successful leaders. But there is no definitive set of rules, no prescription, no fountain of wisdom from which to drink, and no one guru to emulate. Leadership lies within every individual. It lies in the heart of every person's emotional intelligence,[1] or the crucial emotional competencies that permit an understanding of the "human" side of leadership, power, and relationships.

The hallmarks of today's top performers include awareness of self and others, the ability to work with others to maximize productivity, the willingness to embrace change, the courage and skills to resolve conflict, and the vision to stimulate progress.

Despite this fact, the prescriptive literature and guru-based courses on leadership are growing exponentially. This preoccupation with leadership is not hard to understand: it is a wonderfully rich, interesting topic and it sells! Leadership is about people,

---

[1] Daniel Goleman, *Emotional Intelligence* (Bantam Books, 1995).

power, relationships, vision, values, courage, character, and drama on the one side, and politics, corruption, greed, weakness, manipulation, and tragedy on the other.

This rush to discover the leadership secret has created an often singular, narrow point of view. By constantly trying to provide only those in the top management positions with a set of rules, suggestions, and recommendations, we miss something rather fundamental. We miss the rest of the organization and the power that can come from a culture focused on excellence and unified by shared values and attitudes.

In a world where people now work more with brains than with brawn, information and power are dispersed in organizations. Now leaders can be found at every level of the organization: employee, supervisory, managerial, and executive. The leaders with real personal power are the ones whom others count on every day because they can be trusted to get results. They are the ones to whom others turn when problems arise, when a crisis occurs, or when someone just wants to share a creative idea. In fact, this is where the real power in an organization resides—the people and the relationships they share. Without a thorough understanding of people, power, and relationships, considering leadership becomes a rather vacant academic exercise.

Further, by focusing on the top, organizations are left to consider a flow of power that is top-down, one dimensional, hierarchy and control oriented, and unsuited to today's rapidly changing organization. Companies today are searching for new ways to leverage their resources. They want higher quality communication, greater speed in making decisions, increased creativity and problem solving, improved customer service, productivity, profitability, and lower costs, all with a much leaner organization. To achieve this, the flow of power must harness the resources available throughout the organization, and not limit the organization to a forced march behind the chain of command.

Since World War II, trillions of dollars and man-hours have been spent creating vast pools of knowledge, gaining brilliant scientific insights, and discovering incredible technological breakthroughs. Organizations persist, however, in managing with top-down, fear- and control-based leadership styles. People have traded horse-drawn carriages for sports cars but still talk of "cracking the whip" and "pulling back on the reins" when it comes to accomplishing results.

Something fundamental and profound must shift before companies can expect to maximize available resources and generate widespread personal and team commitment. Their view of leadership and power must shift from the view that power resides primarily at the top of an organization and flows down through clearly defined channels in predictable time frames, to something quite different: a view of leadership that is dynamic and interconnected.

The newer view of leadership and power is that both exist at virtually all levels of the organization and people are able to express themselves immediately as the need or situation arises. In fact, the fundamental shift required is from control to freedom—from perceived control to freedom with accountability. People are now seen as the source of vital and responsible energy that can spring into action, not through direction and control, but through their own personal commitment to a common vision and a belief in the values of the organization.

In addition, focusing on leadership in isolation from the organization puts far too much attention and pressure on that one position to achieve results and not enough emphasis and accountability on the organization as a whole. People are willingly seduced by the Chrysler/Lee Iacocca stories because they exemplify the popular theme of "one man against all odds." Yet there are a great many more unwritten stories where one person couldn't do it alone.

The fact of the matter is that most successful leadership strategies are more likely to be systematic rather than dramatic, planned rather than spontaneous, private and low key rather than public and high profile, and integrated with the whole organization rather than championed by one alone.

In their enlightening work, *Built to Last: Successful Habits of Visionary Companies,* Collins and Porras make this point at the outset.

> This is not a book about charismatic visionary leaders. This is a book about visionary companies. What is a visionary company? Visionary companies are premier institutions—the crown jewels in their industries, widely admired by their peers and having a long track record (fifty years or more) of making a significant impact on the world around them. The key point is that a visionary company is an organization—an institution.[2]

History repeatedly shows us that visionary and values-based organizations continue to land on their feet in the difficult periods and surge ahead during the good times.

In fact on the issue of leadership, Collins and Porras debunk a popular misconception:

> *Myth*—Visionary companies require great and charismatic visionary leaders.
>
> *Reality*—A charismatic visionary leader is absolutely not required for a visionary company and, in fact, can be detrimental to a company's long-term prospects. Some of the most significant CEOs in the history of visionary companies did not fit the model of the high-profile, charismatic leader— indeed, some explicitly shied away from that model. Like the founders of the United States at the Constitutional Convention, they concentrated more on architecting an enduring institution than on being a great individual leader. They sought to be clock builders, not time tellers.[3]

When focusing on leadership, if we take into account the whole organization, a number of insights surface and the picture becomes clearer and more real. The whole organization is by far a much larger, more powerful, and more complex dynamic to consider than an examination of just top leadership strategies in isolation would yield. In

---

2 James C. Collins and Jerry I. Porras, *Built to Last: Successful Habits of Visionary Companies* (New York: HarperCollins Publishers, 1997), p. 1.

3 Collins and Porras, *Built to Last,* p. 7.

fact the leader and those being led are such intimately interwoven pieces of the puzzle, that to look at one without the other is of little use.

The focus of this book and the strategy for change and development which follows is to consider the issues of leadership from two points of view:

- To help people understand how others view their behavior, and how to work with and through others to develop teamwork standards of excellence; and

- To help the whole organization understand and capitalize its resources for the decades of changes to come.

When people throughout an organization are involved in learning and practicing new values and strategies at their own individually relevant levels, meaningful leadership development, organizational growth, and change can occur. We are not saying leadership development is unimportant—far from it. What we are saying is that theories, strategies, and tactics for building the health, strength, and resilience of the whole organization are just as important and must be included at the same time.

This comprehensive approach requires a coordinating model, or map, that speaks to every person in the organization from the most senior to the most junior. Speaking in one consistent language, the strategy must encompass the three essential dynamics of organization life:

- understanding self and others;

- understanding how to build and foster sound relationships; and

- understanding how to use power effectively.

Once people throughout the organization understand the dynamics of people, relationships, and power, leadership begins to develop at all levels of the organization, not just at the top. Individual initiative, responsibility, accountability, creativity, and innovation develop in many different ways every day in the form of teamwork. While there are stunning displays of teamwork as a natural phenomenon from insects to the largest mammals, in contrast, its existence in human nature seems rather limited and inconsistent.

Every year in business, sports, and science we hear stories of phenomenal success brought about by "true teamwork." These include stories where, for a period of time, team members came together and found a way to willingly align their personal ambitions to a larger set of team or organization goals.

The puzzling question is, if individuals know that teamwork produces such startlingly positive results, why after thousands of years of living together have they not learned to work successfully in teams as a matter of course? What is the recurring theme or barrier that seems to get in the way of teamwork happening naturally? The answer lies in the continuing debate between freedom and control. The question is asked every day: "Can I trust in the cumulative wisdom and motivation of my team to do the best thing, or must I continually seek ways to ensure, overtly or covertly, that my ideas are followed?" Leaders at all levels constantly wrestle with this dilemma.

As discussed earlier, intellect can find ample evidence and history to support teamwork as the preferred option most of the time. But what happens emotionally when someone has to delegate a crucial task or responsibility to someone else three weeks before an annual performance review? What happens when someone's career success becomes dependent on the results and follow-through of co-workers? That person is now in that a position where logic and facts must give way to trust, respect, forbearance, cooperation, and courage: teamwork.

This pivotal point, where trust invigorates people or mistrust debilitates them, is the moment of truth for teamwork. People face change with the courage to acquire the skills to build relationships with co-workers which establish mutual trust (freedom), or they always seem to step in and take charge in an effort to ensure their outcomes are realized (control). These moments of truth occur constantly in organization life from the work cubicle to the boardroom. Learning to function confidently in this territory where our IQ (logic) and our EQ (emotional intelligence) must combine, is what building effective teamwork is all about.

Three Essential Dynamics

Awareness of the three essential dynamics of organization life—people, power, and relationships—equip people with the skills needed to use pivotal moments to build strength and commitment in teams. They become moments of truth for *maximizing* and releasing energy instead of restraining and wasting it.

People

The world is viewed through a collection of subjective experiences individuals call the *self*. If people know and accept their strengths, weaknesses, values, desires, and fears, they will experience life and view others with the same openness. On the other hand, if individuals are not objective and honest with themselves, they will view life through this distorted lens as well. In order to gain a realistic understanding of others, the first step is to gain an understanding of one's self.

The Leadership Grid© is an extremely powerful tool and framework for enabling people to gain perspective on themselves and the other people in their lives. Like all good tools, it simplifies the complex and provides tremendous positive leverage to personal energy. The theory and strategy give a constant and consistent frame of reference for making sense of the perpetually changing human equation in the workplace.

Power

The second dynamic of organization life is power. *Power* is a highly charged word that evokes various images in the minds of people, many of which are negative. This perception is due to the common abuses of power. But power can also be used fairly and effectively.

Power is the dominant dynamic on the planet. Every relationship at work or at home constantly wrestles with the notion of power. What is the arrangement by which individuals interact? Whether it is with a parent, spouse, boss, co-worker, friend, or acquaintance, is this relationship characterized by control or freedom? Is it healthy or co-dependent? Is it based on fear or on trust and respect?

Relationships based on trust, respect, and freedom are more productive, creative, and enduring than those based on fear and control. The breakdown of the Berlin Wall and the dissolution of the Soviet Empire demonstrated this issue on a grand scale. Understanding power and how it can be used effectively in human organizations becomes the central dynamic of leadership.

In any organization, large or small, people are the individual resources. The character of relationships between these individuals creates the structure that binds them together in a myriad of ways, some permanent and long standing, others more spontaneous and related to specific functions. The quality of these relationships determines the effective use of power in the organization. Is power used in an overt and fair way? Or is it used in a covert, autocratic, or manipulative way? This does not refer to the power to control others, but to the power to create and produce results with and through people by accessing and developing the resources they have to offer. In most cases people welcome the opportunity to contribute their resources on a regular basis. Being able to do so is often a key measure of job satisfaction and commitment.

Power flows between the components of an organization in order to fulfill its purpose. Power is usually released when decisions are made. And when it is used in an open and fair manner, it becomes the energy that produces excellence.

Relationships

The third dynamic of organization life is relationships. The many moments of truth in organizations were described earlier as being a kind of "no man's land" between freedom and control—facts and figures on the one hand, and trust and respect on the other. More broadly stated, it is the gulf between the issues of logic and emotion, or the head and the heart. Both dimensions are essential for all successful human interaction. In fact, either dimension without the other ultimately leads to disaster, not unlike the incomplete nature of the Tin Man (who needed a heart), or the Scarecrow (who needed a brain) in *The Wizard of Oz*.

The structure and support of a relationship allows individuals to negotiate this perilous territory together. Being able to discuss fears, concerns, hopes, and aspirations openly and honestly with co-workers becomes the actual method of developing mutual trust and respect. In turn this trust and respect makes sound relationships possible. Openness, trust, and respect become a self-reinforcing cycle in the development of relationships.

This foundation of sound human relationships is what enables teams to achieve synergy by empowering team members to fully explore and maximize resources with a team focus on greater results than would be possible otherwise.

The organization that understands the potential and power of relationships and takes steps to create the conditions in which they flourish is providing itself with an unparalleled competitive advantage.

The Grid Theory

The Grid strategy for change and development is about learning how to manage people, power, and relationships in organization life effectively and in a manner that continually reinforces the core values of the corporation. The strategy is about understanding and learning how to build and maintain healthy and productive relationships characterized by trust, respect, openness, and candor. Grid is a strategy that provides a framework and practical tools for working with the human side of organization life— people—in the most effective manner possible.

Around the world, corporations and employees are crying out for a set of values that can be deeply held and believed in, and for a vision that can consistently inspire them to initiate, compete, and excel. This book is all about bringing meaningful values and inspiring vision into the workplace, regardless of the size, product, service, or age of the organization.

What follows will articulate an empirically proven theory of human behavior that has been phenomenally effective in leading and managing people the world over for the past 40 years. In addition to providing a model of what's *possible,* a pathway to get there will also be included in the form of a proven methodology for turning concepts, ideas, and values into operational realities.

The Grid as a Framework for Studying Relationships

2

Chapter

This book is about how people relate to one another—how they see themselves, and how others experience them in turn. People maintain a private view of personal effectiveness when it comes to taking initiative, gathering information, advocating views, giving and receiving critique, resolving conflict, making decisions, and bouncing back from failure.

This personal image is seldom objective. Individuals naturally protect and emphasize their own positive characteristics while ignoring or paying less attention to the negative, even if their view bends reality a little. For example, if a person considers himself helpful, but someone tells him what he just did was uncooperative and selfish, his first reaction is to discount or dismiss the comment. He may say, "She took that comment out of context. What I meant was..." People evaluate their own actions based on what they intend to achieve. Rationalization protects that self-image.

This protective reaction is a subtle form of self-deception that everyone experiences to some degree. It is, of course, impossible to be completely objective about one's own behavior. Self-deception creates a gap in awareness between a personal view of effectiveness and the view held by those who experience that person, including coworkers, friends, family members, and others. Self-deception confuses crucial issues and decisions by causing one to avoid a realistic examination of the facts. This confusion is compounded as one moves up in an organization. The higher up a person is, the more people say what they think he or she wants to hear, and the less they confront flaws and problems. Lack of candor perpetuates self-deception and blocks improvement.

When people look at themselves they most commonly consider their intentions, but when they look at others they only see the other person's behavior without the underlying intentions. For example, one team member may think of herself as a confident and capable leader who effectively delivers results. Her actions, however, come across to others as overdemanding and intimidating, and others respond by looking for ways to avoid cooperating. Then she reacts by pushing harder, and so the gap in awareness becomes a gulf where resentment develops on both sides.

An effective way to begin closing the gap between intentions and actions is to discuss, clarify, and define attitudes regarding what sound behavior looks like in everyday interactions. To help do this, the Leadership Grid Theory provides a model of behavior styles—styles that are present anywhere people are working together toward a common goal.

The Dynamics of Teamwork:
R1 Resources, R2 Relationships, R3 Results®

Teamwork includes any activity where people share resources to achieve a common goal. Whenever people work together toward a common result, they participate in three processes, as shown in Fig. 2-1. Each person participating in the activity has something to offer in reaching the result; the people carrying out the activity work together to communicate, set direction, plan activities, discuss alternatives, set priorities, gather and

Fig. 2-1

The 3Rs of Teamwork

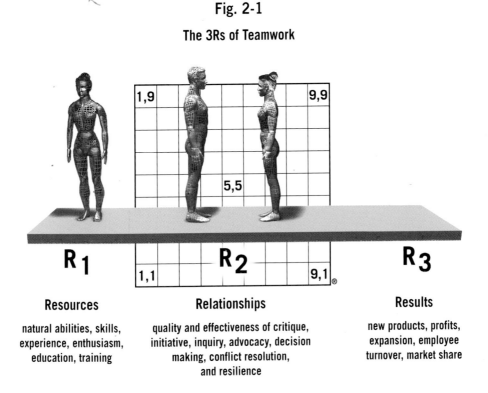

Resources	Relationships	Results
natural abilities, skills, experience, enthusiasm, education, training	quality and effectiveness of critique, initiative, inquiry, advocacy, decision making, conflict resolution, and resilience	new products, profits, expansion, employee turnover, market share

utilize resources, and deal with any obstacles that arise. We call this arena the 3Rs of Teamwork. It is within this arena that human interactions are of vital importance.

R1 Resources: Resources are essentially the "raw materials" that are available to any given team effort. Primarily, R1 is defined by "human" resources such as personal abilities, education, skills, knowledge, experiences, enthusiasm, and confidence. The quality of these human resources can also be affected by the availability of "hard" resources such as time, money, equipment, workload, and ergonomic concerns. A company may recruit and pay a premium price for the most talented group of individuals it can find, but if these talented individuals are hampered by the quality of "hard" resources available, their end result will be of lower quality. Conversely, more money, time, and equipment have little impact when the people involved are not prepared or qualified.

R2 Relationships: R2 relationships represent how people work together to achieve results. Relationships characterize the nature of individual and team commitment and how R1 resources translate into tangible results. It is the domain of relationships that defines, not *what* people do, but *how effectively* they work as a team.

R3 Results: Results represent the outcome of an activity whether it is a product, a service, or an idea. Results can be seen in many forms: productivity, morale, commitment, profits, decreased turnover, company growth, awards, increased market share, acquisition, or expanded capital. This is the "proving ground" for the culmination of R1 resources and R2 relationships. The quality of R3 results defines how effectively resources and relationships have been combined.

Relationships and Quality Results

While the quality and quantity of resources has a direct impact on R3 results, it is the R2 relationships that play the most critical part in the eventual outcome. The finest, most well equipped resources can be wasted if R2 relationships are ineffective. R2 relationships are the conduit through which results are achieved. They are the detailed aspects of how effectively people work together as a team. Are teams able to maximize the contribution of each individual, or are resources being wasted or lost during the

Fig. 2-2

Unsound Teamwork

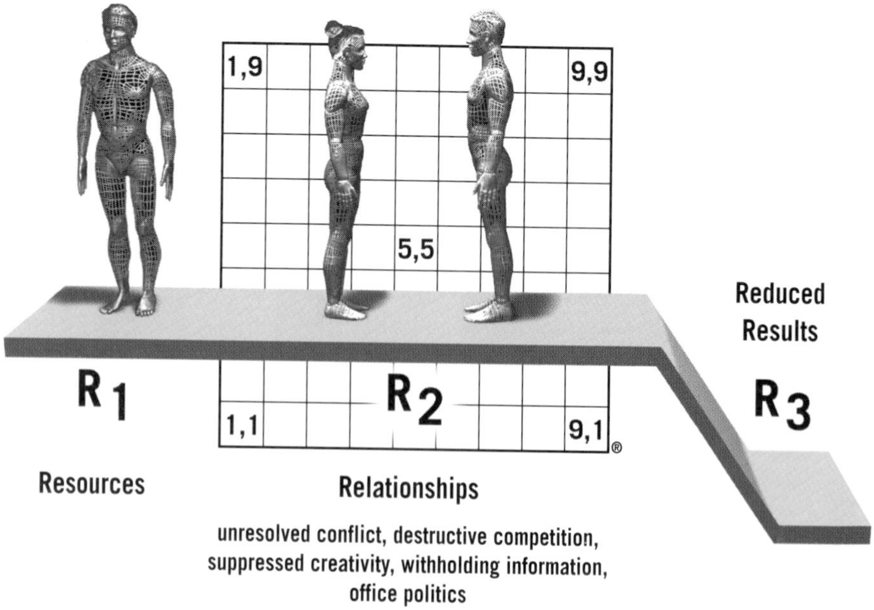

R1
Resources

R2
Relationships

R3

Reduced Results

1,9   9,9

5,5

1,1   9,1

unresolved conflict, destructive competition, suppressed creativity, withholding information, office politics process of working together? This can be answered by examining specific leadership behaviors and team norms: As a team, how effectively do members resolve conflict and react to the conflict resolution of others? Likewise, how do they react to and make decisions, take initiative, gather and share information, advocate convictions, bounce back from failure, and use candid feedback and critique to monitor progress and effectiveness?

The quality of R2 relationships determines how effectively people can translate R1 resources into R3 results. If these relationships are unsound, many available resources are underutilized or even lost as individuals are prevented from or withdraw from getting involved and contributing their best effort (see Fig. 2-2). Unsound relationships lead to unproductive and even destructive practices in organizations that are dominated by office politics, game playing, rivalries, and unresolved conflict.

Unresolved conflicts prevent people from wanting to address weaknesses and tackle problems. Valuable resources are restricted when employees fear retaliation, anger, embarrassment, punishment, rejection, or other negative consequences from colleagues or supervisors. For example, when individuals are angry with each other, they care less about contributing to results and focus efforts on protecting themselves. They may exact revenge, try to prove others wrong, undermine efforts they don't approve of, or sometimes just give up. Creativity is stifled—people won't take calculated risks when they feel little support or commitment from teammates. Unsound relationships inevitably lead to dramatically decreased results.

However, when relationships are sound, a high level of mutual trust and respect exists among team members and nothing prevents them from using resources to their full capacity, and even amplifying them by creating new resources over time. The personal energy used in unsound relationships for making excuses and covering up weaknesses is now available to support and encourage one another toward collaborating, brainstorming, exploring alternatives, and taking calculated risks. When weaknesses are identified with candor, employees are not afraid to address problems and work together openly and honestly to find solutions. The open, supportive environment strengthens the level of commitment among teammates toward reaching the soundest result; such a commitment permits people to challenge, explore, and create without fear of recrimination.

Resources (R1) and results (R3) are objective concepts that easily lend themselves to logical analysis. Relationships (R2), however, are subjective in nature and include emotions, feelings, and notions of fairness and trust. The Grid provides a way to examine this subjective arena in specific, objective, and measurable terms, and provides the framework and guidelines for how to interact with others in an effective and mutually beneficial manner. The real power of an organization lies in the quality of these relationships and whether they are based on trust and candor or mistrust and fear.

The framework focuses on behaviors in an objective way so people can discuss effectiveness without feelings of personal judgment being passed or received. The values presented—openness, honesty, and mutual trust and respect—in the framework are universally accepted as sound and comprehensive, which provides a reference point to use in developing and maintaining standards. Once standards are established, ineffective behavior is easier to address based on the criteria, not on personal judgment. For example, it's much easier and more effective to say, "Your decision was not in line with what we agreed to earlier, and here's why…" than to simply say, "I think your decision was wrong." The latter statement is judgmental and likely to arouse more defensiveness than perspective.

Understanding the basic codes of conduct that underlie *how* people relate to each other in this arena is essential to effectively harness the power of relationships. Just as the principles of mathematics for logical analysis help to make sense in arenas R1 and R3, the Grid provides a framework for understanding the dynamics inherent in the R2 arena. With a common understanding regarding what is sound, teams can begin moving away from results focused on *who is right* to a more objective focus of *what is right.*

The key difference in the Grid approach to change and development is that the primary focus lies in the arena of R2 relationships. When employees work together with high levels of mutual trust, respect, and candor, nothing holds them back from giving their best possible effort. With this assumption in mind, the Grid pays less attention to what people are doing in terms of accounting, marketing, sales, customer service, information systems, etc. Instead, the strategy focuses on how effectively teammates work together to accomplish any task. The values presented apply universally to any industry or culture and at any level of hierarchy. Once the R2 relationships are strengthened, the team always benefits. Personnel can take the energy that had been drained by unsound relationships and start focusing it on the accounting, marketing, sales, customer service, information systems, etc. with renewed commitment.

Fig. 2-3

Teamwork with Synergy

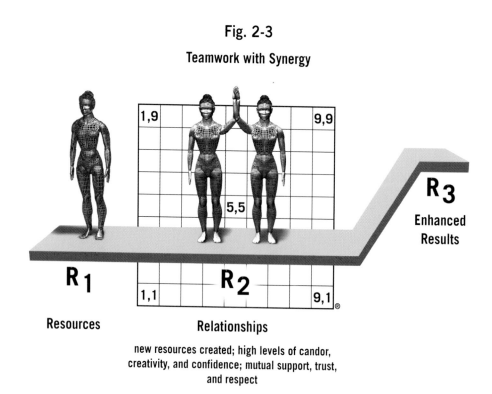

R1 — Resources

R2 — Relationships

R3 — Enhanced Results

new resources created; high levels of candor, creativity, and confidence; mutual support, trust, and respect

Synergy

Synergy occurs when R1 resources expand and multiply in the R2 arena. When teams relate in open and honest ways, results surpass what any individual might have achieved alone. This can also be described as $1 + 1 = 3$, or 5, or something even greater (see Fig. 2-3). Synergy becomes possible when teams clearly define objectives and work together in sound and effective ways to meet those objectives. Synergy happens in relationships where high levels of mutual trust and respect exist, and where candor and critique are ongoing and constructive. If a person does not feel free to say, "Wait a minute, haven't we gotten off track here?" or even something as simple as, "I don't agree with you," then valuable resources can easily fall through the cracks. Synergistic teams are visionary, because they constantly strive for innovation and challenge the limits of available resources. They are courageous because they tackle challenges and take risks. Synergistic teams are also a lot more fun!

Synergy can exist in any type of relationship among any number of people. Synergistic results can happen between two people working together on an isolated month-long project, and they can also happen on a company-wide level involving thousands of employees over decades. Synergy leads to the kind of innovative results present in companies that Collins and Porras describe as visionary, those with "high levels of action and experimentation—often unplanned and undirected—that produce new and unexpected paths of progress."[1]

For example, 3M promoted high levels of creativity in the company by decentralizing and giving researchers fifteen percent of their time to work on any project they wanted. This kind of corporate attitude led to innovations like Post-it™ Notes, waterproof sandpaper, and Scotch™ Tape, all coming from a company that started out in mining. Solutions and results such as these represent synergistic teamwork at its best: capable, creative, and courageous.

The ability to do more with less is not achieved from more people, more hours worked, or more capital. Effective results come from organizations that truly understand the potential for synergy and the methodology to reach and maintain it in the face of constant change and challenge.

A Framework for Evaluating Effectiveness: The Leadership Grid

The Leadership Grid provides the first step toward achieving the kind of sound personal development and change that leads to organization-wide synergy. The framework offers a way to examine the quality of relationships at the individual, team, and organization level by presenting a model of seven styles, or approaches, to leadership. Each style defines familiar patterns of behavior that people experience on a daily basis in discussions, meetings, phone calls, and other communications.

---

[1] James C. Collins and James I. Porras, *Built To Last: Successful Habits of Visionary Companies* (New York: HarperCollins Publishers, 1997), p. 90.

The Grid model is fundamental in providing a critical element of any change effort by addressing the "how to do it" aspect of relationships and change. Significant changes are rarely successful without a clear goal in mind along with a vivid picture of where you currently are. These two points provide the crucial focus to stay on track and reach the sought-after results. A clear framework gives individuals a way to examine *where they are now* in terms of quality relationships as well as *where they want to be* in terms of strengthening them.

Grid styles provide a tangible reference point for defining personal and team standards of excellence. Few people would argue with a personal development goal of becoming more effective in relationships, but many efforts are too vague and general to generate or maintain personal and team commitment. In order to work, a person or team has to be able to define in specific terms what is effective. The Grid framework allows people to focus on specific behaviors such as taking initiative, practicing effective inquiry, or advocating personal convictions. The model can be used to gain support and commitment from people in the best position to help change—those individuals who experience the behaviors firsthand: team members, friends, family, and colleagues.

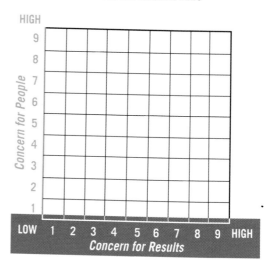

Fig. 2-4

Concern for Results Axis

Once a shared understanding of what is and is not effective is defined, the Grid can be a very useful tool in recognizing and improving ineffective behavior as it occurs. For example, if teammates agree that sound initiative includes actively seeking out information without waiting for others to provide it, addressing unsound initiative is made much easier. A person feels more comfortable commenting on someone's behavior when they have discussed and agreed on what behaviors are effective. This shared understanding makes it easier to say, for example, "I know you have a lot of experience with marketing, but you didn't offer much in that meeting. Can we talk about why?" If starting without a shared understanding, the person on the receiving end is likely to feel defensive or personally judged. In this case, a simple comment can interrupt or even halt progress because of a personal impasse. With a shared understanding, the comment is not personal, but based on what's right for progress. When this occurs, the response is likely, "You're right. I was holding back because..." with an ensuing discussion.

Individual Grid styles are based on how two fundamental concerns interact whenever two or more people are engaged in an activity. These are concern for results and concern for people, as seen in Fig. 2-4 and Fig. 2-5.

Fig. 2-5

Concern for People Axis

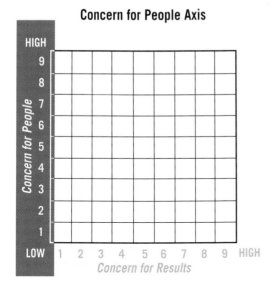

Concern for Results

The term "results" means any consequence, whether immediate or long-term. The degree of concern for results is represented on the horizontal axis from low (1) to high (9). People express their degree of concern for results in many ways. For example, a leader with a high concern for results might define specific guidelines for quotas in the form of minimum daily, weekly, or monthly achievement levels. He or she makes quotas a high priority and exercises influence so they are met. When productivity falls below expected levels, the leader takes immediate action.

A leader with a low concern for achieving results might regard quotas as an incidental priority, and/or even something that might cause resentment and lack of cooperation.

Concern for People

The concern for people also ranges from low (1) to high (9). Concern for people represents the degree to which a person considers how his or her actions affect others. A high level of concern for people means that a person is able to understand and anticipate how others feel, and to consider the impact of certain actions. A person with a high concern for others is the leader who

- is considered "approachable" by making himself or herself available in an understanding way;

- anticipates how a decision may create resentment or confusion and engages in discussions or meetings to address those aspects of the decision; and

- seeks opinions and observations from others in order to maintain a broader perspective than his or her own.

A high concern for people expressed in a sound way instills confidence and allows team members to establish mutual trust and relate openly and honestly with each other.

A person with a low concern for people avoids meaningful discussions or interactions and prefers to limit direct communication whenever possible. He or she may express this by evading, eluding, or ignoring others, or by excluding them from decisions and discussions. This is the leader who

- sends e-mail when a phone call is really needed;

Fig. 2-6

The Leadership Grid®

9,1 Grid Style: CONTROLLING
(Direct & Dominate)

I expect results and take control by clearly stating a course of action. I enforce rules that sustain high results and do not permit deviation.

1,9 Grid Style: ACCOMMODATING
(Yield & Comply)

I support results that establish and reinforce harmony. I generate enthusiasm by focusing on positive and pleasing aspects of work.

5,5 Grid Style: STATUS QUO
(Balance & Compromise)

I endorse results that are popular but caution against taking unnecessary risk. I test my opinions with others involved to assure ongoing acceptability.

1,1 Grid Style: INDIFFERENT
(Evade & Elude)

I distance myself from taking active responsibility for results to avoid getting entangled in problems. If forced, I take a passive or supportive position.

PATERNALISTIC Grid Style
(Prescribe & Guide)

I provide leadership by defining initiatives for myself and others. I offer praise and appreciation for support, and discourage challenges to my thinking.

OPPORTUNISTIC Grid Style
(Exploit & Manipulate)

I persuade others to support results that offer me private benefit. If they also benefit, that's even better in gaining support. I rely on whatever approach is needed to secure an advantage.

9,9 Grid Style: SOUND
(Contribute & Commit)

I initiate team action in a way that invites involvement and commitment. I explore all facts and alternative views to reach a shared understanding of the best solution.

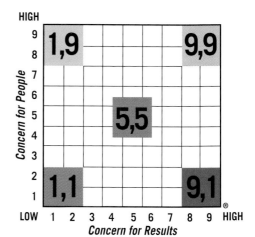

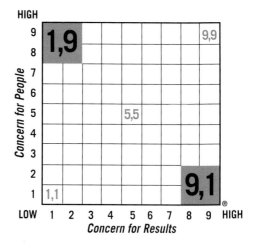

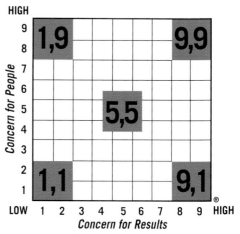

- prefers to make decisions without consulting others; and

- avoids conflict and involvement in meaningful discussions.

How Two Interdependent Concerns Produce Grid Styles

By plotting coordinates on the nine-by-nine Grid, 81 styles are possible. In practice, seven distinct styles stand out (see Fig. 2-6). These distinct styles emerge in a relationship when the two concerns plotted meet at the point of relating with others—working with and through them to achieve results. This "relating" doesn't necessarily mean face-to-face meetings or discussions. Grid styles and relationships come into play, for example, when a leader considers who to recommend for a promotion or who to include in or exclude from a new opportunity. These decisions are based on the relationships already in place.

The two concerns come into focus in relationships in an *interdependent* way, which means each concern cannot be considered in isolation from the other when studying a particular style. Studying how the two concerns relate mutually in relationships is the key to understanding the styles. As an example, a high concern for *people* can come across in very different ways in relationships depending on the interacting level of concern for *results* present. A person with a high concern for people *and* for results behaves in ways that are very different from a person with a *high* concern for people, and a *low* interacting concern for results.

The seven styles presented with the theory encompass the high, low, and medium levels of concerns present in relationships. Although it is possible to define all 81 possible styles, to do so would be impractical, as the distinction between styles would diminish considerably. Because of this, styles that represent intermediate levels of concern like 7,3 or 8,6 are not considered.

Grid Style Motivations

Along with the levels of concern for results and concern for people of each Grid style, the motivational dimension provides another perspective for understanding Grid behaviors. Reviewing each Grid style brings to mind the questions, *What motivates people's behavior?* and *How is certain behavior formed and demonstrated in everyday interactions?* One way to answer the question is to examine what motivates the degrees of concern and how they interact to form a Grid style. Motivations comprise the third dimension of the Grid framework and reflect fundamental values and attitudes that people hold (see Figure 2-7). These attitudes are a product of our environment. Individuals' motivations develop through early experiences with parents, siblings, and other influential family members, and are continually shaped by significant failures and triumphs throughout people's personal and professional lives.

Motivations are often hard to identify and articulate, but clearly reveal themselves in Grid style behaviors. For instance, a person may not realize why he or she insists on controlling every detail of a project instead of trusting others to exercise shared responsibility; he or she may just naturally take charge without realizing how others feel. This behavior is neither consciously connected to the underlying motivation nor deliberately intended to create defensiveness or anger in others. Such behavior may be motivated by a desire to control and dominate others, coupled with a fear of failure and helplessness. This type of leader has an inability to trust others to carry out a task unsupervised.

The motivation profiles in the following chapters offer background and insight into the fears and desires underlying each of the seven Grid styles.

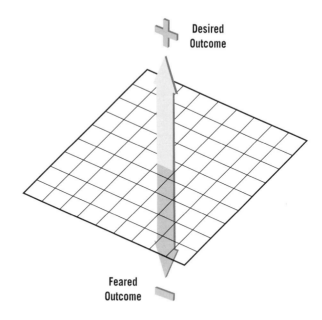

Fig. 2-7

The Grid Motivational Axis

Desired Outcome

Feared Outcome

Grid Style Consistency and Flexibility

Grid styles remain consistent in relationships not just in the short term, but over long periods as well. Regardless of the situation, a leader reacts to conflict in the same way. Whether dealing with an executive, middle manager, or hourly worker, the leader reacts based on values and attitudes that remain consistent. The same applies with regard to advocacy. For example, if a person values candor, he or she offers opinions in clear and forthright terms, regardless of the person or situation. If someone makes personal decisions by assessing popular opinion, then he or she is likely to make business decisions that way, too. If someone has a history of taking initiative only in response to detailed direction and guidance, then that person is unlikely to suddenly take strong and independent action on a new, undefined project.

If people were completely consistent when relating to each other, life would be predictable and boring. There are exceptions to the consistency of a person's dominant style, which make him or her shift temporarily to a backup style. Concerns for people and results never stop pulling and pushing at one another in day-to-day activities. The workplace can be fraught with stress, conflict, crisis, exhaustion, and risk. It can also be a place of celebration, elation, accomplishment, and pride. Personal problems can arise; an illness, death, or other family tragedy can influence work relationships. Although such variations will not cause a person's fundamental values and attitudes to change, they may cause a temporary shift in behaviors from a *dominant* style to a *backup* style. Typically, when the immediate circumstances pass, the person shifts back to the dominant style again.

Dominant Grid Styles

The dominant style is the one that is *most characteristic* of a person. It is the approach known and anticipated as typical for that individual. An understanding and "feel" for a person's dominant style develops as people communicate and establish patterns of relating. Initially, a person may not be sure about how a new team member makes decisions, practices critique, resolves conflict, etc. The person could be friendly and open, reserved and cautious, or even abrupt and rude. As they interact, however, people learn to anticipate actions and reactions based on what they have experienced. This is the process of gradually becoming aware of a person's dominant style.

Dominant Grid styles are not dependent on a single incident or consciously selected according to a particular situation. In fact, dominant styles are based on firmly entrenched values and attitudes and cannot easily be turned on or off according to an isolated situation. People resist change most strongly in the areas they feel most deeply—their fundamental values. For example:

- If speaking openly and candidly is valued, imagine how hard it would be for a person to suddenly withhold an opinion.

- If a person values making decisions based on facts and shared insight, he or she would dislike feeling forced to make a sudden, uninformed decision.

- If a person prefers to complete work without critique, he or she feels uncomfortable when people offer comments and suggestions.

These examples illustrate how behaviors express values and attitudes that people hold and that remain constant over time. Change may occur on a limited basis by adjusting behaviors, but lasting change only occurs when people explore the values and attitudes underlying the behavior. For example, with few exceptions, people with a high concern for results and a low concern for people behave consistently regardless of the situation. They will dominate and control members of a special committee or task force the same way they dominate teammates on a daily basis.

Dominant Grid styles only become apparent when relating to a person over time. An isolated conversation or brief encounter is not a sound way to evaluate a dominant style. It is all too easy to take isolated examples or third-party descriptions out of context and "assign" a dominant Grid style to a person. A person's dominant style is best revealed when people have experienced a comprehensive range of behaviors in direct communication over time, and then evaluated specific examples.

Backup Grid Styles

A person's backup style can be considered the *next most characteristic* style demonstrated by that person in day-to-day relationships. In some circumstances, when a dominant approach isn't producing the desired effect for whatever reason, a person may shift temporarily to a backup style. Backup styles can result from stress, crisis or other negative factors in the workplace, or they can result from celebration or other positive factors. For example, a mild-mannered person who normally relates in ways that accommodate others may suddenly yell in anger at a co-worker. The sudden change probably shocks both people and is likely to be followed quickly by a return to the dominant approach with an apology and explanation for the unusual behavior. This person's dominant style is not changing; it's simply interrupted. Another person may maintain rigorous standards of excellence under most conditions, but after a series of staggering successes, become complacent. The strict standards relax until a setback occurs to shock him or her back into focused attention to detail. There is no particular pattern or coupling of dominant styles and backup styles. Any style can back up any other style.

There are no predictable patterns for how backup styles are revealed. Some people are most consistent in their dominant Grid style and only shift to a backup on rare occasions. This consistency is referred to as a "thick" dominant style. A person with a thick dominant style maintains the approach used, regardless of the circumstances. Others shift to a backup style more often or when certain circumstances arise. For example, a person may shift to a backup whenever conflict arises, or when failure occurs. This person's dominant style is considered "thin" because the shift to a backup occurs on a regular basis.

Building a Foundation

The Grid framework lays the foundation for change by providing a way for individuals, teams, and organizations to discuss and develop shared assumptions regarding what behaviors they agree are effective and ineffective. The natural impulse for many individuals and teams is to jump into the process of working without really examining how effectively they are working or will work together.

People naturally take action based on what is familiar, and getting down to work is often considered easier than taking time to develop a strategy, to discuss standards of excellence, or to establish criteria for results. When these steps are bypassed, people take the attitude that any problems will "work themselves out" in the process of working together, and in the meantime, everyone will move forward in a productive way. This approach is equivalent to asking a group of people in a room to close their eyes and point north and everyone confidently points in a different direction. The same thing happens when teams jump into a project without a shared understanding of how to move forward. This "ready-*fire*-aim" approach is a formula for misunderstandings, poor assumptions, and conflict. And the farther along colleagues work on a task, the more disruptive critique and planning become.

The Grid theory provides a way to develop a shared understanding up front so that people working together can discuss and agree on what behaviors they think are effective *before* beginning a task. With this shared understanding in place, team members' personal and team commitment increases and the team can work naturally toward developing a strategy, discussing standards of excellence, or setting criteria for results.

By using the theory to establish standards, the Grid strategy for change and development gives companies a way to manage ongoing change in a powerful, rewarding way. People can accept or reject the validity of the theory presented and use the concepts to initiate discussions. With the theory as a starting point, teams can begin sharing assumptions and defining criteria for their own change efforts based on personal values and attitudes. With a shared understanding and clear criteria in place, individuals are more willing to make a personal contribution to the change effort because they haven't been held back or cut off from involvement. They can enter into an activity openly and honestly because they have aired reservations and doubts and have had an opportunity to offer ideas. Without such an open forum, change efforts begin with misunderstanding and even resentment still in place which will likely worsen over time.

The theory also provides a starting point for introducing personal change and development. The styles presented help people understand how personal fears block change efforts; why conflict, impasse, and politics emerge in discussions; or why results may be less than expected. The more skilled every person becomes in identifying and correcting or avoiding ineffectiveness early, the better chance he or she has of contributing to team synergy. With the burden of these problems removed, teams are free to explore creative alternatives, test personal limits, take risks, and gain greater rewards.

Chapters 4–10 describe each Grid style in detail. The purpose of these profiles is threefold.

1. The individual styles provide a framework to use in identifying which styles are considered sound and unsound in the workplace and why.

2. The detailed profiles provide a model by which individuals can evaluate their own behavior in the workplace and begin to understand how other people experience them in relationships.

3. The detailed profiles are a model by which individuals can understand the behaviors of others and begin to interact more effectively in the workplace.

Grid Relationship Skills

3

Chapter

Performance measurement occurs every day in the workplace in terms of R1 resources and R3 results. Measurement in these areas is usually based on standards and principles commonly accepted as valid. For example, R1 performance standards are measured with professional degrees, certifications, and specific industry tests. People don't question the soundness of accounting principles or computer programming procedures, and so discussions regarding performance *feel* objective. People feel confident discussing performance with the attitude that, "This is not personal." Measuring R3 results works the same way. Results are measured in tangible terms of the market share, company growth, sales or profits, or employee turnover. Because the standards of measurement are widely accepted, people are more able to discuss performance with an objective attitude.

Measuring R2 behavior is very different. People usually don't share standards regarding what behaviors they think are sound or unsound, making it difficult to discuss with the same objective attitude. With no common understanding, people are left with personal preferences, opinions, cultures and norms as the only basis for comments. To make matters worse, accepted standards of behavior are usually unspoken. It's not *written* in a policy manual anywhere that you don't talk about the boss's temper, but everyone *knows* not to. It's not written anywhere that people can't question authority, but everyone *knows* not to challenge upward in the organization. The unspoken codes of conduct make people even less comfortable discussing personal behaviors in the workplace.

The Grid provides a method for evaluating behaviors with the same sense of confidence and objectivity felt when examining resources and results. The method includes the following two-step process.

1. Defining sound and unsound behaviors in tangible terms of seven relationship skills.

2. Learning structured critique skills that give the ability to assess behavior in objective terms, and most importantly, to make constructive suggestions for improvement without offending or creating defensiveness.

The Grid framework brings the theory into practical use by defining relationship skills in simple and specific terms of what behaviors do and do not work effectively. Grid styles give people a way to build the foundation for objective discussions and to begin thinking in terms of *what's right* rather than *who's right*. Like any sound standard, once effective behaviors are defined, they provide a model for comparing current behaviors with what people agree is soundest. A motivational gap develops as people begin to see the differences between soundest and actual behaviors. And with a model in place, people have a clear understanding of how to change to more effective behaviors.

This motivational gap is the first step toward changing behavior. Because most people want to do their best and improve, the gap in awareness alone is often enough to instill commitment to change. When this level of personal awareness is combined with team involvement and support, however, individual change efforts become team initiatives for excellence. The person in question now has the motivation, a model, and the support of the people most likely to help by challenging unsound behavior when they see it.

Table 3-1

Grid Relationship Skills

Critique	learn from experience by anticipating and examining how behavior and actions affect results
Initiative	take action to exercise effort, drive, and support for specific activities
Inquiry	question, seek information, and test for understanding
Advocacy	express attitudes, opinions, ideas, and convictions
Decision Making	evaluate resources, criteria, and consequences to reach a decision
Conflict Resolution	confront and work through disagreement with others toward resolution
Resilience	react to problems, setbacks, and failure, and understand how these factors influence the ability to move forward

These seven relationship skills arise in the course of achieving results as people work together. Each relationship skill does not necessarily arise with each activity, or in any specific order or pattern in relationships. Some relationship skills arise more than others do, but over time people practice all of them. Answer the following questions to help clarify the relationship skill categories by focusing on your own R2 relationship behaviors.

1. **Critique:** How do you study and evaluate your own effectiveness with others? Do you welcome comments from others regarding your effectiveness? Do you offer critique to others but resist receiving it yourself? Do you prefer to limit critique to positive comments?

2. **Initiative:** How do you start an assigned activity or task? How do you involve other people in your efforts to take action? Do you take action and expect others to follow? Do you wait for others to take action before committing yourself?

3. **Inquiry:** When you need information from someone, how do you go about getting that information? Do you feel uncomfortable being dependent on others for information? Do you prefer that others provide information without offering personal opinions or suggestions, or do you welcome suggestions, even if those suggestions uncover problems? Do you acquire information subtly without revealing your position or do you admit up front what you don't know even if this might make you appear uninformed?

4. **Advocacy:** How openly and effectively do you offer your opinion to others? Do you invite discussion of alternative views? Does your degree of conviction depend on the status of others involved? Do you force your opinion without considering others?

5. **Conflict Resolution:** How do you respond when you disagree or get angry with others? Do you feel compelled to prove others wrong if they disagree with you? Do you withdraw to avoid involvement when conflict arises? Do you seek to soothe feelings and restore a pleasant environment? Do you search for resolution based on *what* is right or *who* is right?

6. **Decision Making:** How do you work with others to reach decisions? Do you try to dominate decisions based on what you think is the best course of action, or do you prefer to wait for others to take the lead? Do you search for decisions that are popular rather than what may be best?

7. **Resilience:** How do you react to setbacks and failure? Is your first reaction to place blame and defend your actions? Do you take responsibility for problems and try to learn from them? Does failure make you not want to take certain actions again for fear of more failure?

Critique

Critique is discussing an event to increase understanding and learning, and represents the single most valuable relationship skill for increasing effectiveness in the workplace. Critique gets information out into the open and creates an opportunity for synergy. When teams can transcend the examination of facts, data, and figures and include R2 discussions about *how effectively* they are working together, productivity increases. For example, teams can include discussions on the best approach to making decisions or establish a strategy for resolving conflict that may occur. The ability to openly express reservations or doubts, as well as creative ideas, allows teams to anticipate and react quickly to resolve problems. These skills are essential for practicing quality critique. There are four components to critique.

Pre-Critique

Pre-critique is used in the early stages of an activity, and addresses the fundamental question, "What are we doing and how are we going to do it?" This stage includes establishing a strategy before jumping into an activity. Many people feel more comfortable rushing into work because the act of working is familiar and feels productive, while planning is sometimes unfamiliar and felt to be time-consuming. This establishes the ready-*fire*-aim mentality where teams are too consumed with *doing* to stop and examine *how* they are going to work together. Pre-critique, however, can be as simple as taking two minutes at the beginning of a meeting to set an agenda, or starting a phone call by saying, "Now, what do we want to accomplish?"

In addition to planning a strategy for the specific steps to take, pre-critique defines a schedule for progress. This step forces people to think in realistic terms of actual implementation. They have to think of all the extra work they are committing to in direct relation to current workloads, resources in place, scheduling, etc. When done effectively, pre-critique is defined in specific terms against clear criteria for accomplishment. When consensus is clear about what progress will look like, it makes getting back on track much easier. When the meeting drifts off topic, it's easier to say, "We've gotten off track," and move forward.

Periodic Critique

Periodic critique is a schedule of critique points set during pre-critique. These preset critique points allow teams to commit ahead of time to stop the flow of work at specific intervals to discuss the quality of progress. The schedule may focus on lengths of time (once a week) or on points of accomplishment (at the beginning of a work cycle). This may include setting a weekly meeting or conference call to discuss a project, ten-minute meetings at the beginning of every day, or quarterly sales meetings. This gives people involved an opportunity to establish planned periods to step back from the detail level of work to look at the big picture. Periodic critique allows people a *planned* opportunity to make adjustments if needed to get back on course.

Concurrent Critique

Concurrent critique occurs spontaneously when someone involved interrupts activity to discuss the quality of work. This may include calling attention to an immediate problem, making changes in a process or procedure, offering a new idea, or simply expressing reservations and doubts. Concurrent or spontaneous critique is critical for uncovering problems that occur outside the more structured forms of critique. This approach demands more flexibility because it means interrupting a process whenever discussion is needed rather than waiting for a scheduled time. Concurrent critique represents a vital form of critique for synergy because problems are caught and resolved *as they occur.*

Concurrent critique is most effective when the comments focus on results and are based on clear criteria set in place during pre-critique. For example, if a person interrupts progress on a new software product to introduce a new feature, the critique can be quickly considered against the desired results and pre-established criteria. The people involved can quickly decide if the benefits are worth the delays and either stop or move on.

In teams where candor and trust are high, concurrent critique provides for instant readjustment with minimal disruption to a course of action. In these cases, the comments are often subtle because the team is functioning at such a highly effective level. If trust is low, a comment such as, "Wait a minute. Shouldn't we check this against the original order?" can result in a large disruption due to resentment or politics. In the team with high trust, the reaction is, "Oh yeah. You're right." The comment doesn't cause any disruption and the adjustment is seamless in the course of progress.

Post-Critique

Post-critique is often the only type of critique used in teams. People wait until after the fact and discuss why an activity succeeded or failed. In teams where mutual trust and respect are low, post-critique may be used as a platform for assigning blame and punishment. It may also be used as a platform for rushing into celebration and praise. In both cases, valuable opportunity for using the experience to learn and improve effectiveness is lost. In post-critique, examining what *worked* is as important as examining what *didn't work*. In this way, teams can reinforce what worked and examine causes of what caused problems.

Post-critique is most effective when it occurs as close to the event in question as possible so that the actions and impact remain fresh and relevant. The most useful comments are given in specific terms and describe actions that took place rather than focusing on personal accusations, blame, or good intentions.

As with the other types of critique, post-critique is most effective when the comments are based on criteria determined in pre-critique. Criteria can be just as valuable for critiquing success as it is for critiquing failure. The outcome of critique is strengthened when teams approach discussions with a clear consensus regarding what they wanted to accomplish. Teams that reach less than expected results can focus on what went wrong and why, and can work to develop a strategy for improvement. Teams that exceed expectations can examine why instead of becoming lost in celebration or complacency. A new resource may have developed that should be examined so teams can assure a repeat of the success. Or success may have resulted from an underestimation of what they could accomplish, and they need to raise expectations next time. In either case, post-critique is valuable for keeping teams focused on continuous improvement.

Anonymous Versus Open Critique

A common method for avoiding candor is to use anonymous critique as opposed to face-to-face critique. The argument for anonymity is that people are more likely to give and receive honest critique when a comment's origin is unknown. However, the opposite is usually true. The first reaction to an anonymous comment is, "Who said that?" because *who* said it is as important as *what* was said. As an example, negative comments from a close and respected supervisor make a very different impression than comments from an envious colleague who rarely works directly with the person in question.

Anonymous comments reduce the ability to learn from experience in a self-convincing way because there is no opportunity for discussion, clarification, and new insight. People learn by discussing assumptions and perspectives, and providing specific examples. Without discussion, individual perspectives remain independent and are only valid as isolated opinions. This reduces the possibility for synergy because there is little opportunity to clarify understanding with the other person and to generate new learning.

Anonymous comments are also difficult to consider objectively because people are not held accountable for what they say. When the person being discussed is addressed directly, comments are more likely to be thoughtful and sincere as opposed to casual and less focused. If a person has a grudge, he or she can use anonymous critique as an opportunity to let the person in question "have it," regardless of whether or not the comment is true. For teams to develop mutual trust and respect, the people involved need to clarify what each person thinks to develop a shared understanding.

Using Criteria to Build a Foundation

Criteria provide a foundation for critique by defining up front what teams plan to accomplish and how. Criteria can take many forms, like setting short and long term goals, or developing strategic plans and timelines. Once established, these agreed-to criteria provide focus and allow people to move forward with common objectives.

Criteria are usually developed in the pre-critique stage when planning, goal setting, and strategies are mapped out, but they can be developed or revised as issues come into focus or as new learning occurs. They are also used throughout the process so each stage of critique tests the validity of the criteria that has been set. Criteria provide a clear idea of where you're going, what you're doing, and how you're going to proceed by establishing

- an objective reference point for moving forward, and

- an objective perspective for personal behavior based on *what's* right not *who's* right.

For example, if the goal is to outline a production schedule, sound criteria for achieving that goal enable any deviations to be quickly addressed so people can move on. "I thought this meeting was about our production schedule, but you're discussing a marketing strategy." Concurrent critique is especially effective in helping to maintain focus on the goals in place. "We don't all need to be in this discussion. Can the two of you have a private meeting to work out the details?" With no criteria in place, such comments cause much more of a disruption.

Behaviors can also be addressed more effectively with criteria in place. If the meeting is running late because one person is talking too much, any comment can focus on the criteria rather than the person. If a person says, "You're talking too much and we need to move on," he or she is likely to feel judged and insulted. With criteria in place, it's much easier to say, "We agreed to cover 15 topics; discussing this level of detail is putting us behind." The latter statement focuses on how the *behavior* impacts the goals instead of evaluating the *person* as good or bad.

Criteria are only useful for critique when they are vivid in people's minds. Writing down goals, posting them in a visible place, and revisiting them regularly makes them *real* and *tangible* to those involved in a discussion or meeting. The written statements keep the criteria current and relevant and provide a starting point for initiating critique.

As well as occurring at different times during an activity, critique can occur at many levels. The effort can range from involving many people in a formal series of meetings to a moment of introspective review by one person to reflect on the activity in question.

Characteristics of Effective Behavior Critique

Effective critique includes specific examples to support observations. "I think you're unqualified," is not specific. "This is the third time today you have asked for help with this. Do you feel comfortable with these responsibilities?" is specific, objective, and helpful.

Here-and-now: In any situation where feedback and critique occur, the most effective comments relate to immediately observable, here-and-now events. Here-and-now critique has the advantage of using specific examples that are fresh and vivid. For example, by saying "Your positive comments this morning helped me focus on the next phase of the project with confidence," the person gets immediate feedback about what works well. There is also great advantage to capturing feelings while they are fresh to gain a more immediate and timely understanding of how behavior impacts others. Even anger and frustration help focus discussions by capturing the feelings that the behaviors cause. For example, if a person can say, "When you contradicted me without taking the time to get all of the information, I felt cheated," then he or she feels immediate relief, and the other person feels the impact of the behavior.

The exception to the effectiveness of here-and-now critique is when tempers are so high that people cannot discuss issues objectively. One or both people may be so angry that they risk doing more damage than good by confronting the situation immediately. Then a temporary cooling-off period may be necessary to give people a chance to gather thoughts and express them more objectively. This may take an hour or a day, depending on the person and situation. The key to making the cooling-off period work is to use the time to gather thoughts so that discussions can be objective. The emotions are valuable and should be expressed, but in a way that encourages an open, two-way discussion.

Non-judgmental: Feedback and critique are most effective when offered spontaneously, with a nonjudgmental restatement of the events that took place and a statement of how that behavior affected the person in question. "When you cut me off like that, it really shuts me down and makes me want to stop offering any suggestions in these meetings." This method does not pass judgment on the individual being critiqued—it doesn't say "You're bad," but instead lets the person know how the behavior affects others, and all in the spirit of helpfulness.

Criteria-based: Many teams resist deliberately incorporating critique into activities because they have an image of nonproductive, lengthy conversations with everyone involved. Even the word critique sometimes brings sighs of resignation at falling behind schedule. However, when critique is used effectively, quite the opposite is true. Effective critique increases efficiency in every aspect of relationships. A lengthy meeting with every team member pulled off-line can easily become a five-minute phone call or a meeting between only a few people. The key to making critique succinct is having predefined criteria in place as a point of reference for discussions. Members should be able to compare where they are against a clear schedule of where they need to be and make any necessary adjustments. This makes the discussion clear, focused, and based on facts.

Initiative

Initiative occurs whenever a person takes action to either establish a new activity or to move a current activity forward. Initiative is characterized by *how* a person embraces a new assignment or opportunity. A person with strong initiative skills moves ahead with confidence to define a course and direct action. This may be seen in efforts to offer suggestions, begin planning strategies, rally involvement from others, and to maintain momentum once progress is under way. This person needs less direct supervision and instruction, and is confident enough in his or her abilities to take the risk of being the first to step forward with an idea.

The character of initiative taken by individuals sets the tone of relationships by being the starting point for establishing and maintaining productive momentum. The character of initiative is critical for gaining involvement from others. When done effectively, strong initiative can rally people into action with enthusiasm and confidence. They feel a personal stake in the outcomes because they have been considered in defining the initiative.

When done too forcefully, however, initiative can inhibit involvement by setting up resentment and defensiveness. This usually occurs because the initiator is plowing ahead without considering others involved, forming and announcing a clear plan without giving people an opportunity to comment. Resentments can also occur when a person asks for comments without considering them sincerely. He or she is simply "going through the motions" with a clear course already in mind.

When initiative is weak, involvement is low because people sense apprehension and caution and so feel less confident about stepping out themselves. This is especially true when a leader demonstrates weak initiative. Weak initiative in leaders has the same contagious effect as enthusiasm and confidence.

Sound initiative develops naturally in relationships based on mutual trust and respect. This focus eliminates the need to jockey for recognition by outperforming colleagues. The fear of failure is replaced by the confidence that each person is doing his or her best with all the available information. When people trust each other, initiative focuses on *what's right* rather than *who's right*. Team members seek out and share information and discuss weaknesses and barriers openly. With all the information out in the open, when initiative is taken, it is comprehensive, objective, and motivating.

Inquiry

The simple act of asking a question can do more to set the stage for effective discussions than any other action. Inquiry occurs whenever a person gathers information with others, and may take the form of one-on-one questions, group "brainstorming" discussions, or a special task force.

Questions represent a critical starting point for any discussion because they initiate two-way discussions. *How* a question is asked can promote enthusiasm and openness or defensiveness and resistance. Teams that base actions on the *what's right* approach to inquiry usually operate on one basic assumption: *question everything.* No tradition is sacred; no past practice is unchangeable. Effective inquiry focused on *what's right*

- promotes insight into all relevant perspectives, and leads to new understanding;
- allows people to share personal insights openly and spontaneously so that all relevant information is considered;
- encourages rather than punishes people for sharing information; and
- establishes the foundation for an objective evaluation of facts.

In teams operating on the *who's right* approach, inquiry is restricted to accommodate one or a few people. The objective in the *who's right* approach may be for the people in authority to look good. Information, facts, and evidence are presented in ways that advance the *person* rather than the best possible course. Any facts, data, and logic that don't fit the sought-after objectives of that person are overlooked. Effective inquiry bases research, questions, discussions, and strategies on standards of excellence that everyone involved understands and feels committed to achieving.

Effective Listening

The key to sound inquiry is to create a two-way process of asking *and* listening. In fact, the most simple and effective way for a leader to acknowledge people and ensure participation is to listen effectively. Learning to listen effectively makes inquiry work better by closing the loop of communication. When asking questions, put yourself in the other person's shoes and listen to his or her ideas with respect and objectivity. A really great question can be immediately undermined when the person asking the question does not listen to the response. The objective is to obtain as much information as possible for consideration.

Effective listening requires thinking through questions more thoroughly ahead of time. If time does not permit the thorough discussion that is needed, then delay the question. If an interruption prevents listening, then explain the circumstances and make arrangements to follow up.

Another key for sound inquiry is listening with objectivity. Sound listening skills permit the other person to express opinions openly and honestly so every view is clear. It's impossible to turn off personal opinions, preconceptions, prejudices, and biases, but you don't have to. The goal is to "hear" and understand the other person's views, whether you agree or not.

Criteria for sound listening:

- Try to understand the speaker's point of view, even if you don't agree. This may mean restating what the speaker has said to ensure correct interpretation. For example, "This is what I hear you saying . . ."

- Encourage the speaker to talk more, that is, look at the person with comfortable yet direct eye contact. Include "tell me more" expressions and body language.

- Clarify your own understanding of the speaker's feelings by asking, for example, "Is this how you feel?" followed by your interpretation of the speaker's opinion.

Another strategy is to critique the quality of listening on a continuing basis. Then distortions can be identified immediately and brought to a listener's attention to increase awareness. "Am I still making sense here? I get the feeling I lost you on that last point." Once several examples are available, the person is able to strengthen personal listening skills.

Advocacy

Advocacy is revealed initially when people articulate convictions to others, and continues as people maintain those convictions over time and under pressure. Are they willing to shift their thinking as new, sounder ideas emerge? Individuals and teams that follow the *what's right* approach to advocacy practice open and objective discussion of ideas with a focus on results. Convictions are advocated in ways that clarify opinions while also inviting alternative views. Teammates are encouraged to openly discuss personal experiences, ideas, and fears so that a topic is explored thoroughly. The result is that the *soundest* idea presented prevails, regardless of *who* offered the suggestion.

Sound advocacy is not just practiced by individuals; teams with an objective of exploring every view seek it out. Teams practicing sound advocacy take responsibility for ensuring every member's view is expressed and explored thoroughly before moving on. Silence can do just as much to express convictions as pounding a fist on a table. It's very easy for the loudest person to be heard, but anyone knows that loud does not always mean best. If a team member is very quiet during a discussion, others are responsible for stopping the discussion to pull him or her in: "You haven't said anything about this topic, Robert. What are you thinking?" Over time, the team can help the person advocate convictions more effectively. This approach assures complete utilization of resources, while increasing commitment to the team's effort.

The key to making advocacy work is to use strong critique skills to establish criteria for discussions and then keep the discussions focused on results. Critique provides a guideline for people to follow when advocating an idea. For example, a team may define the criteria for a specific meeting in the following way.

- We will identify three possible courses of action in this meeting.
- We will support each suggestion with at least two examples.
- Every member will voice a point of view before we reach a team decision.

The criteria for the meeting immediately provide a focus for how to advocate by defining the outcome (three possible options), and limiting suggestions to only ones that can be backed up by two examples. With these criteria in place, it makes it easier for people to say, "You've advocated this view for ten minutes but haven't been able to come up with examples." The team reaches agreement quickly and moves on because the person immediately knows that the advocacy is not focused on the objectives. If another person remains quiet during the discussions, others can say, "We agreed that everyone would offer a point of view, but we haven't heard from you yet."

Constructive and candid advocacy can dramatically increase personal commitment in teams. Individuals naturally want to share personal views and offer opinions that improve the quality of results. The act of expressing convictions relieves tension, clarifies underlying assumptions, and addresses fears. The need for personal fulfillment increases the value of individual contribution to the team result by creating a win/win scenario. The personal connections felt by each individual lead to a heightened interest and awareness regarding team progress.

Decision Making

Decision making includes how effectively individuals and teams consider all of the available resources to define a course of action. The two keys to taking sound, decisive action are

- having strong relationships in place to support the decision, regardless of who makes it or under what circumstances, and
- establishing criteria up front for measuring the effectiveness of the decision.

Consensus decision making occurs when all of the facts, data, experience, and criteria are explored openly and objectively to reach a solution that everyone supports. This does not means everyone is involved with the decision, or even that everyone agrees, but that everyone can *support* the chosen course.

Characteristics of Sound Decision Making

The idea of "team decision making" often creates misunderstandings regarding what makes a decision sound. A common misunderstanding is that the only way to make sound team decisions is to involve every member in every step of the process. This approach can not only consume time, but also wastes key resources by overextending people. Only those people who have experience and skill to contribute to the decision need to be involved. Another common misunderstanding is that one-alone decisions are *never* sound. This idea is also unrealistic in the fast-paced business world where crises arise and quick responses are vital.

Sound decision making can take many forms and depends on the size and configuration of teams, the team's criteria for the use of power and authority, and the complexity of the decision being made. Consensus decisions may include one-alone decisions, one-to-one decisions between two individuals, one-to-all decisions made with an entire team, or one-to-some in which more than two but not all members are involved. The fundamental key to making sound decisions is to involve every resource *necessary* to make the right decision.

Consensus decision making occurs naturally in teams that share mutual trust and respect. The reason individuals are able to support a decision they may not agree with is because they have had the opportunity to contribute to the process either directly or indirectly. Although direct involvement is effective for developing commitment, it is not always possible or even practical with the fast pace and time pressures of most companies. Strong relationships reduce the need for ongoing direct involvement by establishing shared trust between people responsible for the decision. One team member, for example, may only endorse decisions when historical trends have been considered. Another may rely on projected earnings and production volumes, while another always considers new, creative ideas that haven't been tested. All of these values are understood in the team, and the team addresses each when making a decision.

When teams operate based on ongoing mutual trust, respect, and candor, the person taking action makes an *informed* decision. He or she has maintained communications with the people involved, and makes the decision with the whole picture in mind. This means that if he or she knows a decision may offend one person, an effort is made to inform that person as soon as possible to provide rationale. For example, if a one-alone decision leads to a strategy that does not consider historical trends, the people involved know they have to provide a sound rationale to the member who values trends. This simple but profound step of considering all views protects valuable relationships from being damaged by one-alone decisions. The frustration felt by the person relying on historical trends is reduced by hearing the rationale directly and in a timely fashion from peers. If a consensus decision turns out to be incorrect, a thorough understanding of all views ahead of time dispels the temptation for one team member to say, "I told you so."

Keep in mind that people quickly see through veiled attempts at consensus decision making. Just going through the motions of calling a meeting and asking for suggestions does not automatically create commitment in people. They have to believe that their convictions are being considered based on merit. For example, if a leader goes through the motions of asking for new ideas every month, but always decides in favor of his or her own ideas, people will stop offering ideas.

To generate lasting commitment, leaders and team members must not only ask for involvement, but also honestly consider and weigh information in objective terms. Simply going through the motions causes more resentment because ideas were not simply ignored, but ignored after someone took the time to advocate them. John Humphrey, chairman of the Boston Ballet Company in 1990, observed problems in the ballet's management. He pointed out to managers that revenues were down because of messy conditions in the upper balcony seats.[1] Customers had to walk past old scenery props stored in hallways. In addition, sloppy masking tape, which marked stage positions for dancers, was not visible from floor seats but was an eyesore for people in balcony seats. And finally, dancers bowed to every seating section except the balcony seats following performances. Managers thanked Humphrey for his suggestions and promised to do something again and again, but nothing changed. Finally, Humphrey invited one of the managers to join him for a performance in the balcony. Decisions and changes followed, and within a week conditions improved and profits followed. Humphrey was in a leadership position that warranted listening and he was persistent. Many people would not be so persistent in getting a point across, especially in a company culture that doesn't welcome challenge.

Mutually supportive relationships make it much easier to explain the rationale after the fact, in order to learn from the experience and recover from possible damage. With shared assumptions in place, any team member can make a decision with the entire team in mind with less need for direct consultation.

Conflict Resolution

The opposite of conflict is not peace and harmony, but apathy. Conflict resolution is how people anticipate and react to conflict when it occurs. Conflict is defined as a difference of opinion between people and can range anywhere from a passing comment of disagreement to openly arguing and challenging another person in anger. The dynamics are the same whether in a marketing team making a crucial presentation, a research team laboring to develop a new product on time, an operations team wrestling with day-to-day problems, or an executive team establishing a long-range plan. Conflict can quickly and effectively halt team progress. People often do not know how to react and seek to cut off conflict, withdraw, smooth it over, encourage compromise, circumvent it for private gain, or admonish it as disloyal. These approaches may be effective in a limited, short-term way, but rarely resolve conflict, leaving it to fester and ultimately resurface later.

People often avoid conflict instead of viewing it as a positive source for productive energy. Yet controversy is vital for progress and growth because its accompanying diversity of views breeds creativity and ultimately synergy. Conflict enables people to feel personally challenged, committed, and capable of maximizing resources. Conflict focuses issues and motivates people to explore differences to generate new ideas and learning. The Grid strategy for change and development is not about trying to eliminate conflict from the workplace. That would be impossible. The Grid strategy is about providing skills to manage and resolve conflict with an objective focus on *what's right*. Conflict inevitably arises in the process of working together, and differences are invaluable for communicating and clarifying goals.

---

[1] Richard C. Whiteley, *The Customer Driven Company* (Reading, MA: Addison-Wesley Publishing Company, 1991), pp. 186-187.

Conflict is like an iceberg with only the tip showing above the surface—the majority of the controversy remains unexpressed. Many work groups operate under the illusion that because no one is openly fighting or apparently angry, no conflict exists. There is a strong tendency to overlook comments or situations because of the fear of conflict and the fallout that may follow. When leaders avoid conflict, they create the perfect setting for resentment, frustration and indifference.

When conflict is handled with openness and remains focused on the best possible solution, the improved results surpass those achieved by win/lose approaches, suppression, or avoidance. This ability to enhance results through effective conflict resolution leads to synergy at its best, and is a master key to successful leadership.

The Grid provides a way to use conflict to align goals, focus issues, and clarify convictions with productivity in mind by giving people the skills to confront differences objectively. In effective relationships, people know and use conflict resolution skills to reach mutual understanding and ensure shared commitment. This does not mean conflict becomes easier or fun; it just means that conflict becomes manageable and its resolution can be constructive.

People in sound relationships still experience the fear and apprehension in surfacing and addressing conflict, but they do it because they understand the benefits and have a sound strategy for resolution. Their apprehension is relieved by the confidence and support of others involved and by a successful history of resolving conflict. Like any group of people who successfully work through a crisis, they have experienced the surge of energy and creativity that occurs when a problem is identified, confronted, and resolved.

Resilience

Resilience is measured by how individuals and teams handle setbacks and failure when R3 results are lower than expected. Resilient individuals and teams face failure directly and embrace all of the disappointment and anger that come with it for understanding and learning. No matter how high the level of mutual trust and respect and candor, failure is never easy to take. The Grid does not pretend to make it easier, but it gives people the skills to learn from the experience and strengthen effectiveness in the future. The simple act of standing squarely in the face of failure and accepting responsibility is the only way to benefit from the learning experience it offers. Many teams cannot take this step because they make excuses, blame others, smooth over weaknesses, and rush ahead to the next task, leaving the failure behind to "go away."

Resilience is a critical relationship skill for achieving success in a constantly changing business world. The ability to learn from a setback, regardless of how devastating, and to translate the failure into valuable learning is powerful. This is where sound R2 relationships based on mutual trust and respect pay off. This is where consensus decision-making pays off. This is where having sound criteria in place for critique pay off. In order to recover and move on, individuals and teams must be able to discuss and explore what went wrong in candid, objective, and constructive terms that focus on recovery and improvement.

If handled in a responsible and objective way, failure can be a most provocative ingredient for motivating people to change. People risk settling into complacency with too much success. They may loosen standards and feel they can do no wrong. In the meantime another team alongside them with high resilience is digging in and finding creative ways to succeed the next time around. Recovery is swift when mutual trust and respect is high and the failure causes people to pull together, regain strength, and move forward. Teams that operate based on high standards of excellence and a high concern for results will not settle for less.

Summary

Any change effort undertaken by a team is strengthened by a shared understanding not only of the R3 objectives, but also of how the team will get there. The R2 relationships and the Grid relationship skills provide that crucial path. Effective relationship skills are critical for leveraging all of the team's resources. It's often much easier to examine the value of a contribution by examining it in the context of everyday actions like decision making or conflict resolution. In this manner, Grid values can be applied in day-to-day terms. The relationship skills can also be used to track improvements in these specific areas until sound values and effective management of behavior becomes second nature. Individual actions with regard to each relationship skill are based on deeply held values that most people do not question or examine. Individuals simply carry them out like shutting off a light switch or turning off a car ignition. They are not even aware of why they take initiative or advocate a certain way—they just do it.

Examining the critical relationship skills in specific and objective terms is fundamental for beginning any change effort. These relationship skills are not so deeply ingrained that they cannot be changed; most people simply have no effective method for discussing behaviors objectively. These behaviors can be changed, but only after people become aware of them in day-to-day relationships and have a clear picture of where they want to be. To work successfully, personal change takes clear understanding, goals, and support from people who experience behaviors on an ongoing basis.

The 9,1 Style: Controlling
(Direct & Dominate)

4

Chapter

Overview

The 9,1-oriented[1] style is found in the lower right corner of the Grid figure (see Fig. 4-1). This person demonstrates a high concern for results interdependent with a low concern for people. The high concern for results present in this style brings determination, focus, and drive for success to any team. The person operating from the 9,1 orientation is usually highly trained, organized, experienced, and qualified to lead a team to success. He or she also has the confidence and courage to demand high standards and takes calculated risks as needed to reach them. The low concern for others, however, limits the ability to reach synergy because the effort to involve others is low and results in an overly forceful approach. The person with this style approaches relationships with an underlying assumption that the two concerns work against each other in the workplace. He or she believes that demonstrating a concern for people diminishes the ability to achieve results, and so actively works to play down and suppress the "people" side of relationships.

Fig. 4-1

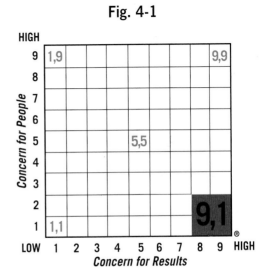

9,1 Grid Style: CONTROLLING
(Direct & Dominate)

I expect results and take control by clearly stating a course of action. I enforce rules that sustain high results and do not permit deviation.

The low concern for others prevents the 9,1 person from being aware of others involved in an activity beyond what is expected of them in relation to results. The overriding focus lies in results, often leaving others lost in the wake of his or her forceful

---

[1] A person is not "9,1"; rather, his or her behaviors are oriented to a Grid style. The correct phraseology for describing an orientation is, "the 9,1-oriented person." In order to make this a more readable text, we have chosen to introduce the style in chapters 4-10 with the "oriented" phraseology, but succeeding references are in the format of "the 9,1 style."

initiative. The 9,1 person expects everyone else to "keep up" with his or her efforts, and so moves ahead, intensely focused on results.

The 9,1 person can come across as pushy and demanding without considering how his or her behavior impacts others. "People" concerns such as benefits, training, flexible work hours, social meetings, and personal discussions are often given low priority. In short, this person is unapproachable in a personal sense. Human qualities of relationships (candor, openness, mutual trust and respect, personal goals) are often seen as issues that slow down the main focus of maintaining high standards and achieving results. If costs need to be cut, the "people costs" are the first to go, often with little awareness of important developmental work which eventually might have to be reinitiated later with increased expense and under-motivated and perhaps less knowledgeable employees. The 9,1 person does not mean to attack people, but truly believes a singular focus on results is the only way to get the job done: "All that other stuff is frills, anyway."

9,1 Controlling Style at the Team Level

The following examples represent typical 9,1 responses in the workplace.

The 9,1 response when a team member fails to accomplish his or her share of the workload:

The 9,1 person confronts the team member with an accusatory tone. Criticism might include statements about the person being lazy or incapable. Personal attacks may occur, such as a suggestion that the team member is really not cut out for the job. The team member's explanations are not tolerated, or are accepted in a limited way, with dismissals like, "That may be true, but...," "You may think that, but...," " or "That's not relevant." Finally, conditions for conforming are outlined in detail, accompanied by an ultimatum.

The 9,1 response to constructive critique from a team member:

The 9,1 person immediately defends his or her actions. Even if the comment is valid, the 9,1 person wants it acknowledged that despite the consequences, his or her thinking was sound and quickly assigns blame to someone else or to some other cause beyond his or her control.

The 9,1 person stands out in a team because he or she is typically "in everyone's face," imposing a position and taking control of results from the beginning of an activity. He or she takes pains to define, plan, and set in motion a clear course of action, but without involving others, often even those responsible for carrying out the actions. No matter how sound the proposed strategy, the impersonal approach often limits commitment from other team members. Personal stake and commitment are reduced because people feel disconnected from the assigned objectives they carry out. The attitude created in teams is often, "Why should I put so much effort into this when he gets all the credit, especially when I disagree and my suggestions are ignored?"

The 9,1 team is only as strong and effective as the person at the helm. No matter how talented, skilled, and experienced the 9,1 team leader is, the low concern for others leads to a monopoly over team resources because alternative views, challenges, and even questions are discouraged. The 9,1 leader's idea of "working with and through others" is to have everyone comply without question. Alternative views and objections are often overlooked by the forcefulness of 9,1 convictions and are treated as interruptions or deviations that keep the team from moving ahead. Work is arranged so that others have little chance to challenge or offer ideas, share critique, or advocate personal convictions.

Relationships are approached with decisive but narrow-sighted determination that reduces the possibility for losing control of the critical path to results. Instructions are announced with statements like, "This is what we're going to do," "You need to . . ." and "I have already come up with a plan." The 9,1 person prefers to define the action to take and then announce it to others with little opportunity for discussion or creative involvement. Others are then expected to jump into action without question. This approach minimizes the opportunity for synergy, as other team members are restricted from personal involvement.

A 9,1 team leader wants to achieve the highest possible results, which is a challenge in any workplace, but the challenge is increased when strong relationships are not in place to support the effort. If team members are discouraged, they do not pass on information that might prevent a major setback; the team member with an idea that could eliminate an obstacle remains quiet. The attitude is, "Why should I speak up and help out?" The only way to optimize available resources is to get people to support each other and speak up when they see a problem. This kind of support gets the team back on course with new ideas that offer further improvement. Even if the leader is phenomenally qualified and experienced, one person cannot possibly anticipate every problem or come up with every creative solution. Goals can be difficult to achieve even when team members are actively sharing information. Problems multiply when people withhold information or even work against one another.

The 9,1 individual works at a disadvantage by suppressing involvement, preferring instead to assure success by maintaining unilateral control. Additionally, the 9,1 leader doesn't want to spend a great deal of time explaining, discussing, and evaluating his or her actions. In order to accomplish this feat, the 9,1 stretches his or her own resources by constantly monitoring to assure compliance and feels ultimately responsible for identifying and resolving every obstacle, setback, and problem. The 9,1 person often and accurately sees himself or herself as the hardest working person on the team, but the quality of work is often lowered when the 9,1 person overextends himself or herself by excluding others. The 9,1 person doesn't see this discrepancy, however, and doesn't understand why everyone else is not working as hard for the same goals. When problems do arise, he or she increases the focus on results and pushes colleagues to work even harder.

R2 Relationships and the 9,1 Controlling Style

The 9,1 style contradicts a natural desire in individuals to communicate, offer ideas, and contribute to outcomes. Personal commitment comes from mutual trust and respect, and the opportunity to make a personal contribution; these qualities are strained in 9,1 relationships (see Fig. 4-2). When the 9,1 leader announces a unilateral decision that affects the entire team, the message often heard by others is, "You can't think for yourself," or "Your ideas are not important."

Fig. 4-2

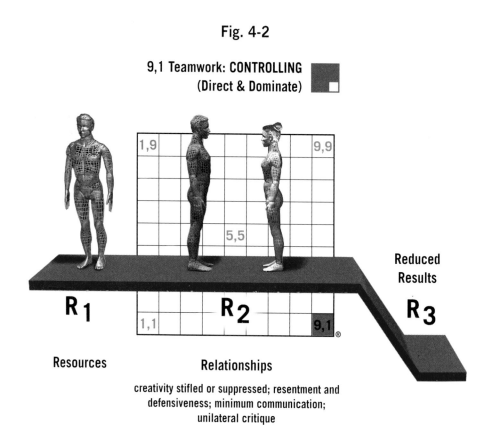

9,1 Teamwork: CONTROLLING
(Direct & Dominate)

Resources   Relationships

Reduced Results

creativity stifled or suppressed; resentment and defensiveness; minimum communication; unilateral critique

It's natural for people to want to go home at the end of the day feeling that they have made a contribution to the workplace, and the 9,1 approach polarizes rather than meshes resources. When suggestions are repeatedly cut off or criticized, people eventually develop the habit of saying, "Fine, I don't care what happens. What I do or say makes no difference anyway," and start looking for a transfer or another job altogether. Apathy and lack of commitment may develop in the team as an "us against them" attitude develops. In the worst situations, team members begin to work against the 9,1 person by undermining efforts, even relishing the thought of seeing him or her suffer setbacks: "It serves her right. Any one of us could have told her that would happen, but she never listened." With such a resentful team, the 9,1 person has moved even farther away from establishing shared objectives and has lowered any chance for mutual trust and respect by team members.

9,1 Controlling Motivations

The 9,1 person sees an inherent contradiction between the concern for results and the concern for people. He or she believes that expressing a high concern for people reduces the ability to achieve sound results. This contradiction is seen in 9,1 motivations in the form of a desire for control and domination and a fear of failure and helplessness (see Fig. 4-3).

Fig. 4-3

9,1 Motivations: CONTROLLING (Direct & Dominate)

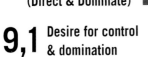

9,1 Desire for control & domination

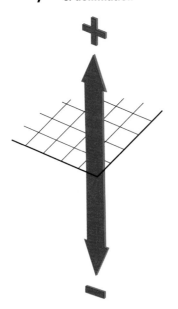

9,1 Fear of failure & helplessness

Positive Motivation

The positive motivation for 9,1 is control and domination in his or her relationships. This positive motivation brings a vital determination and focus to teams wanting to forge ahead to tackle change and increase success. While many people may resist setting high standards and demanding goals, the 9,1 person relishes the challenge. He or she is usually organized and is not afraid to jump in and take initiative regarding strategy, planning, and allocating resources. This is the person who comes to the meeting with a complete strategy already thought through and planned down to the last step for each person involved. This level of personal commitment to results is vital for team success.

However, with the 9,1 approach, others are treated as workers instead of individuals with personal goals, ambitions, and unique abilities. The 9,1 person expects people to treat his or her decisions as final and believes that if everyone would focus on work in the same singular fashion that he or she does, results would soar. The 9,1 person seeks to impose that focus on everyone involved. The low concern for others means that this person is not aware of how his or her approach may have a negative impact on others.

When deviations occur which shift the focus away from results, the 9,1 person seeks to get people back on track as soon as possible rather than openly address the underlying reasons why. He or she is not interested in why a person may have walked off the job, or why one team member repeatedly makes mistakes. The only focus is for the other person to fulfill responsibilities or be removed so the team focus can return to results as soon as possible.

Negative Motivation

The negative motivation for 9,1 is a fear of failure and helplessness. The 9,1 person gambles a great deal on his or her own abilities by forcing them on others. This means that the solutions offered must be strategically sound enough to assure success. This is why a 9,1 person is usually very thorough and methodical in thinking through an issue so that when the solution is presented, it is clear and concise and requires little or no question or discussion. People can simply get down to work.

The message sent through this unilateral approach is, "I have all of the experience and answers needed to achieve success." This attitude cannot be maintained unless he or she can back it up with success. This gamble ultimately creates a high degree of pressure on the 9,1 for the ideas to work, which creates a fear of failure and helplessness. When a 9,1 suffers failures and setbacks, he or she feels vulnerable because people are not as compelled to obey without question the next time.

In order to regain control, the 9,1 person is forced to solicit and consider alternative views when planning strategies, and to appeal to people on a personal level, which is extremely difficult for the 9,1. The low concern for others has kept him or her out of touch with the personal side of R2 relationships including candor, mutual trust and respect, humor, personal feelings, and ambitions. This means the 9,1 person must begin building these skills from a point of disadvantage. This human side of relationships is unknown and intimidating, making the 9,1 feel weak and dependent.

Relationship Skills and 9,1 Controlling Behaviors

CRITIQUE

I give my opinion of others but resist attempts by others to evaluate me. I comment on weaknesses and assign blame so that people learn from their mistakes. I withhold praise because I fear people will become complacent.

The 9,1 approach to critique is one-way. He or she takes strong initiative to point out mistakes, errors, and weaknesses in others. This is meant to instill learning and increase productivity, but it is done in a judgmental fashion that often does not consider the other person's feelings and the personal impact of the comments. He or she may announce errors and problems in a group setting "so that everyone in the group can learn from the mistake at the same time." Although the 9,1 believes this is simply efficient (because one announcement saves time), this approach can be humiliating and *de*structive rather that *con*structive.

The 9,1 approach to critique is one-way because it resists participation from others. These kinds of comments threaten control and credibility, so they are usually cut off, countered, or rationalized away: "You're wrong—and let me tell you why," "I had nothing to do with that," and "You don't know what you're talking about."

Positive comments are withheld by the 9,1 person or given only begrudgingly. He or she expects people to succeed and so sees positive comments as weak and solicitous distractions which risk making people complacent.

INITIATIVE

I clearly understand my responsibilities and take decisive action to demonstrate my determination. I expect others to follow my direction without question. I cut off or suppress conflict that threatens progress.

The 9,1 exercises forceful initiative based on the following fundamental assumptions.

- I already know the best way to proceed.
- I will look weak and risk loss of control if I seek out alternate views.
- I do not trust people to exercise independent initiative.

Enthusiasm and willingness to jump into an activity without reservation characterize 9,1 initiative. He or she thrives on methodical details that others dread when it comes to initiating a project. This is the person who comes to the planning meeting with a clear strategy ready for implementation. However, the low concern for people comes through in the 9,1 approach used for introducing this plan to others involved. Once developed, the plan is announced to others with confidence and determination. The attitude conveyed to everyone else is, "Okay, now that we have this settled, let's get down to work!"

The forcefulness of 9,1 initiative often has a negative effect on others. He or she is often off and running with a project before anyone else has had time to digest the information and develop any kind of shared understanding regarding how to move forward. Others may not understand what he or she is explaining, but feel uncomfortable asking questions. The material covered may encompass an area with which the 9,1 person is extremely familiar but which others are not. The materials may represent new, unfamiliar roles and responsibilities that raise new and unwelcome questions. Regardless of the reason why people feel left behind, the 9,1 person is largely unaware of the impact this kind of initiative has on others. The low concern for others also assures that the 9,1 person is not receptive to the kind of involvement most people need in order to understand and fully contribute to a project or activity.

INQUIRY

I question others but I resist being questioned by others. I ask pointed questions meant to test understanding while also limiting possible responses to only the information I want. I reject inquiry that explores ideas different from my own.

The high concern for results makes the 9,1 person practice inquiry that is focused and detailed but limited by a lack of objective involvement. He or she takes proactive steps to gather information and organize it in ways that support his or her initiative without involving others to the extent that is needed. For example, if the 9,1 leader is responsible for selecting a new office, he or she immediately takes steps to gather information. He or she conducts extensive research to secure a location, but probably never talks to the people who will be working in the new office. What do they need? What problems are they having with the existing office? What would they recommend? These are the people who will ultimately make the new office a success or failure, but consulting them is probably seen as unnecessary and unproductive: "It would be a waste of time. They would probably just complain anyway, and I know what is needed."

9,1 inquiry includes one-way questioning that gathers information but discourages discussion and involvement from others. He or she uses inquiry to gain assurance that those responsible for carrying out initiatives understand the defined responsibilities. The 9,1 maintains control by closely monitoring and questioning people about progress, problems, or misunderstandings, and taking action as needed.

The 9,1 approach to inquiry does not encourage people to engage in a discussion. This one-way inquiry is accomplished by asking questions that promote "yes" or "no" answers or that require a person to simply repeat something to assure understanding. The 9,1 person also discourages inquiry by talking to people in terms that come across as final and not open to discussion. For example, he or she may say, "This is what we need to do," or "You should ... " These kinds of statements do not invite people to challenge or offer new ideas. This is especially true if the 9,1 person is in a position of authority over the people involved. In this case, people tend to follow the lead of the person with authority anyway, so they are even less likely to challenge or question this person.

Such a unilateral approach to inquiry prevents mutual trust and respect from developing in relationships. People become wary of questions for fear of being trapped into admitting something, and the entire team suffers the consequences. What 9,1 perceives as inquiry often feels like interrogation to others. This approach often becomes a barrier to gathering information rather than a way to obtain it. People begin withholding valuable information that could ultimately increase team effectiveness. The attitude that develops is often, "You think you're so smart—figure it out yourself."

ADVOCACY

I express my point of view with authority, conviction, and an air of finality. I resist attempts to challenge or question my point of view. If opposed, I reject other views. I rarely change my mind, even if a more effective alternative emerges.

The 9,1 excels when it comes to advocating convictions. The same valuable determination and focus in taking initiative are present when the 9,1 person advocates a position. There is no holding back or uncertainty of where he or she stands on an issue. Convictions, when expressed, reflect thorough research and rationale, and are based on facts and evidence. Statements are delivered in absolute, even passionate terms that do not invite challenge: "This is the only way," "That will never happen," "Everyone knows," etc.

Convictions are advocated so forcefully as to discourage discussion. Suggestions, opinions, and alternatives are viewed as instigation and are met with counter arguments and criticism, with little regard for the validity of the points being raised. Those who do challenge are often worn down and exhausted by the intensity of counter arguments or criticisms. They frequently give up, feeling that it is not worth the fight. This is especially true if the 9,1 position is one of authority, making people even less willing to challenge or question.

The 9,1 perspective of advocacy is more about winning or losing (control) than about introducing a new perspective for team consideration. This competitive attitude means that even when sounder evidence comes along, it rarely changes 9,1 convictions. Backing off from an opinion looks like uncertainty and weakness, two characteristics that the 9,1 avoids. He or she is often too busy arguing a position to consider the soundness of the views presented. On the rare occasion that convictions do change, the 9,1 concedes begrudgingly, and often with conditions attached: "Fine. If that's the way it's going to be, I guess I have no choice."

DECISION MAKING

I prefer to make decisions alone and announce them to those involved with little discussion. I discourage or cut off attempts to question my judgments or to offer alternatives. If controversy arises, I vigorously defend my decisions.

The 9,1 approach to decision making is one-way, one-sided, and final. The 9,1 brings strength to a team by being unafraid to make tough decisions in timely terms. This makes the 9,1 person invaluable in crisis and problem-solving settings because he or she can be counted on to take action, even under intense pressure.

However, 9,1 decisions are made with little discussion, then proclaimed with an air of finality, specifying clear instructions for everyone involved. Others are considered only in terms of how they will carry out the decision as described. A few questions for clarification are acceptable, but challenges and alternatives are rejected.

The 9,1 person prefers to make decisions alone based on personal knowledge, experience, authority, and responsibility. He or she approaches decisions with a highly focused attitude and follows logical steps valuable in any team setting. This strict, one-alone approach, however, often reflects an incomplete or unrealistic picture of what is needed to implement the decision.

The 9,1 person often does not involve the people responsible for carrying out a decision in the planning stage. He or she may ask indirect questions or ask for a summary report so that necessary information is obtained, but does not involve people in discussions or even tell them why they are being asked to give the information. The rationale is "I know what's best." He or she wants the *facts* from people—not their *opinions*. This approach invites an incomplete picture for the 9,1 decision because people can only respond to issues when they are given a comprehensive overview of the issues involved and the implications of their answers.

CONFLICT RESOLUTION

I see conflict as a threat to productivity. I react by taking control to suppress or cut off conflict so progress can resume.

Conflict threatens control, and so, as with other perceived threats, the 9,1 approach to conflict is to attack rather than seek resolution. The 9,1 suppresses conflict by making decisions in isolation and then taking strong initiative to implement them while forcefully advocating convictions. This approach is meant to leave no room for questions, uncertainty, or mistakes, and maintains 9,1 control.

Fig. 4-4

9,1 Conflict Resolution: CONTROLLING
(Direct & Dominate)

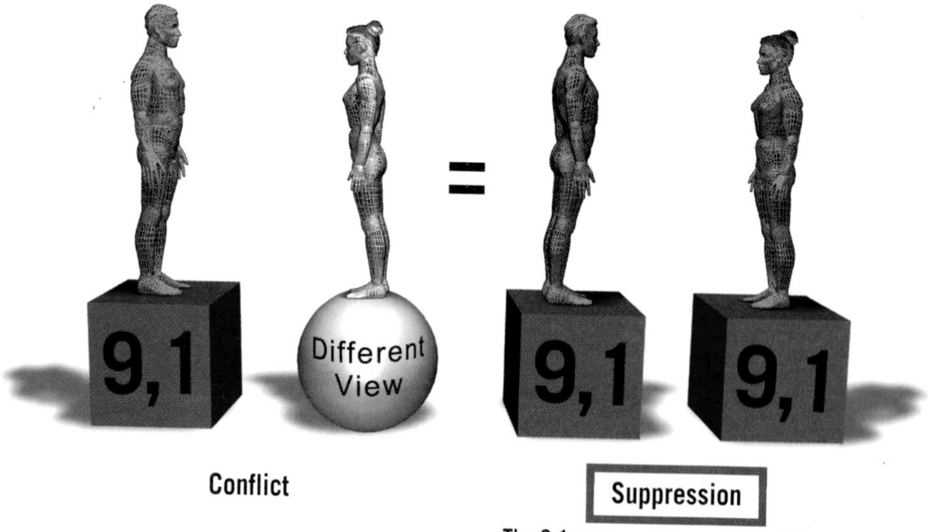

9,1   Different View   =   9,1   9,1

Conflict

Suppression

The 9,1 person suppresses the different point of view. The 9,1 view prevails.

When conflict occurs, the 9,1 seeks first to suppress it so that productivity is not threatened (see Fig. 4-4). This may be done by forcefully restating instructions, along with threats of consequences for noncompliance. Another approach is to simply replace the troublemakers so that work can continue. Still another approach is to reject counter arguments while staunchly defending the 9,1 point of view in an effort to prove others wrong.

The 9,1 is not likely to back down if challenged, so another form of conflict ensues if someone refuses to comply. If the challenger cannot be forced into submission, a standoff results (see Fig. 4-5). Regardless of how sound the challenging view may be, the 9,1 person can't give in for fear of looking weak. Such a standoff is likely when a 9,1 leader cannot use authority to "pull rank" and order compliance.

When conflict cannot be avoided, the 9,1 person attempts to maintain credibility and authority by assigning blame. He or she may do this by singling out those responsible as a warning to others; their punishment may be a demotion, assignment to undesirable duties, or withholding benefits. By doing this, the 9,1 person re-establishes authority and compliance while also instilling fear.

The 9,1 approach overlooks the potential benefits of confronting conflict for resolution. Conflict can be invaluable for clarifying issues and uncovering weaknesses in teamwork, but the 9,1-controlled team never reaches that point because conflict is cut

Fig. 4-5

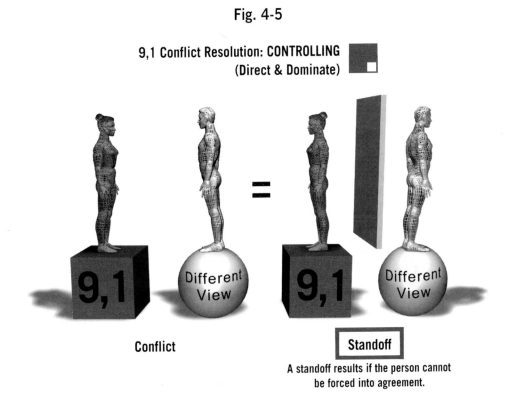

**9,1 Conflict Resolution: CONTROLLING
(Direct & Dominate)**

Conflict

Standoff

A standoff results if the person cannot
be forced into agreement.

off and suppressed. Instead of exploring differences and discussing solutions, the primary focus for the 9,1 is to cut off the conflict and get back to work. To accomplish this, the human aspect of conflict is often overlooked and problems are dealt with in mechanical and impersonal ways. People in disagreement are separated and unhappy people are isolated or removed.

RESILIENCE

*I expect success and persist in focusing my energies on winning.
If confronted with failure, my priority is to deflect responsibility
away from me and redouble my effort to be fully in charge.*

The 9,1 approach to resilience follows the one-way, win-or-lose approach of the other relationship skills. The 9,1 person works hard to assure success by exercising strong initiative, forcefully advocating convictions, and quickly dealing with problems as they arise. He or she often simply outlasts the opposition by remaining focused and determined toward results with relentless counter arguments.

The 9,1 is determined and therefore very resilient as long as setbacks can be handled "mechanically." He or she excels when setbacks can be resolved by changing a procedure, repairing or replacing a piece of equipment, or simply dictating an answer. Resilience flounders when he or she is forced to deal with "human" issues. Problems arise when the failure involves relationship differences that he or she can't control, such as falling productivity due to low morale or employee standoffs.

When failure occurs, the 9,1 first seeks to assign blame and make excuses rather than to acknowledge the failure and move on constructively. The 9,1 person often uses overt statements meant to "rub in" his or her point: "I told you that would happen . . . ," "You should have known . . . ," or "How could you miss such an error?" These statements create distance between the 9,1 person and responsibility for the problem while asserting his or her abilities, experience, and knowledge.

When the failure or setback rests squarely and unequivocally with the 9,1 person, he or she is often devastated and isolated. Without strong relationships with colleagues, he or she cannot rely on a support system to restore and reinforce confidence. In fact, people often relish the opportunity to finally see him or her fail. Sometimes, they even go so far as to seek revenge, making it even more difficult for the 9,1 person to recover from setbacks or failure.

Recognizing 9,1 Controlling Behavior

9,1 behavior may be the easiest of the Grid styles to identify. The style is reminiscent of post-World War II western management where individuals outside the immediate realm of authority had little influence over decisions, policy, and strategy; a few people held sole responsibility for decisions and others were expected to conform. This style is still common in the workplace, but it is much less acceptable in a world that has learned to see the severe limitations of autocratic behavior.

Fig. 4-6 provides key words and phrases that help identify 9,1 behavior. They are presented on the motivation scale to show how the behaviors reflect the positive and negative motivations at work.

Window on 9,1

Steve had enjoyed a successful career at a large dairy. Since getting into management he had progressed rapidly through the ranks, rising to his current position overseeing 360 people as manager of cold storage. He had developed a reputation of being hard on people, but he always got the job done, so the other problems were overlooked. In his new position, however, the "people" problems were starting to surface more and more, especially since he was now charged with the responsibility of designing and constructing a new 4-million dollar, automated cold storage facility.

He began by hiring a team of engineers, architects, and construction people and proceeded to finalize plans. Each updated plan was approved by the executive committee and others above him, but no input was solicited or received from those who were to work in and service the new facility.

Problems arose as news of the intended plans leaked to the employees and they realized that a number of basic design flaws which would significantly affect their working environment would be *built into* the project.

The outflow area for the conveyors from cold storage to shipping did not take into account the increased speeds and was far too small for the anticipated higher volumes. During peak shipping times (early mornings and late afternoons) a large marshaling area was required to facilitate multiple product loading. The existing area was already too small, and to further complicate things, a large new food store chain was coming on-line as a client in one month. In addition, the workers from the floor also raised concerns about pallet sizes, warehouse door sizes, and proposed coolers.

Steve had recently become aware of the need to critique and the value of listening to other points of view. He scheduled a meeting where all concerns and opinions could be formally heard. In doing this, not only were the above problems articulated and addressed, but numerous other issues surfaced that would have delayed the project start time by six months had they gone unrecognized.

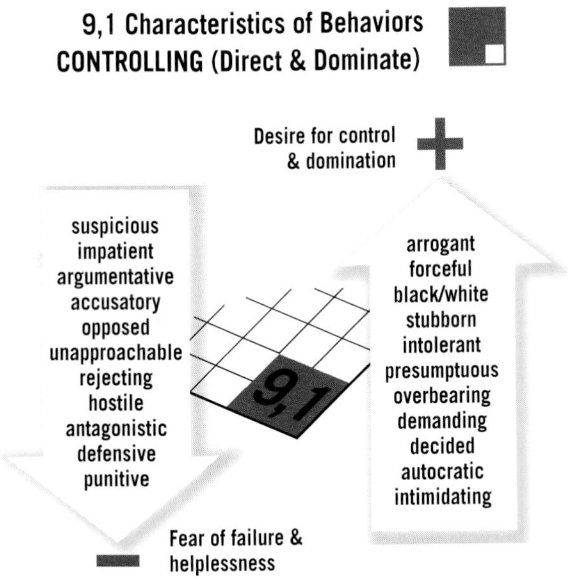

The result of this consultation was at first difficult for Steve to engineer personally, and was a source of frustration with his design team and the board, but resulted in a substantially re-designed cold storage warehouse. In the end, the project was completed on time and $400,000 under budget. The on-time completion was due largely to the cooperation and collaboration of the work force that had to undergo significant dislocation (shift changes, split shift, job changes) during the construction and transition periods. The employees were very enthusiastic about being a part of the decision-making process and motivated to make "their" warehouse work.

Fig. 4-6

9,1 Characteristics of Behaviors
CONTROLLING (Direct & Dominate)

Desire for control & domination **+**

suspicious
impatient
argumentative
accusatory
opposed
unapproachable
rejecting
hostile
antagonistic
defensive
punitive

9,1

arrogant
forceful
black/white
stubborn
intolerant
presumptuous
overbearing
demanding
decided
autocratic
intimidating

Fear of failure & helplessness

The facility opened with only a few minor problems and was producing at 130 percent of designed capacity within three months. In retrospect, it was also discovered that by consulting ahead of time with those who would be most heavily affected by the new design, two major flaws in Steve's original concept had been uncovered and resolved.

- A major conflict with the union, which had been brewing under the surface, was avoided altogether.

- Although Steve's original design was excellent, it simply would not have worked under these particular circumstances.

Steve's willingness to incorporate suggestions from those in a better position to see outcomes proved to be the rallying point behind the success of the entire project. An additional "fringe" benefit turned out to be an increase in employee morale and ownership of the project and tremendous pride in their "team" accomplishment.

Summary

The 9,1 person brings determination, focus, and capability to teams. This person can be counted on to get results in the short term, but the overly forceful attitude and narrow focus have negative effects on relationships. The low concern for people often works against the vital resources that he or she can bring to the team. The 9,1 person appears fearless, not afraid to speak up, and not afraid to tackle tough issues and make tough decisions. He or she is organized, seemingly thorough, and advocates convictions with confidence, even passion.

The low concern for people, however, can work against the high concern for results in two distinct ways. First, the 9,1 person is unaware of the value that involving people on a relationship level can bring to a team. The primary focus is on taking R1 resources directly to R3 results. The contribution others can make in terms of offering creative ideas, mutual trust and respect, and personal support (R2 relationships) is overlooked. This means that valuable 9,1 determination and drive are often based on a narrow and incomplete picture of how to achieve sound results. The second way the 9,1 person's low concern for people can work against results is through the alienation of others by implementing unilateral decisions that impact them directly. Rather than feeling strong personal commitment and a personal stake in results, others feel only a distant connection with the work they are expected to carry out.

The 1,9 Style: Accommodating (Yield & Comply)

Overview

The 1,9-oriented style is found in the upper left corner of the Grid figure (see Fig. 5-1). This person demonstrates a low concern for results with a high concern for people. The high concern for people brings to teams a valuable quality for building relationships. The individual operating from a 1,9 orientation maintains a heightened awareness of personal feelings, goals, and ambitions of others, and always considers how proposed actions will affect them. He or she is approachable, fun, friendly, and always ready to listen with sympathy and encouragement. The interdependent low concern for results, however, works against the high concern for others in the workplace by shifting the focus away from work achievement. This makes the relationships, although warm and friendly, too shallow and superficial for synergy to occur because full candor is lacking.

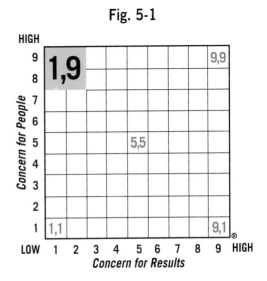

Fig. 5-1

1,9 Grid Style: ACCOMMODATING (Yield & Comply)

I support results that establish and reinforce harmony. I generate enthusiasm by focusing on positive and pleasing aspects of work.

This leads to individuals and teams that are ultimately unprepared for the kind of challenges that arise in the pursuit of improved productivity and change.

The 1,9 and 9,1 styles are diametrically opposed in their perspectives. Each of these orientations leads in a narrow and singularly focused manner by trying to diminish the other primary concern in the workplace. The Achilles' heel in 1,9 thinking is, "As long as I'm keeping people happy, they respond by working hard to achieve results." The evidence shows the opposite: relationships suffer when employees are not challenged in the workplace. People become bored with work and frustrated with each other because something is missing in the relationships. Further, productivity decreases when the concern for results is low.

Some cornerstone phrases of the 1,9 attitude are "Let's talk about it. What can I do to help? Let me know what you think." The main weakness, however, lies in the *focus* of the discussions. Instead of focusing discussions in specific terms of causes and solutions, 1,9 discussions include an overwhelming emphasis on personal feelings and preferences. The *discussion itself* becomes the goal, so conversations can meander in any direction. If an individual is angry, the 1,9 person follows the comments and offers sympathy and encouragement whenever appropriate. If an individual is pleased, the 1,9 person offers compliments and celebration. He or she uses discussions to constantly gauge morale levels and quickly offer encouragement, support, and praise as needed.

1,9 Accommodating Style at the Team Level

The following examples represent typical 1,9 responses in the workplace.

> The 1,9 response when a team member fails to accomplish his or her share of the workload:

> *Since the 1,9 avoids conflict at all costs, the first approach will probably be to address the problem at a personal level. The focus of the conversation is not on resolving the problem itself, but on what can be done to ease the tension. The 1,9 belief is that by talking to the team member on a personal level, he or she will feel more motivated to contribute. However, the actual lack of contribution may never be addressed directly in hopes that the gentle hints and suggestions given help the other person "figure it out" alone. Even if the problem is repeated, direct confrontation is seldom used. When team members are unhappy, the 1,9 individual may even take on the burden of completing the slacking person's share of work to ease tension. If direct confrontation cannot be avoided, the 1,9 abdicates responsibility by delegating action or by making any action taken so weak as to be inoffensive—and ultimately unlikely to produce change.*

> The 1,9 response to constructive critique by a team member:

> *The 1,9 reacts by apologizing for the mistake, with possible self-criticism: "I feel terrible for letting you down. That was stupid of me." This reaction assures that no one will see this leader as argumentative or disagreeable. He or she then asks for and praises alternative views, and encourages others to decide the best way to move forward.*

The 1,9 team is one that has a lot of fun, but does not reach its potential for results. Members do not believe that relationships can survive conflict, and so constantly work to maintain a pleasant environment. 1,9 teams want everyone to be happy, and so spend a great deal of time discussing how each member feels. Differences are smoothed over, disagreements are solved with positive encouragement, and any accomplishment is cause for celebration. The attitude of the 1,9 culture is, "If you can't say anything nice, don't say anything at all." This may seem effective in the short term, but in the long term, being able to resolve conflict and overcome adversity motivates people on a deeper, more personal level and encourages even greater commitment and accountability. Full candor strengthens relationships more than praise alone ever can.

The overwhelming focus on people and relationships creates a 1,9 culture where team members are out of touch with hard facts, business acumen, and logic. Teams are unprepared to react to, confront, and resolve problems effectively because they are afraid to face the controversy that may ensue. Continuous praise also leaves members feeling overconfident about their performance, and thus farther out of touch with their actual effectiveness. Since ineffective behavior is played down or completely overlooked, team members unwittingly perpetuate bad behavior and mistakes until conditions deteriorate and their actions have serious consequences.

Complacency is another key feature in 1,9 relationships. Teams take on the quality of a "mutual admiration society," offering constant praise and encouragement. Individual and team accomplishments are celebrated, but in shallow terms that do not focus on specific learning strategies or criteria. Instead, the focus is on offering support and encouragement, even if actions were flawed or results were less than expected. Members who try to confront ineffectiveness are thought to be "bringing the team down" or "trying to hurt the people involved," and are often ignored or somehow isolated from the rest of the team. With complacency, malaise sets in as members increasingly feel unchallenged and unmotivated.

R2 Relationships and the 1,9 Accommodating Style

The 1,9 style leads to relationships that are warm and friendly, but are more superficial than strong relationships based on mutual trust, respect, and candor. Colleagues may work side by side for years and talk every day, but often remain as near-stranger acquaintances, because mutual trust and respect is low.

The 1,9 person is a constant source of praise. Even when an idea posed is unrealistic or unsound, he or she is not likely to issue a challenge. "Find something nice to say about it," is the attitude. Relationships always come first, are kept on a friendly level, and are focused on keeping individuals happy. This makes conflict a dramatic obstacle to overcome because people are so afraid of losing approval and acceptance. Teams scramble to smooth over differences by holding parties or other positive distractions in the face of unpleasantness. The stronger personal relationships become, the less likely people are to confront problems. Their attitude is, "I don't want to jeopardize the strong relationship we have; I don't want to alienate anyone" (see Fig. 5-2).

Inability to confront ineffectiveness and problems in relationships leads to reduced R3 results. Valuable resources are left on the table as teams move ahead without exploring differences and taking calculated risks. As a consequence, teams never achieve the powerful, motivating experience of reaching the other side of a problem; therefore they

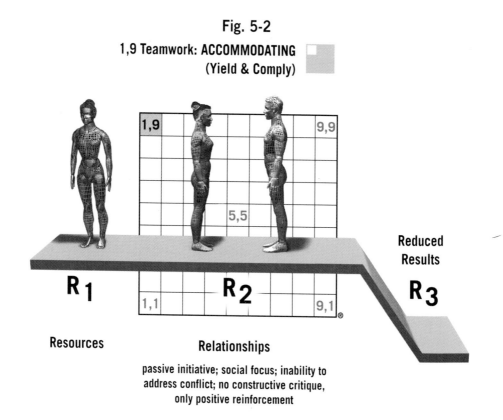

Fig. 5-2

1,9 Teamwork: ACCOMMODATING
(Yield & Comply)

passive initiative; social focus; inability to
address conflict; no constructive critique,
only positive reinforcement

never experience sound resolution and synergy. Instead, the 1,9 person treats relationships as if they were fragile dolls that would break if handled incorrectly.

1,9 Accommodating Motivations

When it comes to expressing concern for people and results, the 1,9 person sees the reverse perspective from the 9,1 person. The 1,9 believes that expressing a high concern for results reduces the ability to achieve sound relationships, and so works to promote a "good enough" attitude regarding results (see Fig. 5-3). This attitude is seen in 1,9 motivations as a desire for agreement and approval and a fear of rejection and abandonment.

Positive Motivation

The 1,9 person desires agreement and approval from others. He or she is a nurturer who wants everyone to be happy, and expresses this by focusing attention on relationships. He or she puts people first, above any other concern in the workplace. Successful R3 results for a 1,9 person are measured by the satisfaction of others, so he or she constantly works to please. This is accomplished by making himself or herself available at any cost, and always offering support and encouragement, even at the expense of work production. This may even be done to the point of being a martyr for others, but without manipulation; the desire to please is genuine. The 1,9 person offers services, help, and even makes personal sacrifices in order to gain the agreement and approval of others and to maintain happiness.

This motivation creates a selfless approach that often makes the 1,9 person come across as over-enthusiastic and solicitous. As a result, colleagues can find him or her an easy target, often taking advantage because the 1,9 person doesn't usually fight back. He or she is too motivated to please others to cause a disturbance.

Negative Motivation

The 1,9 negative motivation is fear of rejection and abandonment. One of the most difficult actions for a 1,9 person is to stand in the face of controversy and endure anger and criticism from others. Even when the anger and criticism does not involve the 1,9 person, he or she wants to restore peace.

Fig. 5-3

1,9 Motivations: ACCOMMODATING (Yield & Comply)

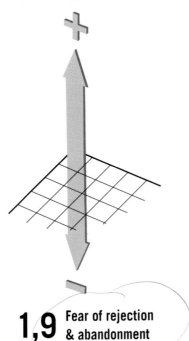

1,9 Desire for agreement & approval

1,9 Fear of rejection & abandonment

The 1,9 fear of rejection and abandonment comes across most apparently in behaviors regarding critique and feedback on performance. Personal feelings of regret overwhelm discussions regarding personal weaknesses. Any form of critique that does not include positive praise, even when constructive and well intended, is taken as rejection by the 1,9 person. This is also true when giving any negative critique to others. The 1,9 person has difficulty addressing personal weakness or failure and often smothers comments in praise so that any constructive learning is hidden. For example, "You worked very hard on that project. The results were a little less than we expected, but I'm sure we can make up for it next time," is the kind of comment that leaves a person thinking, "Gee, I did pretty well after all."

The 1,9 person's worst-case, most feared scenario is that relationships and all of the efforts that went into them will be lost as people abandon him or her due to a mistake, flaw or failure. Rather than enduring and exploring the comments as opportunities for improvement, the 1,9 expresses guilt and regret for letting others down. He or she makes immediate efforts to regain agreement. Statements made are often over-solicitous and self-critical. For example: "I don't know how I could have done something like that," "What was I thinking? I should have bounced this off you before I started," or "This is all my fault." These kinds of statements are meant to motivate others to reassure the 1,9 person that everything is okay because he or she has regained the coveted approval of others.

The 1,9 negative motivation overlooks the opportunities for learning in conflict. The problem, weakness, or failure is smoothed over and quickly put in the past with as little discussion as possible so those in conflict can begin mending the relationship. Once the 1,9 person recovers, team members no longer want to go through the ordeal of offering anything other than positive critique. They may opt to overlook weaknesses or address them indirectly since direct critique is too devastating for the 1,9 person to accept objectively.

Relationship Skills and 1,9 Accommodating Behaviors

CRITIQUE

I give encouragement and offer praise when something positive happens but avoid saying anything negative. I appreciate positive critique and apologize when I have to say anything negative.

The 1,9 person uses positive critique in an active and ongoing way. The high concern for people makes him or her critique actions spontaneously in order to maintain awareness of morale. This is accomplished by being available and approachable for discussion on a one-to-one basis. As a leader, he or she establishes an "open-door policy" and encourages colleagues to come and talk anytime. No problem is too small. The 1,9 is quick to recognize and acknowledge accomplishment, notice problems, and offer support. He or she is also valuable for anticipating what people feel and for offering sympathy and help. This approach makes the 1,9 person appealing to others because he or she listens to and has high regard for them.

The quality and depth of 1,9 critique is limited to an overwhelming focus on personal feelings, morale, and preferences. Specific criteria for accomplishment and standards of excellence are rarely included. As a result, most discussions are conducted in a limited way by focusing on only one side of the work process. Comments are limited to positive aspects of work. When individuals express concern or unhappiness, the 1,9 serves as a cheerleader. He or she cheers them up, persuades them to focus on positive aspects of the current conditions, and builds confidence to overcome the problem. The basic attitude is "grin and bear it." This effort is meant to smooth over differences rather than confront them for resolution.

If the cheerleading approach is unsuccessful, the 1,9 backs away from further involvement. He or she offers sympathy but avoids engaging in any discussion that threatens peace and harmony. At this point, the 1,9 person will attempt to create as much distance as possible from the controversy to avoid looking responsible. He or she listens but encourages people to resist taking actions that may cause problems. The 1,9 person will go to great lengths to create this distance by remaining "blind, deaf, and dumb" to negative actions rather than critiquing them openly.

This narrow view is reinforced by the ongoing and always positive critique. The more problems arise, the harder the 1,9 person works to compensate by building confidence and pointing out strengths in other areas. Personal weakness and ineffectiveness are overlooked, and teammates are told how talented, skilled, and valued they are. Negative critique—even when constructive, sincere, and supported—is discouraged because it represents the possibility for rejection. When mistakes and problems cannot be overlooked, the critique focuses on building the the the other person's confidence with comments like, "You had a small and insignificant setback but you're so talented. I wouldn't worry about it at all." This glossing over of problems leaves people misinformed and provides little opportunity for improvement.

INITIATIVE

I invest time securing the approval of others before taking action. I exercise initiative enthusiastically when the issues promote a pleasant experience, and when team-wide support is evident. I will abandon or divert initiatives when conflict arises.

The 1,9 person exercises strong initiative when it comes to reinforcing relationships and taking care of people. This person demonstrates a keen awareness of people and their needs and doesn't hesitate to take action that helps others. The 1,9 is also first in line to initiate actions regarding well-received activities like announcing achievements, bonuses, pay increases, new hires, and capital expenditures. These are actions that he or she does for the others and that are undertaken with pride and enthusiasm.

The 1,9 person resists taking initiative when controversy is involved and prefers to let others take charge in settings where controversies are likely to develop. This prevents him or her from being connected with any activity that may cause resentment, rejection, or abandonment. The 1,9 is also reluctant to take proactive initiative in other areas because he or she does not want to be seen as pushy. The preferred approach to taking initiative is to talk to people first to find out what they want and then take action based on that information. What people want is always preferred over what is best, regardless of the negative effect the actions may have on R3 results. The 1,9 person is willing to lose R3 results if it means keeping relationships intact.

The message 1,9 initiative gives to others is, "I value your opinion more than my own judgment." As a result of 1,9 fears, initiative often comes across as weak, tentative, or reluctant in statements like, "This idea may not work, but I'm just going to make the suggestion," or "I'll tell you what I'm thinking, but stop me if you don't agree." These kinds of statements allow the person to back away from an idea whenever conflict arises, to avoid being held responsible. He or she gains approval by asking questions like, "I was thinking about doing this, but want to know what you think?" and "What do you think I should do?" The initiative taken flows from whatever course will cause the least amount of controversy, and will make people happy.

The 1,9 person does not incorporate strict standards of excellence when taking initiative. The overwhelming concern for people keeps the 1,9 person out of touch with resources, innovation, and bold trends. Standards of excellence and specific criteria for success also represent pressure on people that he or she is reluctant to impose. Instead, the 1,9 person presents a positive and often watered-down view of what is expected while offering encouragement and support to achieve these standards. Unappealing standards or criteria which are considered over-demanding are often overlooked or omitted by the 1,9 person. The rationale is that he or she is protecting the people involved by not worrying them with these kinds of details. If overtime is expected, for example, the 1,9 person may think, "It probably won't be necessary anyway, so why mention it?" Keeping criteria and standards of excellence very loose decreases the odds that *any* initiative others take will be seen in a negative light. If standards are low and loose enough, it follows that there is less necessity for constructive critique. This, in turn, gives the *appearance* of more positive actions that can then be praised by the 1,9 person.

INQUIRY

I inquire in an informal way to enhance morale and friendliness among team members. I seek out and encourage discussion about information that creates positive feelings. I discourage inquiry that surfaces negative or controversial issues. I embrace inquiry and opinions different from my own, even if I disagree.

The 1,9 approach to inquiry is valuable for building strong relationships in the workplace and addressing change efforts. He or she makes it a point to talk with people often, asking many questions in a friendly and open way to stay in touch with morale levels. This enables the 1,9 person to maintain a deeper understanding of where people stand on issues and to anticipate how they are likely to react to specific actions. The goal of 1,9 inquiry, however, weakens its effectiveness. The fundamental objective of 1,9 inquiry is *not* to evaluate soundness, but to assure that agreement and approval continue. The 1,9 person actively uses inquiry in the workplace to address the fundamental question, "What do you think of me?" rather than, "What is the best course of action?" Questions asked express sympathy, understanding, and encouragement by focusing on each person as an individual. This is accomplished by spending a great deal of time talking with people about what they want, think, and feel.

As with initiative, the 1,9 person uses inquiry to discern what actions are acceptable and then takes initiative accordingly. The 1,9 practices an indirect approach to avoid coming across as pushy or accusatory. If someone makes a mistake on a project, the 1,9 person does not make a direct inquiry. He or she first addresses how that person feels about what happened in order to react in a way that offers support and encouragement: "I heard there was some kind of problem this morning?" This allows the 1,9 to let the other person define the course of the discussion. The best-case scenario for the 1,9 is for the other person to admit to the problem first. When this happens, the 1,9 can completely avoid saying anything negative, and can move right into restoring morale: "I'm sure it wasn't that bad. I know how hard you worked. This is a small glitch!"

This indirect approach to inquiry wastes time by waiting for others to volunteer information they may not even be aware of and usually leaves the 1,9 uninformed or misinformed. This indirect approach to inquiry leads the 1,9 to make inferences about what people think and feel instead of basing reactions on facts and logic. Since only positive remarks feel safe, the 1,9 is likely to edit what was said to put a positive spin on findings: "He is a little disappointed in the results, but feels very optimistic and enthusiastic about the steps taken now," or "I don't think we have anything to worry about. All of the differences have been worked out."

ADVOCACY

I advocate ideas openly and with conviction when they support friendly relations and positive benefits for the people involved. When opposition is evident, I withhold my convictions or attempt to smooth over any differences.

The 1,9 person advocates convictions with passion and enthusiasm when the outcome clearly boosts morale and strengthens relationships. He or she expresses deep convictions and loyalty to people and relationships and serves as a crusader and "defender of the people" in teams by fighting for salary and other benefits. The 1,9 sees to it that colleagues are recognized for achievement and offers help in any way necessary.

When issues involve controversy or conflict, 1,9 advocacy is weak. The 1,9 person resists advocating his or her own position in the face of controversy until support (acceptance and approval) is evident. This approach often slows progress as the 1,9 person assesses everyone's personal feelings regarding an issue. Another reason this approach is slower is because discussions do not center on specific criteria for standards of excellence. Instead of focusing on *how* and *what* people will accomplish in specific terms, 1,9 discussions center on personal preferences and opinions. This leaves little opportunity for a deliberate, shared effort toward results because people are operating on independent assumptions. The alternative of working to develop shared assumptions about what is expected and how to get there is too risky for the 1,9 person.

The 1,9 person further protects relationships by asking people for advice before advocating a position: "What do you think I should do?" "I want to know what you think before I make any statements," and "I value your opinion and don't want to do anything to damage our friendship." These kinds of statements make it clear to others that peace and harmony are the overriding concerns.

Even when support is evident and the 1,9 person feels confident, advocacy expressed is further weakened by the 1,9 fear of appearing pushy. The result is that he or she comes across to others as tentative, even wishy-washy, with statements like, "This is only a suggestion..." or "This may sound ridiculous..." Statements often include qualifying words: perhaps, maybe, possibly, by chance, etc. This tentativeness makes it easier for the 1,9 person to back off of a position if controversy arises.

DECISION MAKING

I rarely make decisions without discussing issues at length with others first to find out how they feel. I make decisions with an emphasis on considering the impact on the people involved. I delay or delegate controversial decisions that could jeopardize relationships.

1,9 decisions are slow in coming unless a positive response is obvious and no obstacles are in the way of implementation. In all other circumstances, the decision-making process is slowed down by lengthy discussions, often with more people than necessary, and without clear criteria in place. As a result discussions float along, taking whatever course emerges. A meeting to decide on a new software package can easily turn into a two-hour discussion on many topics because there is no structure or criteria in place. The 1,9 person wants as many people as possible to approve of the decision before taking a risk. To accomplish this, he or she spends a great deal of time asking questions and soliciting advice. This process is carried out until the 1,9 feels confident that there is adequate support for a decision.

The 1,9 person is dependent on others when it comes to decision making. He or she prefers to have criteria defined by higher-ranking people in order to distance himself or herself from personal responsibility. This relieves the 1,9 from having to suffer the consequences of a contestable decision.

The 1,9 person often feels torn between this desire for authority and loyalty to others when it comes to making decisions. He or she wants to make decisions that please team members and subordinates, but that also satisfy the requirements of higher-ranking authority. Since the concern for individual relationships is strong, decisions more often benefit team members and subordinates with whom he or she is directly and more closely involved.

When decisions involve controversy, 1,9 decision making becomes even slower or stalls altogether. If discussions reveal problems, the 1,9 person searches for alternatives that colleagues will accept. This invariably involves more discussions, usually on a one-on-one basis, to plead a case and solicit approval. This entire process is stressful and draining on everyone as decisions are delayed and often diluted. When a peaceful alternative cannot be found, the 1,9 person may take several courses:

- make a decision which serves the people involved but sacrifices R3 results;

- postpone the decision and hope it's forgotten; or

- delegate the decision to an outsider, allowing the 1,9 person to "wash his or her hands" of responsibility for whatever fallout may follow.

CONFLICT RESOLUTION

I avoid generating disagreement and avoid conflict whenever possible. I attempt to divert attention away from conflict when it arises by offering encouragement, comfort, and reassurance.

Conflict pacification is a more appropriate description of the 1,9 approach than is conflict resolution. Conflict is avoided by encouraging support and agreement and by rarely disagreeing; this is accomplished by staying in touch with morale levels and offering reassurance when needed. Even when he or she disagrees, the 1,9 may yield to other views in order to maintain harmony. Conflict itself is rarely explored or evaluated based on the facts involved or the merits of the differences. Instead, the 1,9 person considers conflict "resolved" when people are placated (see Fig. 5-4).

Fig. 5-4

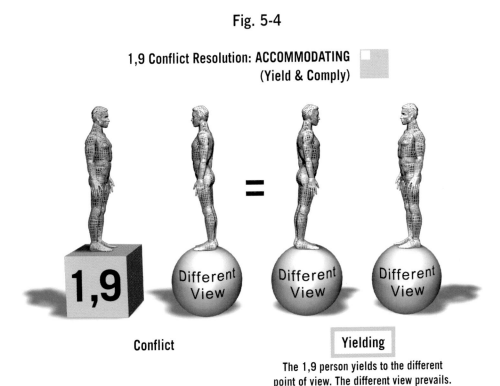

1,9 Conflict Resolution: ACCOMMODATING (Yield & Comply)

1,9

Different View — Different View — Different View

Conflict

Yielding

The 1,9 person yields to the different point of view. The different view prevails.

When conflict cannot be avoided, the 1,9 person first attempts to smooth over hard feelings between colleagues. He or she is very persuasive and creative in convincing people to shift attention onto the positive aspects of issues so that conflict does not erupt. This may include making excuses to discount or minimize problems: "He's been under tremendous pressure," or "I know that's not what she meant." Attention may be diverted to less controversial subjects with lighthearted humor: "Hey, don't be so serious!" Another approach includes a campaign for tolerance: "It's hard enough to survive around here so let's focus on supporting each other," and "Can't we let this go for now?" Finally, the 1,9 person may personally offer to take the blame or make up for the problems in order to reestablish cooperation and good will.

When attempts to smooth over differences fail, the 1,9 creates distance from the conflict by abdicating responsibility with statements like, "I had nothing to do with this," or "This decision was out of my hands." The 1,9 person sees conflict as the ultimate threat to good relationships.

The 1,9 person sees no benefit in strengthening relationships through confronting conflict. Even when the 1,9 knows a conflict exists, he or she takes comfort in maintaining even temporary or superficial peace, rather than enduring open antagonism. The overwhelming attitude is, "We can deal with that later," or "Maybe they just need some time to cool off."

Another factor in 1,9 behavior is the "see no evil, hear no evil, speak no evil" approach, where ineffectiveness and problems are hidden or ignored and thus not subject to discussion. This unwillingness to confront problems often results in more serious consequences later.

1,9 conflict resolution is made more difficult because teams rarely sit down and define clear criteria for performance ahead of time. They prefer to begin work with positive enthusiasm and feel that planning strategies and strict criteria lower that enthusiasm. The attitude is "If people are talented and enthusiastic, everything else will fall into place." As a result of the lack of sound criteria, a comment or action is more likely to sound like a personal opinion rather than a description of specific behavior that deviates from what everyone agreed was acceptable. This makes confronting ineffectiveness more difficult because members have no standards against which to compare ineffective behavior. For example, if members feel someone is not doing his or her fair share of the work, that person, if confronted, can easily say, "Says who? Where does it say that I had to do this?"

RESILIENCE

I am thrilled by success and take great joy in celebrations with others. When confronted with failure, I feel personally responsible and guilty for letting others down and seek to make everyone feel better. I have trouble overcoming setbacks without support and encouragement from others.

1,9 resilience is fragile and can be described as "high maintenance" in terms of the level of effort needed to maintain it. The 1,9 person can always be counted on to make people feel better in the face of setbacks and failure. This quality makes him or her valuable for building morale and restoring confidence in others following problems. The 1,9 is generous with encouragement and praise, and always takes time to find benefits within losses and to recognize individual contributions and achievement.

The level of resilience expressed by the 1,9 regarding his or her own performance, however, depends on the level of support expressed by others involved. If colleagues are sympathetic and supportive, the 1,9 can bounce back with restored confidence and move on. Without that support, the sense of failure and guilt paralyze the 1,9 person from being able to move forward.

1,9 lack of resilience is evident during activities in the form of insecure comments and solicitations for approval. He or she interrupts progress to assure continued agreement and approval with statements like, "Is this going okay?" or "I was thinking about doing this. Would that be all right?"

When the 1,9 person suffers setbacks, guilt and shame prevent coworkers from being able to provide constructive criticism because he or she is already taking it so hard. A 1,9 seeks support by expressing self-criticism and guilt for letting others down. The message heard is, "I can't bear criticism." Because of this, team efforts can come to a complete standstill while members stop to bolster confidence and offer reassurance to a 1,9 person instead of offering constructive comments. Eventually, co-workers often learn to "work around" a 1,9 person to avoid upsetting him or her with bad news.

Recognizing 1,9 Accommodating Behavior

The 1,9 represents a kinder, gentler, and less challenging workplace. Although others may feel comfortable and content in the short view, the likelihood for personal reward through contribution is limited. Beyond feeling understood and appreciated, people want to be challenges and make a contribution with their skills and talents. The 1,9 suppresses the concern for results which creates such challenges and instead creates relationships where individuals are complacent and afraid to take risks and confront problems.

Fig. 5-5 provides key words and phrases that help identify 1,9 behavior. They are presented on the motivation scale to show how the behaviors reflect the positive and negative motivations at work.

Fig. 5-5

1,9 Characteristics of Behaviors
ACCOMMODATING (Yield & Comply)

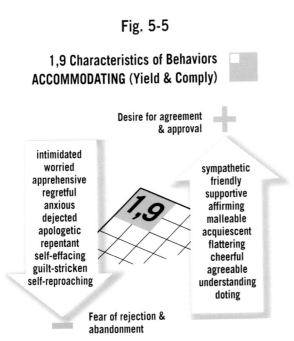

Window on 1,9

John had been in the investment business for 13 years. He began as a stockbroker and progressed through three management positions up to a partnership in the firm where he managed a division of seven offices and 75 people. He was clever, articulate, and humorous. Though he had a serious side and could work hard, most people thought of him as a good guy and a great person to have at a party. He saw himself as a hard driving young executive who had done very well for himself until one day when his boss asked for his resignation.

He wasn't able to make sense of this decision until a year later when he found himself receiving feedback from a group of people and began for the first time to see himself as others saw him: yielding and compliant. For example, they said, "Whenever you get into a crunch (conflict), you back off," and "You are engaging and persuasive, but you seem to avoid making the tough 'people' decisions." At first this revelation was extremely difficult for him to accept. He had a great deal invested in his own self-image; seeing himself as 1,9 was unpleasant, humiliating, and hard on his ego.

However, the more he opened up to this point of view, the more sense it made. His fear of rejection, avoidance of conflict, and his difficulty in taking a strong position and sticking to it were characteristics of his behavior that became more and more apparent as he reviewed his career. His persuasiveness and creativity had gotten him out of jams at lower levels of management, but as the stakes rose in his business career, he could see how his inability to make tough decisions regarding people had seriously undermined his effectiveness.

In retrospect, it was precisely because he was so well-liked by everybody that he lasted as long as he did in his last position. In fact, he spent more time projecting himself as fair and a "good guy" than he did on determining the soundest actions. He never got mad and was always ready to have another conversation with someone about his or her low production to see if he could help. He went to great lengths to avoid conflict. "There were times when I would see a pattern emerging for conflict to erupt around a situation weeks ahead of time, and so I would make arrangements to be out of town."

Some years later, John talks now about "being able to hold the tension." "Sometimes it takes only a matter of seconds to look someone in the eye and say, 'No, we are not going to do that.' They *feel* your intention, accept your position, and together, you begin looking at other alternatives. I couldn't do that before. What's even more amazing is that nine times out of ten, the other person just says, 'Oh, okay. Well, let's find another way.' Before, I would have expended an inordinate amount of effort to avoid confrontations that might have been over in a matter of seconds!"

John says now that the moment he was able to see himself as 1,9 was the moment he also began to become a more effective leader. He laughs and says, "It's a long journey, and I'm still working on it. The tendency to give in is still there. I'm just able to recognize it now and adjust accordingly."

Summary

The 1,9 person makes a valuable contribution to any work place by focusing attention on the "human" side of leadership and change. This perspective is vital for building the kinds of relationships that must be in place to meet the challenge of change and achieve synergy. Most companies underestimate the power of individual influence on the process of change, but the 1,9 person sees it with "super-defined" clarity. He or she knows the value of maintaining an awareness of how people feel, their personal opinions, goals and ambitions, and to what degree they feel like they "fit in" to corporate objectives. The 1,9 also knows how important it is to have teammates support you when introducing any change if that effort is going to work.

Like the 9,1 approach, however, the overwhelming concern in one area weakens concern in the other. This inevitably backfires, negatively affecting results. Both concerns are always present in a team setting. Neither concern can be eliminated without crippling a team's ability to achieve both high quality results *and* individual team member satisfaction.

Just as the 9,1 person tries to take R1 resources directly to R3 results, the 1,9 person does the opposite. The 1,9 approach tries to ignore the R1 resources and get to R3 results with R2 relationships as the starting point. Both styles view the concerns as working against each other in the workplace. The 1,9 person believes the only way to get results is through strong relationships. What happens, however, is just the opposite. The more effort expended to protect individuals from conflict and to build up a picture-perfect relationship, the more disappointing the relationships become. Like spoiled children, people become bored with ongoing praise and long for more challenge. As time passes, 1,9 teams lose touch with how their behavior impacts others. All they hear is how great they are. This makes it even harder to take harsh reality when it hits.

The 5,5 Style: Status Quo (Balance & Compromise)

Overview

The 5,5-oriented style is located in the middle of the Grid figure, indicating a medium level of concern for both people and results (see Fig. 6-1). Like the 9,1 Controlling and the 1,9 Accommodating styles, the person operating from a 5,5 orientation believes there is an inherent contradiction between the two concerns. But unlike 9,1 and 1,9, neither concern is valued over the other. Instead, the 5,5 person sees a high level of either concern for people or results as too extreme and takes actions to moderate both in the workplace. This is accomplished by balancing the needs of people with the need for results through compromises and tradeoffs. The overwhelming attitude is, "Good enough or a little better is okay."

The objective of the 5,5 person is to play it safe and work toward *acceptable* solutions that follow proven methods. This is a politically-motivated approach that seeks to avoid risk by maintaining the tried and true course that follows popular opinion and norms. The 5,5 does not *strive* to settle for less, or to reduce R3 results, but that is what happens as a consequence of the 5,5 approach. Creativity, personal commitment, and mutual trust and respect are found only at the high end (level 9) of concerns. These characteristics are found in the kind of strong convictions, bold ideas, disagreements, and deep commitment people experience when

Fig. 6-1

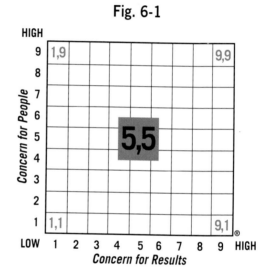

5,5 Grid Style: STATUS QUO
(Balance & Compromise)

I endorse results that are popular but caution against taking unnecessary risk. I test my opinions with others involved to assure ongoing acceptability.

sound relationships are in place. These qualities are diluted in the 5,5 approach through an overdependence on these criteria:

- relying on history, precedent, and past practices to guide action;

- following the majority rule and popular opinion; and

- adhering to the norms and standards in place whether they are sound or not.

The 5,5 person is often the best informed person in the team. He or she reads company policies, periodicals, and other sources of information, and maintains a historical knowledge of events. A 5,5 can often quote detailed history at length and is well-versed regarding existing reservations, doubts, and dangers. The 5,5 person also tracks norms by regularly observing and talking to people about progress and expectations. All of these efforts can provide strength in evaluating a calculated risk and in progressing at an acceptable pace. These efforts are weakened, however, because the information gathered is not used to challenge standards and search for creative solutions. The objective is to identify popular patterns and trends in order to maintain the *status quo.*

Another key aspect of the 5,5 approach is maintaining popular status within the team and organization. He or she must be intelligent and informed enough to persuade people and companies to settle for less than they want—less than they could achieve. This is done by being well liked, staying well informed, and effectively convincing people that the consequences are not worth the risk. On the surface, this may make the 5,5 appear unbiased and impartial, but more accurately, the 5,5 approach represents a narrow view that underestimates people, results, *and* the power of change.

5,5 Status Quo Style at the Team Level

The following examples represent typical 5,5 responses in the workplace.

The 5,5 response when a team member fails to accomplish his or her share of the workload:

The 5,5 person waits before addressing the problem, hoping it corrects itself. Any action taken is indirect and diluted. For example, a 5,5 leader may call a meeting and raise an issue indirectly, saying, "It has come to my attention that our team has fallen below expectations. Does anyone have any comments?" This kind of platform allows him or her to raise the issue without taking responsibility for instigating conflict or singling out anyone. He or she hopes someone else speaks up instead. If the 5,5 person is singled out or addressed directly, he or she avoids providing specific critique and defers to company rules and policies. Another approach of the 5,5 may be to ask the group how to move forward. This way, if an unpopular idea emerges, he or she is not responsible for bringing it up.

The 5,5 response to constructive critique from a team member:

> *The 5,5 person avoids negative critique by retreating to the safety net created by majority thinking. This is accomplished by presenting the majority (or authority-directed) idea to the group and then asking for others' opinions. This makes the 5,5 feel less responsible for personally advocating an unpopular proposal. If the majority supports the point made, the 5,5 endorses that directive. If the idea presented is unpopular with some team members, he or she encourages the minority to compromise toward the majority view for the sake of progress.*

The 5,5 person is friendly and approachable in teams, but often operates as a facilitator instead of a true team member. This role allows him or her to relate to people as equals while also maintaining the safe distance of an authority figure. He or she talks to people frequently, especially on a one-to-one basis, in order to maintain an understanding of current politics, progress, and expectations. As a facilitator, the 5,5 person can step in and mediate when people start to waiver from the "proven" path. This may include conflict and disagreement on the positive side, or indifference on the negative side. The 5,5 person attempts to bring people back in line with the accepted norms.

The 5,5 team often works at having fun. Like the 1,9 team, members socialize together and spend time discussing both personal and work-related issues. These are the teams that often make fun out of work by creating games and other activities that shift the focus away from hard-driving production. On a personal level, team members usually enjoy each other's company, and may even spend a great deal of personal time together. Like the 1,9 approach, however, the relationships tend to be shallow and superficial because trust, respect, and full candor are suppressed. People may be friendly, but they are not willing to confront conflict openly or share in a personal risk.

The 5,5 team is grounded in politics and precedent. The "right" people move ahead in the organization based more on who they know, who has seniority, or how well they "play the game," while everyone else waits in line for a chance.

Caution and protocol dictate team action. Trust and respect exist, but only at moderate levels. This leads to tentativeness and caution, which slows down response time and dulls personal commitment. People feel disconnected from the processes they share. Creative ideas are lost or watered down through mechanical comparison with traditions and current expectations, or are passed over in deference to majority decisions.

R2 Relationships and the 5,5 Status Quo Style

Relationships in the 5,5-led team seem strong on the surface, but reveal weakness on closer examination. Accomplishment is measured according to how well people fit in with group norms, which undermines the sense of individual contribution and creativity. No one wants to be held responsible for stepping outside the mold and causing unrest. Although team members often share friendly relationships, they resist confronting problems openly, especially when conflict is anticipated. As a result, unrest builds as people become frustrated by being unable to speak candidly or carry out creative ideas (see Fig. 6-2).

Gossip runs rampant in 5,5 relationships, because the 5,5 prefers to talk to people one-to-one before bringing up potentially controversial issues in a group setting. Issues

Fig. 6-2

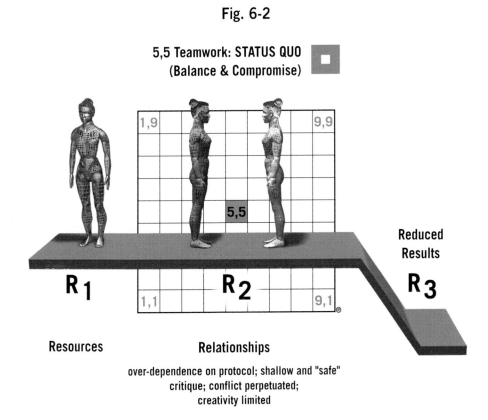

**5,5 Teamwork: STATUS QUO
(Balance & Compromise)**

1,9   9,9

5,5

**Reduced
Results**

R₁   R₂   R₃

1,1   9,1

Resources   **Relationships**

over-dependence on protocol; shallow and "safe"
critique; conflict perpetuated;
creativity limited

are dealt with indirectly through third-party comments and private conversations instead of being confronted openly and directly. However, most people are attentive enough to know when something is up. The cautious nature of the 5,5 approach leads to misinformation as people jump to conclusions and make assumptions based on hearsay. People may become so paranoid that, by the time the issue is addressed openly, much more damage control is required to restore relationships and progress.

Since the example has been set, others follow, and gossip replaces open and honest give-and-take discussions where people work through disagreements. In group settings, the only acceptable methods of discussing issues include compromise, concession, and following majority opinion—all meant to diminish the possibility of conflict. A stifling structure is often imposed to facilitate discussions instead of letting people explore issues with openness and candor. People who stir up controversy in group settings by not fitting in are criticized for making trouble, holding up progress, or not showing team spirit. In reality, they are simply disrupting the polite, amiable, and stifling atmosphere in which no one can challenge norms.

Following protocol provides confidence and a feeling of acceptance for the 5,5 person. Others, however, realize that protocol is being used as a shield to deflect controversy. People feel unable to make an individual difference when sound ideas and creativity are passed over in favor of following established guidelines or going with the majority voice. Commitment levels suffer when "What's the soundest course of action?"

is replaced by "That's the way we do it around here," "That's the most popular view," or "That's what worked in the past."

The 5,5 person believes that balance and compromise represent a sounder R2 relationship approach than taking the kind of risk that high degrees of concern represent, even if potential R3 results are lost. When conflict arises, the response is not to evaluate the facts based on evidence, but to automatically suppress the controversy by using compromise to balance the needs of everyone involved.

The 5,5 views compromise as win/win, because it means that everyone gets *part* of what they want. However, this approach provides half-hearted, short-term solutions at best, and people ultimately feel cheated. The 5,5 person would rather have two people in disagreement receive *something* rather than have one person get nothing. Regardless of how sound the solution may be, the 5,5 person avoids the extremes of having an outright winner or loser. Others may feel temporarily appeased by the compromise, but conflict eventually reappears if left unresolved.

5,5 Status Quo Motivations

The 5,5 person never experiences the full benefits of true synergistic teamwork because of an overly cautious attitude. He or she sees a contradiction between the concerns for people and results and reacts by attempting a balancing act between them. The underlying motivations reflect this in the form of a desire to maintain continuity and belonging, and a fear of embarrassment and humiliation (see Fig. 6-3).

Positive Motivation

The 5,5 desires continuity and a sense of belonging in the team, and so demonstrates a strong resistance to change, especially the spontaneous and continuous kind of change that characterize the workplace today. The 5,5 person is willing to change, but only when the strategy fits into the criteria of middle ground found in traditions, precedents, and norms. He or she believes that the best approach to change is to meet production needs and people needs halfway so that everyone gets a little bit of what they want.

The 5,5 wants to be looked up to as impartial and objective, but does not dig deep enough into issues to accomplish true objectivity. The positive motivation for continuity and belonging also limits the ability to remain objective. The 5,5 balances options against a standard of status quo instead of basing actions on soundness. When controversy arises, he or she takes pride in evaluating both sides on equal terms, but the process used is too shallow. Extreme points of view are discounted or put on hold so that order can be restored as soon as possible. Instead of exploring alternatives in depth, the 5,5 person gathers just enough information to recommend a compromise.

Negative Motivation

The 5,5 negative motivation is a fear of embarrassment and humiliation. He or she avoids this reality by always fitting in with the crowd and by relying on popular, proven

Fig. 6-3

5,5 Motivations: STATUS QUO (Balance & Compromise)

5,5 Desire for continuity & belonging

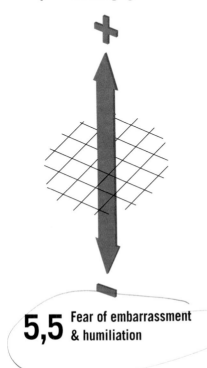

5,5 Fear of embarrassment & humiliation

methods. He or she does not want to be singled out as an underachiever or an overachiever. Overachievement has the potential for embarrassment and humiliation by singling him or her out for future scrutiny. Overachievement can also lead to envy and isolation from team members which makes it even harder to cope with the pressure of high-level performance. The 5,5 person would rather play it safe and fit in, even if it means giving up the rewards of greater importance.

When continuity and belonging are threatened, the 5,5 feels vulnerable because he or she *needs* membership in order to survive. The 5,5 relies heavily on protocol and guidelines instead of trusting his or her own experience and knowledge. The lack of mutual trust, respect, and full candor prevents the 5,5 person from building strong relationships based on shared commitment and personal stake. Instead, he or she builds relationships based on fitting in and emulating others.

Maintaining a certain image for others keeps the 5,5 person from consistently developing and demonstrating personal convictions. Instead, convictions shift with popular trends and the norms of other people. If they cut him or her off from being able to echo their opinions, the 5,5 person becomes tentative in offering views. Since 5,5 relationships are based on appearances, he or she does not have the confidence that the relationships can survive an embarrassing and humiliating setback.

Relationship Skills and 5,5 Status Quo Behaviors

CRITIQUE

I give informal or indirect feedback to keep others moving forward at a reasonable pace. If I have to say something negative, I prefer an indirect approach so that I, personally, am not seen as the bad guy. I actively solicit ongoing critique to assure my actions remain acceptable.

The 5,5 engages in critique to assure that progress occurs at a reasonable pace. This is most often accomplished through informal, one-to-one discussions and comparisons with history and traditions. Discussions do not go beyond confirming acceptable progress, however, and may even discourage creative ideas that could lead to synergy. Alternative and unplanned ideas represent a threat of disruption and risk and are usually met with polite disregard: "That's an interesting idea. Keep it in mind for the next project."

Critique is less than effective in the 5,5 approach because he or she does not come right out and ask for or state specific information. Instead, vague and open-ended questions and statements are meant to direct conversations so that others volunteer information. This is especially true when the issue at hand is controversial and potentially explosive. For example, if one person is chronically late for meetings, the 5,5 leader may call a meeting of the entire group and initiate vague critique: "Are we having any problems with organizing our meetings?" or "What would you think about moving our meetings to the afternoon?" Another example would be if one person is abusing vacation and sick leave. Instead of addressing that person directly, the 5,5 person's approach would be to propose a total revamping of the vacation and sick leave policies. In both of these cases, the entire team suffers because he or she is unwilling to confront the individual at fault.

The "sandwich" approach is another critique technique used by the 5,5 person to limit controversy. He or she does this by couching negative statements between two positive statements to lower the chances for conflict. For example, if a team member makes a mistake on a project, the 5,5 person says, "You worked really hard on your research and it showed. There were some key issues overlooked, but I know you were working under pressure and didn't have enough support, so I wouldn't worry about it." This sandwich approach leaves the other person without a clear picture of what went wrong, why, or how to strengthen his or her effort next time. This approach increases the chances that the mistake might recur.

The 5,5 person's approach to critique has three fundamental characteristics. First, personal convictions are not revealed or only tentatively revealed until a compromise can be reached. This distance allows the 5,5 to actively participate in and facilitate the discussions without making a commitment. As the leader, he or she also has the advantage of withholding a personal view until a solution has been reached by the rest of the team. Then he or she can confidently state the position most likely to be well received, presented with an equitable "I'm in total agreement on this."

Second, he or she focuses attention on minimizing conflict by asking for opinions and then restating them to others involved. This allows the 5,5 to edit comments so that they sound more acceptable. For example, if a disgruntled manager states, "This is the third time John has taken my ideas, made minor changes, and passed them off as his own," the 5,5 person would take the statement and diffuse it in the following way: "Teri is a little disappointed in the way the presentation was carried out, John, but I talked to her about it and everything is okay now." This statement is much less controversial than the original; unfortunately, it is also vague and inaccurate. Specific critique, even when controversial, is the most effective way to surface underlying differences. By watering down or editing comments, the 5,5 leader limits people from reaching resolution based on facts.

Finally, team members are encouraged to bargain, settle, and compromise for the sake of progress rather than critique actions openly and honestly. Progress sounds appropriate but the perspective is short-sighted and, ironically, often leads to more controversy in the long run. By encouraging compromise, the 5,5 person is basically telling people to withhold critique, hoping grievances or disagreements will go away or emerge at a more acceptable time later. Unresolved conflict, however, usually goes underground until addressed openly and honestly through critique.

INITIATIVE

I take low-risk initiatives based on a comparison of expectations with history and precedent. I avoid surprises by discussing possibilities with people in order to prepare for reactions to initiatives. If an unpopular action is required, I carry it out but cite rules, procedures, and history to explain myself.

The 5,5 person takes very deliberate, even swift action when a course is clearly outlined by someone else or by history. So long as someone else, like an authority figure or team member, is dictating the course, the 5,5 can be effective and efficient in relationships. He or she is not taking a personal risk because the objectives belong to and originate with someone else. This relieves the 5,5 of personal responsibility if something goes wrong. As long as the circumstances unfold in a predictable way while carrying out the activity, the 5,5 person is effective. If problems arise, he or she stops and awaits direction before proceeding further.

The 5,5 approach to taking independent initiative is overcautious and often delayed. He or she resists taking initiative without excessive information, including majority thinking, tradition, and history. If controversy is involved, he or she delays action further until a middle ground becomes evident. People involved are encouraged to make concessions for progress, but this appeal has more to do with avoiding disagreement than a genuine concern for progress or quality. He or she simply does not want to commit until the right (politically correct) course is clear.

In order to avoid disruption when conflict arises, the 5,5 person exercises swift initiative to intervene, but at a shallow level. He or she takes the "no risk" role of an outsider or mediator to reach a compromise and restore order without taking a personal stand. This initiative is quickly abandoned if controversy arises or increases and makes it difficult for him or her to keep a safe distance. The 5,5 is more *willing* to take initiative than a 1,9 so long as the actions are popular and widely supported. Regardless of how popular an initiative may be, the 5,5 cites rules and guidelines when conflict arises, to avoid becoming a target. This includes statements like, "I don't agree with this, but my hands are tied," and "I agree with what you are saying, but it's not up to me to decide." This allows the 5,5 to feel loyal to both sides. In reality, the 5,5 effectively weakens his or her own authority or the authority of others. The message given is, "I'm not committed to this initiative, so why should you be?"

INQUIRY

I inquire extensively to keep in touch with other people's opinions and suggestions so that I can maintain popular status. When issues are controversial, I facilitate inquiry without revealing my personal opinion. I acknowledge inquiry and opinions different from my own but resist stating a clear position.

Like the 1,9 person, the 5,5 exercises a great deal of inquiry, but at a more superficial level. The objective of this person's inquiry is to isolate majority thinking and trends rather than to explore the best approach. 5,5 inquiry is carried out in two ways. The first is through private and indirect discussions, like one-to-one meetings; this allows the 5,5 person to appeal to others individually. Questions asked may encompass a wide variety of subjects:

- morale: "How do you feel about this."

- current trends: "So what have you seen going on lately?"

- norms: "What do you think of what is happening in our team?"

- popular thinking: "It seems like everyone is in favor of this. What do you think?"

In each case, the 5,5 person has a tendency to withhold personal convictions until the popular or dictated course is clear.

The second method of inquiry requires staying informed of current trends in the industry through reading, memberships, or other forms of networking. This research has the potential to bring strength and focus to teams, but the 5,5 person does not evaluate facts in a sound way. Instead, he or she evaluates the facts based on the same limiting criteria—current trends and popular, high profile cases are favored, and controversial information is played down. The 5,5 person uses the information to persuade others to compromise and follow trends. The assumption is that people will defer to his or her opinion because of demonstrated knowledge of current information. This approach is only effective in teams where other members defer to the 5,5's recommendations without question.

The 5,5 person often uses indirect methods of inquiry to gather information from people without getting involved or making a meaningful commitment. Individuals with direct experience may be consulted to determine precedents before posing a question. These consultations are limited by the fact that the 5,5 person keeps the discussion vague, and his or her comments are usually neutral and non-binding: "I heard you had some experience with taking a product into new territory," or "We don't know what direction we're going in yet." These kinds of comments invite discussion without getting others too deeply involved, and without informing them of why they are being consulted.

5,5 questions have two characteristics. Questions are usually open-ended and vague to avoid being pulled in if controversy arises. For example, if one team member confides to the 5,5 that another member is angry about a specific aspect of a new policy, he or she may inquire in the following roundabout way: "I've been reading a lot about this new policy we're considering. What do you think about it?" or "I hear you may have some concerns about this new policy we're considering." A more direct and effective approach is, "I heard that you disagree with the reporting structure stated in the new policy. What are your specific concerns?" The 5,5 person wants people to volunteer information, and so it may take several vague statements or questions to guide the conversation where he or she wants.

The other characteristic of 5,5 inquiry is that he or she resists revealing private convictions until a clear course is evident. This follows the "no-risk" mediator or teacher role that he or she wants to assume. The 5,5 person does not discuss personal opinions about a new policy. This cautious approach prevents him or her from risking embarrassment before all of the information is gathered. To compensate, if asked directly, he or she may make vague statements like, "Well, I can only say what I've heard and read so far," or "I sympathize with both sides. They each have strong points." These kinds of statements free up the 5,5 to jump on whichever side comes out as most acceptable in the end.

ADVOCACY

I compare my point of view with expectations from superiors, history, and current views before advocating a position. I withhold expressing convictions if support is unstable or the outcome is unclear. I usually advocate a popular and reduced-risk position and make concessions if challenged.

Whenever possible, the 5,5 person resists stating private convictions until the majority view is clear. This allows him or her to couch statements in terms acceptable to those in authority as well as subordinates, such as, "Based on this new evidence, I can see your perspective."

The 5,5 person withholds advocating a position until he or she can ensure widespread acceptance and popularity. Advocacy is not determined by privately held convictions or by a belief in what is the soundest course; 5,5 convictions are dictated more often by politics. This tentative approach allows the 5,5 to evaluate views and tailor his or her advocacy to be acceptable to the majority.

The 5,5 may advocate strongly when his or her convictions reflect the status quo. When challenged, however, he or she often backs off of these convictions, or places responsibility on others to avoid conflict. Typical statements might include, "Don't kill the messenger, here! I'm only passing on this information," or "We may not like it, but this is the way it has always been done, so we have no choice." These statements relieve the 5,5 of the responsibility for the convictions expressed. If criticism follows, he or she may back away from involvement completely until a more opportune time. This may include statements like, "We're not getting anywhere by arguing. I think we should drop this for now until we cool off." Otherwise, the 5,5 person's standard facilitate-and-mediate approach prevails. He or she subtly shifts the position expressed away from controversial views and encourages compromise. This may include statements like, "Maybe we should all think about how we can reach an agreement. For the sake of progress, I think we should meet each other halfway." The goal is not to make progress, but to end the conflict.

DECISION MAKING

Majority thinking and agreement are the keys to making decisions. I am willing to make compromises for the sake of progress, even if the decision is less than fully sound. I usually avoid supporting decisions that are unpopular, risky, or not proven with the team.

Most 5,5 decisions are simple and straightforward because they are based on what has been done in the past, what is popular, or what he or she is told to do by someone in authority. As long as a decision is not controversial and clear precedents are established, he or she makes timely decisions and carries them out with reasonable effectiveness. When decisions are not so simple, the 5,5 person relies on a variety of techniques that provide the safety net needed to move forward.

One approach is to follow majority thinking. The 5,5 discusses the circumstances and alternatives one-on-one with others to get a feel for the most acceptable course. This may be followed by a group discussion to assure majority agreement. The 5,5 is also careful to find out what those in authority expect. His or her own conviction is always carefully hidden in these discussions until the majority preference is clear. Then he or she can say, "That is exactly what I think, too!" In 5,5 thinking, safe outranks sound. A minority opinion expressed in discussions may present an innovative and creative idea, but will be quickly dismissed without investigation: "That is simply too risky at this time," "We don't have any evidence to prove it," or "That's an interesting idea, but it simply won't work here."

The second 5,5 decision-making method is to ground the decision firmly in history. The 5,5 does not want to put his or her neck on the line and so depends on protocol. He or she seeks the views of people involved with similar decisions in the past. If no clear precedent exists, he or she looks for patterns in past actions that provide an acceptable course. Finding out what people think and conducting research before making a decision are both sound qualities; however, the motivation behind 5,5 research is questionable and not apt to produce the best possible decision.

Another characteristic of 5,5 decision making is the belief that everyone should be treated equally, meaning duties are delegated equally among team members. Bonuses and benefits are given across the board rather than rewarding actual individual or team performance. One person may be more qualified to take on an area of a project but the 5,5 assigns the task to another, unqualified person in the interest of equal distribution of work. This approach slows down team effectiveness by overlooking individual strengths and weaknesses and undermining personal commitment. The 5,5 prefers simply to treat everyone as "interchangeable parts" rather than facing potential objections and resentment.

CONFLICT RESOLUTION

I prefer to remove myself from direct conflict by taking a neutral position and facilitating a solution. I search for solutions that cause the least amount of controversy, often relying on what has worked before and encouraging people involved to compromise for the sake of progress.

Conflict *mediation* is a more appropriate description than conflict *resolution* for the 5,5 approach. Like the other relationship skills of the 5,5 style, conflict resolution is based on compromise (see Fig. 6-4). To avoid conflict the 5,5 person exercises caution at every turn. By relying on tradition, precedent, past practices, and majority thinking, he or she avoids being singled out. Fundamental 5,5 attitudes are, "It's better to be safe than sorry," and "If this backfires on me, at least I won't be alone."

Although conflict is unpleasant at times, it is vital for focusing issues. Conflict provides an opportunity to compare opinions and convictions against standards of excellence. The soundest idea can emerge and be embraced, regardless of who suggests it or how angry it makes someone else. Confronting conflict at its inception also allows teams to resolve problems quickly instead of wasting valuable time and resources perpetuating conflict through compromise. But the 5,5 person avoids conflict because he or she sees it only as destructive.

Fig. 6-4

5,5 Conflict Resolution: STATUS QUO (Balance & Compromise)

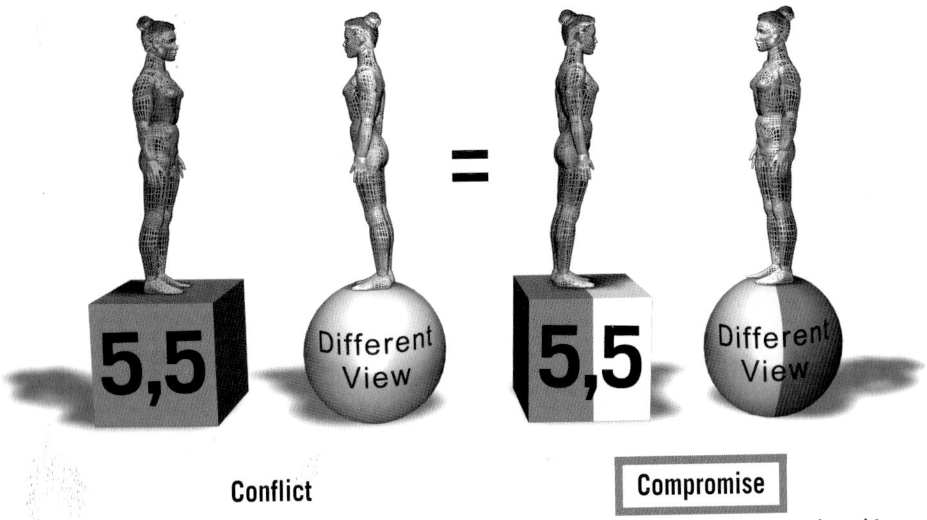

Conflict = **Compromise**

The 5,5 person works for compromise with different point of view. A mixed solution emerges.

To the 5,5 person, conflict means someone must win and someone else must lose. Since this outcome seems far from being equal and fair, he or she feels compelled to balance the two extremes. This avoidance of confrontation is at the core of the 5,5 person's negative motivation: the 5,5 person knows that the loser may cease to accept him or her as a member. In the worst case, the entire conflict could escalate, resulting in everyone being angry at him or her.

These fears compel the 5,5 to seek compromise as the best solution. If everyone gains even a little of what they want, that is better than someone being completely left out, at least in the 5,5 way of thinking. The question asked for any situation is not, "What is *right*?" but "What is *acceptable*?"

If conflict remains, the 5,5 person's reaction is to distance himself or herself as far as possible. Ironically, 5,5 people think they are confronting conflict; they see themselves doing it in a very objective fashion, but instead they are using past practice and precedent as standards. The rationale may include statements like, "Why don't we agree to disagree?" or "We need to defer this to an outside party." Another 5,5 approach is to interrupt the conflict by separating the people involved. This action is meant to end the disagreement once and for all and restore peace to the team. At best, this approach brings the conflict to a standstill. At worst, the conflict intensifies because people are not allowed to express their opinions or reach resolution.

RESILIENCE

I strive for progress by minimizing risk. I do not want to be singled out, either by failing or overachieving. I take a proven course in pursuing goals. This allows me to share success and failure equally with others involved. If confronted with failure, I take comfort in knowing I'm not alone.

The level of resilience expressed by the 5,5 depends on how securely he or she feels a part of the majority. Like the 1,9 person, the 5,5 person depends on endorsement from others to move on. The difference, however, is that the 5,5 expresses stronger resilience when it comes to controversy and conflict. As long as the majority suffers the same consequences, he or she bounces back with confidence. The attitude is, "Whatever happens is okay as long as I'm not alone."

Caution also defines how 5,5 resilience is expressed. Since the 5,5 person does not want to be singled out in any way, every opportunity is taken to decrease that possibility: "We need to spend more time studying all possible outcomes before taking action," or "We have to prevent these kinds of surprises by doing more research." Studying outcomes and conducting research are admirable and necessary steps, but the 5,5 undertakes them to reveal the safest, most acceptable course. When the 5,5 suffers a setback, these efforts are redoubled to assure that the same problem is not repeated.

Potential success is approached with the same caution as potential failure; overachievers as well as underachievers draw the attention and scrutiny the 5,5 wishes to avoid. In addition, overachievement means he or she risks others feeling jealous and competitive. This threatens his or her feelings of continuity and belonging.

Recognizing 5,5 Status Quo Behavior

The 5,5 person demonstrates an overcautious attitude in relationships that prevents people from exploring possibilities beyond the commonplace. Every action taken is compared against the fundamental criteria of maintaining the status quo, which effectively reduces the opportunity for synergy to develop.

Fig. 6-5 provides key words and phrases that help identify 5,5 behavior. They are presented on the motivation scale to show how the behaviors reflect the positive and negative motivations at work.

Fig. 6-5

5,5 Characteristics of Behavior
STATUS QUO (Balance & Compromise)

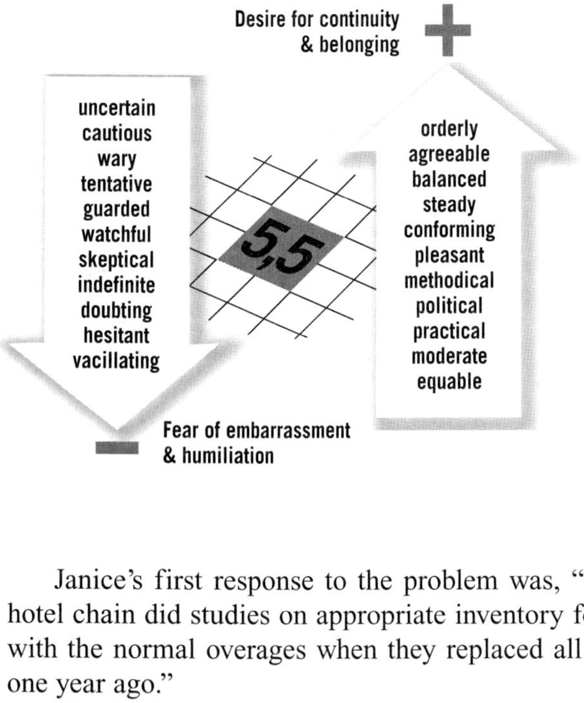

Desire for continuity & belonging **+**

uncertain	
cautious	orderly
wary	agreeable
tentative	balanced
guarded	steady
watchful	conforming
skeptical	pleasant
indefinite	methodical
doubting	political
hesitant	practical
vacillating	moderate
	equable

5,5

Fear of embarrassment & humiliation

Window on 5,5

The problem first surfaced with room service in a large top-rated downtown hotel. Guests were complaining that room service orders were taking 45 minutes to an hour or longer.

When questioned, Janice, the manager of room service, revealed the problem was a shortage of cutlery, flatware, and glassware. Sometimes the hotel had to send its staff members down two floors to the dishwashing area to wait beside the machine to find clean plates or utensils as they came out. They had learned the trick from one of the hotel restaurants where people had been doing this for some time.

Janice's first response to the problem was, "These shortages are ridiculous. The hotel chain did studies on appropriate inventory for hotels of our size and supplied us with the normal overages when they replaced all the cutlery, flatware, and glassware one year ago."

The hotel had just come out of a prolonged slump and was in its second year of increased earnings. Things were working well, and Janice really did not want to rock the boat at this time, preferring instead to keep everyone focused on their new convention business strategy which had them at 110 percent occupancy for the next two months. The owners were finally happy, and she wanted to keep them that way.

But complaints continued and Janice was forced to investigate deeper. The investigation turned out to be a simple one, taking only a day's time by two senior managers.

The dishwashing machine was more than 20 years old, and had to be set on the slow cycle to clean the new glassware without leaving water marks. The upsurge in convention business meant that because the hotel was serving more meals than ever before, especially during large conventions, the banquet and catering departments were running out of plates and glasses.

For days leading up to a series of large convention lunches and dinners, the banquet and catering departments were swooping through the hotel and hoarding all the excess plates, cutlery, and glasses. They went so far as to set up skirted tables in wide-open hotel spaces, put floral arrangements on them, and hide their booty underneath until it was needed. It was during times like this that everybody else experienced their shortages.

An investigation revealed a classic 5,5 culture. The hoarding had been going on for a long time but had only surfaced with the recent upsurge in business. The culture in the hotel was to "make do." In one person's words, "You have to do this to get your plates; everybody else does it, so we do too."

Nobody wanted to complain too loudly and be seen as a non-team player. So a whole series of informal, 5,5 decisions flowed from an outdated dishwasher and a cultural norm that operated under "acceptable" conditions. Two other departments took action that worked for them, but that did not address the overall problem, and the hotel manager moved only when complaints from hotel guests forced her to.

Summary

The 5,5 person demonstrates all of the potential for bringing strength and perspective to the team, but he or she does not go far enough in the R2 relationships to maximize R3 results. The 5,5 person seeks to establish equilibrium between seemingly competing concerns in the workplace, which ends up diluting both concerns.

The point of reference for maintaining this equilibrium in relationships is conformity, which causes the 5,5 person to stop short of digging deep enough to reach synergy. Without mutual trust and respect in relationships, the consequences of stepping outside the lines are not worth the risk. This leads to an overwhelming attitude of keeping up appearances, fitting in, and maintaining the status quo.

The 1,1 Style: Indifferent
(Evade & Elude)

7

Chapter

Overview

The 1,1-oriented style, located in the lower left corner of the Grid, represents the lowest level of concern for both results and people (see Fig. 7-1). The key word for this style is *neutral*. The person operating from a 1,1 orientation is the least visible person in a team; he or she is a follower who maintains distance from active involvement whenever possible. A 1,1 person carefully goes through the motions of work, doing enough to get by, but rarely making a deliberate effort to do more.

1,1 survival is enabled and even inadvertently caused by highly structured workplaces where the boundaries of effort are rigid and communication is minimal. Over time, the entire culture of a company can become firmly entrenched in a 1,1 style because of an overbearing structure that blocks independence and creativity. A stereotypical example of this is the government

Fig. 7-1

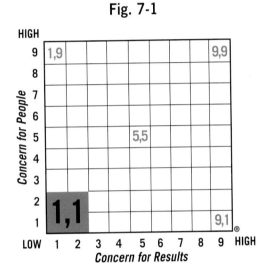

**1,1 Grid Style: INDIFFERENT
(Evade & Elude)**

I distance myself from taking active responsibility for results to avoid getting entangled in problems. If forced, I take a passive or supportive position.

agency where everyone is treated like a number. This sort of workplace allows the 1,1 to blend in without attracting attention. In fact, he or she often seeks work that can be done in isolation in order to carry on without being disturbed.

The 1,1 relies heavily on instructions—he or she depends on others to outline what needs to be done. Reliance on instructions prevents the need to take personal responsibility for results: "No one told me to do that." If problems arise, the 1,1 ignores or overlooks them (unless the instructions specify how to react), or points them out to someone else, but with little or no effort to offer a solution. With no instructions, he or she simply carries on with the attitude that "This is not my problem." If the 1,1 person were to suggest a solution, others might expect him or her to carry it out, which is not worth the risk. The 1,1 feels it is safer to wait for someone else to notice and take action.

People do not usually start out embracing 1,1 values, but end up changing into that style over time as a way to recover from an ineffective and/or dominating person or culture. The 9,1 leadership style, for example, often forces people into the 1,1 corner. The low concern for people present in the 9,1 style can be devastating to individual and team morale, leaving people feeling trapped into submission. A 9,1 leader who lashes out or discounts people for suggesting creative ideas eventually breaks the spirit of others involved. The resulting attitude is, "I give up. Let him do what he wants—I'll just do my job and keep my mouth shut." People will only fight back and defend themselves so many times before retreating into a 1,1 corner as a way to survive.

The 1,1 style can also develop when R1 resources are lacking. This can include a person who is promoted but is unprepared for the new responsibilities. He or she may have always had direct supervision in the past and may now be expected to start exercising more independent initiative and individual leadership. Without the necessary resources in the form of training, experience, or skill, a previously proactive person can become immobilized by the pressure to perform and gradually end up changing into 1,1.

The lack of available R1 resources can also create a 1,1 style in people who become "burned out" from overwork. A person can start out in a company with a highly effective, proactive style of leadership, but either voluntarily takes on or is given too much work until the original style is overcome through burn-out and exhaustion.

The 1,1 style can also develop when a 1,9 or 5,5 leader constantly discourages people from tackling tough issues and taking risks. Over time, with little reward for increased participation, people become indifferent: "Why should I work harder when no one else around here cares about results?"

1,1 Indifferent Style at the Team Level

The following examples represent typical 1,1 responses in the workplace.

The 1,1 response when a team member fails to accomplish his or her share of the workload:

Because self-isolating 1,1 is unaffected by others not carrying their share of the workload, he or she ignores the ineffectiveness. If his or her own work suffers, there is still little concern, because the 1,1 attitude is, "It's not my fault so I can't be held responsible." No action will be taken by the 1,1 to address the ineffectiveness of others.

The 1,1 response to constructive critique from a team member:

The 1,1 person would not volunteer suggestions for how to proceed with an activity in the first place. The 1,1 offers an opinion only when asked. If others object to a suggestion made, he or she quickly backs off, relieved to be off the hook of being held responsible for results.

With little commitment to achieving results or maintaining relationships with others, the 1,1 person is easily the weakest link in a team. The 1,1 attitude is expressed by "Whatever you think is fine with me." Other team members cannot count on the 1,1 to do any more than the minimum, so they learn to "work around" him or her. They only give the 1,1 person tasks that are simple and straightforward, requiring little personal initiative, because they know he or she can't be counted on to handle problems that might arise.

The 1,1 leader presents overall expectations and waits for others to take responsibility for carrying them out. As long as the minimum expectations are met, he or she is content to follow the lead of others. Under these circumstances, even the most committed team members become tired and restless. Commitment suffers a serious drain because the 1,1 leader seeks to achieve only minimum results. With no shared commitment from the 1,1 leader, motivated team members who challenge themselves and set high standards are left unfulfilled.

R2 Relationships and the 1,1 Indifferent Style

Relationships become polarized between those people taking proactive initiative and the reclusive 1,1 person. Resentment builds as others take on the responsibilities of the 1,1 person as well as their own. The 1,1 does not feel included in the team and so

Fig. 7-2

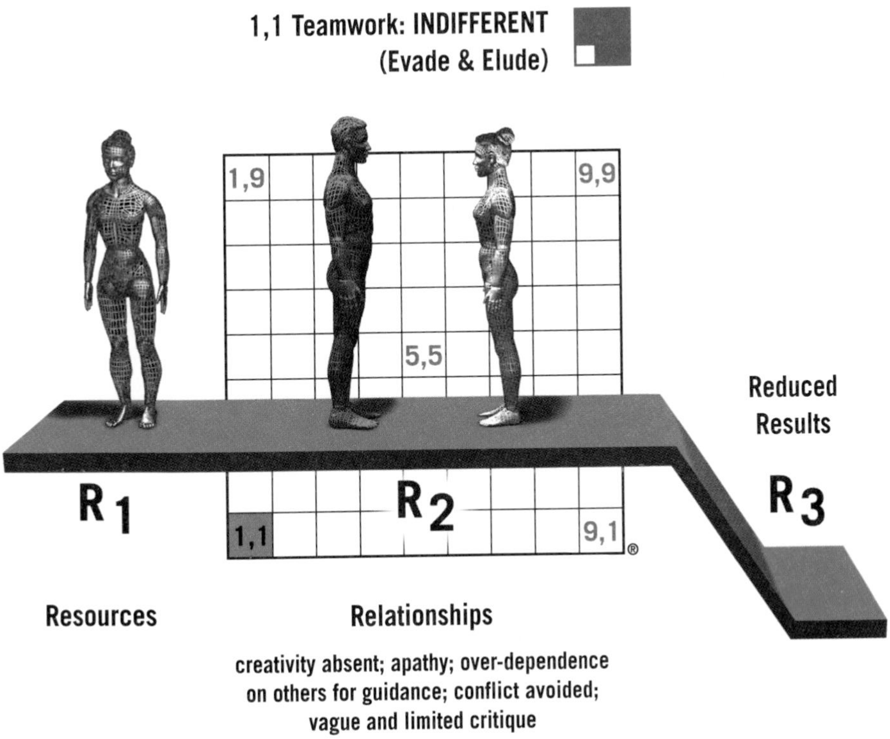
1,1 Teamwork: INDIFFERENT
(Evade & Elude)
1,9
9,9
5,5
1,1
9,1
R1
R2
R3
Reduced
Results
Resources
Relationships
creativity absent; apathy; over-dependence
on others for guidance; conflict avoided;
vague and limited critique

remains distant and guarded from proactive responsibility. As time passes, this polarization increases as the team does more and the 1,1 person does less. Responses to the 1,1 can range from subtle disappointment, "I thought she cared more about what happened here," to outright condemnation, "He is dragging the whole team down."

Over time, the 1,1 becomes a constant target. Depending on the team culture, the criticism may include blaming him or her for problems and mistakes. The 1,1 is also an easy target because he or she usually does not offer much of a defense, but simply gives up when challenged, using as an excuse, "No one told me what to do" (see Fig. 7-2).

Without realizing it, team members often drive the person farther into the 1,1 corner by pointing out with criticism and judgment the discrepancy in the person's contribution. Increasing scrutiny in this way often makes the 1,1 person withdraw further by making him or her feel even less a member of the group. Efforts to force the 1,1 to take more initiative only cause him or her to retreat deeper because it is often forceful actions that caused the 1,1 style to begin with. Without the benefit of the support that team membership represents, the 1,1 person is left alone to survive the only way he or she knows how—by taking neutral actions and trying to remain invisible.

1,1 Indifferent Motivations

The 1,1 person sees little connection between the concern for people and the concern for results. The low level of concern felt for both diminishes the opportunity for him or her to feel any real benefit from relationships and sound teamwork. The motivations underlying these low levels of concern are a desire to simply survive and remain uninvolved, and a fear of entanglement and expectation (see Fig. 7-3).

Positive Motivation

The 1,1 person desires survival and uninvolvement in the workplace, and thus seeks to establish a predictable routine with as little interaction as possible. He or she has found a way that works and is acceptable, and resists change by creating a cocoon around that routine. The 1,1 protects routines by following them closely and by ignoring both problems and opportunities. Policies or rules become a neutral shield used to avoid further involvement and complications: "You cannot hold me responsible for that. That's not part of my department." The 1,1 may also avoid change by taking a pessimistic view of the consequences: "If we start making changes, we'll probably do more harm than good."

The 1,1 person nurtures the predictability of his or her own routine by making it clear that he or she cannot be counted on to do more. No benefit is seen in stepping outside the cocoon to explore possibilities; the attitude is that involvement only leads to trouble. This dependence on routine often comes from repeated and devastating criticism for stepping out in the past. If asked to participate more, he or she may give vague answers such as, "Maybe," "We'll see," or "I'll see what I can do." Team members and subordinates may make an effort to pull him or her into more involvement for a while; however, this constant effort becomes a burden, so they often move on. This abandonment leaves the 1,1 where he or she wants to be: isolated and unencumbered.

Fig. 7-3

1,1 Motivations: **INDIFFERENT**
(Evade & Elude)

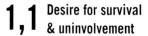

1,1 Desire for survival
& uninvolvement

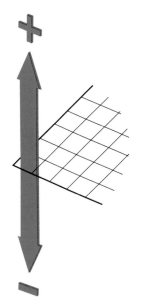

1,1 Fear of entanglement
& expectation

Negative Motivation

The 1,1 person maintains a pessimistic view of relationships and what they have to offer. The low level of mutual trust and respect creates an uncertainty and fear of entanglement. He or she views involvement as an invitation for scrutiny and criticism and assumes the worst: "They are looking for a reason to remove me. They are just waiting for me to make a mistake." The 1,1 person steadily accomplishes enough to remain a member, often with an underlying rationalization that people owe him or her. The 1,1 will not give anyone ammunition and so comes to work on time, arrives at staff meetings prepared, and maintains an acceptable level of results. The character of the relationship, however, is always guarded and limited. He or she does not offer an opinion unless asked, and then often offers a neutral position, or whatever view causes the least controversy.

Over time, people tend to maintain the 1,1 values even after the conditions that caused the damage have changed. For example, an outgoing and creative person may evolve into a 1,1 style because of a 9,1 supervisor who demoted him five years ago. Even though the supervisor has long since gone and other opportunities have become available, he remains withdrawn and neutral.

Relationship Skills and 1,1 Indifferent Behaviors

CRITIQUE

I avoid giving feedback and rarely critique the work of others or myself. When compelled, my critique tends to take the form of complaining to a third party without directly seeking resolution.

The thought of using critique seldom occurs to the 1,1 person. The level of concern is so low that reflection of any kind is not seen as valuable. When the 1,1 does offer it, critique is impromptu, shortsighted, and given only in response to an explicit request. If someone requests critique, the 1,1 usually responds with a vague answer: "Sure, we can talk about that," "I thought everything went fine," "I wouldn't worry about it—things will probably work out next time." The main objective of 1,1 critique is simply to get it over with as soon as possible.

One reason the 1,1 is uncomfortable and ineffective with critique is because he or she has so little information to use as a basis for analysis. Effective critique comes from observing and conversing with people, and comparing their behavior with performance standards or goals. A person conducting effective critique uses specific examples and states observations in an objective and helpful way. The 1,1 takes the safe path of participating in critique only by concurring with other statements made, or simply observing critique without active participation.

The weakness of 1,1 critique is that it creates a work environment where any learning that *does* take place just "happens." There is little deliberate effort to review performance before, during, or after an activity. Any consequence is treated as a *fait accompli:* "It happened. There's nothing we can do about it now."

INITIATIVE

I cautiously exercise the lowest acceptable initiative based on established expectations. I rarely exercise independent initiative outside these expected boundaries, but respond to requests when asked. I back off initiatives when conflict arises.

The 1,1 approach to initiative is minimal and passive. The 1,1 exerts effort at a steady pace to complete the work that is expected. He or she rarely goes beyond that and prefers to let things happen rather than take proactive steps to influence a course of action. This low level of initiative is maintained by operating "by default" in following instructions and guidelines. When addressed directly, he or she answers with enigmatic statements such as "That's not a bad idea," or "That might work." Words like "perhaps," "maybe," and "I don't know" are used, because these statements allow the 1,1 to deny involvement if problems arise: "I never said I liked the idea," or "I never said we should adopt that idea."

One characteristic of 1,1 initiative is delegation. To avoid further involvement, the 1,1 delegates whenever possible. When this person observes problems, he or she may address them indirectly by delegating resolution to someone else: "Jerry is having a problem setting up the new schedule. Why don't you give him a hand?" As a leader, this person over-delegates, leaving the minimal amount of work for himself or herself. If problems arise, he or she can deflect attention by blaming the person who took the initiative.

1,1 initiative is reactionary; that is the 1,1 reacts to problems—usually by pointing them out for someone else to address. Even when the 1,1 knows that something needs to be done, he or she waits to be told. There is no decisive effort to influence the results by anticipating or addressing problems, or to otherwise strengthen results. For example, if a 1,1 person notices a problem in someone else's work area, he or she says nothing. The thinking is, "It's not my problem." If a 1,1 sees another team member struggling with a project, he or she pretends not to notice: "If I get involved, I'll probably end up having to do all the work myself." If a co-worker needs to leave work suddenly, the 1,1 person feels no responsibility to help him or her by taking on some of the work. If asked, or if it's expected, the 1,1 may take on the work, but he or she would not likely volunteer.

Another form of 1,1 initiative is the "I'm too busy to be bothered" deflective approach to avoid being drawn into more involvement. He or she accomplishes this by simply not being available for involvement. The 1,1 carries this out by immersing himself or herself in a one-alone activity that discourages people from interrupting. For example, the 1,1 may close his or her door to discourage interruption, deliberately spend more time away from the office than is necessary, or simply plunge into tasks like paperwork. The message broadcast to everyone else is, "Don't bother me."

INQUIRY

I inquire in an indirect way through third-party questioning rather than going directly to the source. I resist asking or answering direct questions centered on controversial issues, because I don't want more responsibility or trouble. I go along with different opinions even if I disagree.

The 1,1 person rarely initiates anything beyond a superficial inquiry. Since knowledge leads to obligation, the attitude is, "The less I know, the better." He or she questions only enough to reach the minimum requirements. For example, if a new project is assigned, the 1,1 asks only questions that define his or her responsibilities. Even if he or she does not understand the instructions, the 1,1 remains quiet to minimize communication.

The 1,1 person often gathers information indirectly through informal channels and conversations. This allows him or her to stay informed without being drawn into direct involvement. The last thing the 1,1 wants to hear in response to a question is, "You've raised a great point! Why don't you go ahead and take the lead on that." When a new project comes along, the 1,1 waits for someone else to devise a course of action and instructions, and then follows. If the project fails, the 1,1 can plead innocent. The 1,1 attitude is, "I cannot be held responsible. I was only doing what I was told."

The information given out by the 1,1 is often cautious and vague to avoid taking responsibility later. Responses may include statements like, "I don't know," and "I think so, but I'm not sure. You'd better ask someone else." This passive approach becomes tedious and frustrating for other team members, because it makes them have to work harder to gather information from the 1,1 person. The result is exactly what the 1,1 wants: they move on and stop asking questions!

ADVOCACY

I advocate my convictions only when I am explicitly asked and when support is clearly established. Otherwise, I resist expressing convictions and prefer instead to wait as long as possible before agreeing. I quickly change my mind if challenged.

The 1,1 approach to advocacy is noncommittal and reticent. He or she rarely expresses convictions regarding an activity, or expresses them in a neutral way that offers little insight: "That is probably fine" or "I could probably go along with that." The 1,1 believes the best approach is to withhold information until asked, and then avoid saying something that attracts scrutiny or obligation. Because of this attitude, even when convictions are stated, they are fuzzy or vague to help the 1,1 avoid being pinned down by others. He or she may reply, "I would rather not say what I think at this point," or "I don't have any preferences at this time."

The 1,1 person tends to follow the crowd with regard to advocacy. When expressed, convictions often reflect the popular view so that he or she blends in: "Whatever we decide, the results are what count," or "If that's what you think we should do, I will go along with it." This tentativeness leaves the 1,1 free to criticize others' actions when problems arise: "I had my reservations about this."

The 1,1 approach to advocacy is characterized by a reserved or sullen attitude that creates a self-fulfilling prophecy regarding problems and obstacles. When the result of an action is untried or unknown, the 1,1 expresses reservations and doubts. For example, if the team is discussing whether to upgrade a computer system and create a network, the 1,1 person points out only the negative aspect: "We'll have to take the whole system down to accomplish this. We'll all have to get up to speed on the new computer software. Orders will be held up. Can we really afford that?" This negative attitude works as a defense mechanism, so that if problems arise, he or she can say, "I knew this would happen." By expressing such reservations, the 1,1 reduces the probability that he or she will be held accountable.

DECISION MAKING

I prefer to have others take responsibility for decisions. I am more or less indifferent about how decisions are reached and usually go along with whatever suggestions are agreed to by others. I resist participating in controversial decisions with the team unless forced.

The 1,1 maintains a short-term outlook and, as stated earlier, prefers to let decisions "happen." He or she waits for the circumstances to dictate a course of action; what appears to be patient perseverance is actually indifference. Like the 5,5 approach, the 1,1 person relies on precedents and tradition to dictate action but at a more extreme level. While the 5,5 person would make a decision with confidence where a precedent exists, the 1,1 person prefers to have someone else make the decision. Again, the worst-case scenario is perceived: "I am not about to get caught out on a limb." "They may agree now, but if I make this decision, it could come back to haunt me." When forced, decisions are made in strict accordance with precedents in place.

A 1,1 leader may argue that delegating is good leadership: "She needs the experience if she wants to move up in the organization." The problem with this approach is that the 1,1 leader over-delegates to people who may be unprepared. Since the 1,1 person keeps communication to a minimum, he or she is not likely to make an informed decision regarding who is capable. An enthusiastic employee may be eager but unqualified, or someone else may be contending with competing projects and doesn't have time; the 1,1 leader is not likely to notice these distinctions, and will give them the work anyway: "Sure, if you want to do it, great!"

Another 1,1 approach is to delay or defer a decision in the hope that the need will go away or someone else will take charge: "Let's not worry about that now." "We need more information" or "Let's wait and see what happens."

The 1,1 person creates a catch-22 situation with regard to decision making. He or she does not want to make decisions that will lead to increased attention and obligation. Additionally, he or she stays uninformed about people and issues and avoids getting involved enough to review the facts and ask questions. This leaves the 1,1 ill-prepared to make sound decisions. Since he or she resists involvement, the only option is to delay, delegate, or endorse someone else's view.

CONFLICT RESOLUTION

I avoid direct conflict by making indirect comments in the form of complaints, or quietly go along with others taking action. I refuse to tackle controversial issues alone, but may consider agreeing with others if support is evident.

"Conflict? What conflict?" is the standard 1,1 attitude regarding conflict resolution. He or she ignores conflict as long as possible, hoping it will go away. The 1,1 takes the position of a bystander seeking neutrality: "This is your battle. Don't pull me in," or "Do whatever you want, but count me out" (see Fig. 7-4).

In teams, this lack of commitment to resolve conflict often creates resentment. Team members soon learn that they cannot depend on the 1,1 when problems arise. This alienation appeals to the 1,1 because he or she wants less involvement, but it increases the animosity already present in the relationships. Trust and respect suffer as the 1,1 moves farther and farther away from experiencing the benefits of sound teamwork. Team members begin to say things like, "Don't even bother asking him. We know what the answer will be."

The 1,1 person uses several strategies to avoid getting involved in conflict. The most common, described above, is to ignore it. On the surface, the 1,1 gives the appearance of being involved by following the rules, looking busy, and adhering to acceptable norms. This allows him or her to blend in and not draw attention. For example, the 1,1 may arrive at work and meetings on time, turn in reports that reflect the minimum requirements, attend social functions just long enough to make an appearance, etc. When problems arise, however, he or she becomes invisible, speaking up only occasionally, or offering vague comments: "Yes, I hear what you're saying" or "That sounds like a problem that should be dealt with."

Another related strategy is to be unavailable for conflict resolution. This is where "looking busy" becomes a valuable strategy. People are less inclined to interrupt the 1,1 when he or she appears immersed in an activity. He or she may also use subtle strategies like responding to requests via voice-mail or e-mail when direct contact would be

Fig. 7-4

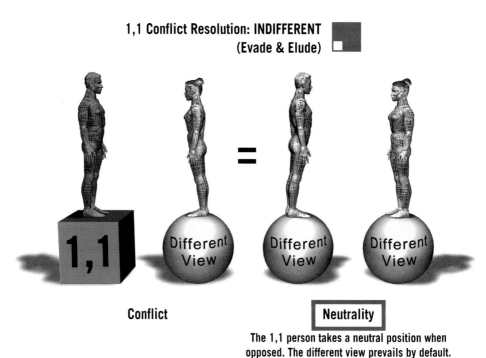

1,1 Conflict Resolution: INDIFFERENT
(Evade & Elude)

Conflict **Neutrality**

The 1,1 person takes a neutral position when
opposed. The different view prevails by default.

better. The 1,1 may purposely time a response for when he or she knows the other person is not there, such as returning calls during lunch: "I called you back, but you weren't in," or "I tried to reach you but you were away from your desk." Another strategy may be to volunteer for activities that remove him or her from active involvement with others. The 1,1 may react to conflict by requesting vacation, taking business and sales trips, or engaging in other activities that physically remove him or her from the conflict.

Another strategy for the 1,1 is to pass along information to people he or she thinks will take action. The 1,1 person depends on others who feel committed to achieving sound results. He or she knows that by mentioning a problem, others will take responsibility for seeing it through to resolution. When relating information, the 1,1 person is careful not to offer interpretations or edit information; the preferred method is to repeat what was heard, verbatim. If queried, he or she says, "You know as much as I do. I can only tell you what I heard."

Information is passed along in this way so as to play it safe if problems arise. This abdication of responsibility often occurs when the information being passed generates conflict. The 1,1 reasserts a neutral stance by pinning responsibility on someone else: "I'm only passing on what they told me. If you have a problem, you'll have to take it up with them."

When conflict continues, the 1,1 person removes himself or herself from the discussion as soon as possible, ostensibly remaining neutral: "Fine, if that's the way you feel, do whatever you want." He or she may make a statement that shifts attention, such as, "Why are we wasting time fighting over this? Let's just do it your way and move on."

On the rare occasion when the 1,1 does take direct action to resolve conflict, he or she often does more damage than good. Since the 1,1 remains uninformed, the action taken does not reflect a sound understanding of facts, and often reflects a short-term view that simply seeks to halt the immediate controversy. The 1,1 person rarely makes a genuine effort to understand the facts involved to reach a sound resolution.

RESILIENCE

I take comfort in being dependable and achieving what is expected of me. I avoid taking risks because I do not want to be singled out and blamed for any problems. When confronted with failure, I try to deflect criticism and withdraw further.

The 1,1 demonstrates weak resilience. Working so hard to avoid responsibility makes the 1,1 unprepared to bounce back with any kind of effectiveness. In addition, the 1,1 person gains very little benefit from the relationships in place, and so cannot count on mutual trust, respect, and support from others: "They think I just let things happen" or "They probably blame me for the whole mess." Whether or not this view is accurate remains untested, because the 1,1 person offers little defense, explanation, or challenge to this perception.

1,1 resilience is often low because he or she is not comfortable conversing with people, and therefore constantly operates from a point of disadvantage when it comes to relating with others. This is especially true when the issue at hand is controversial. He or she is so disconnected from others that when involvement occurs, it often misses the mark. This may include humor that doesn't fit in or comments that people do not understand or may even find offensive.

The 1,1 person works from a great disadvantage when it comes to resilience because he or she remains so distant and disconnected. The low concern for results leaves him or her uninformed and unprepared for the operational challenges of the job. The low concern for people leaves the 1,1 person unprepared to open up and share feelings with others and build the kinds of relationships needed to bounce back from failure.

Recognizing 1,1 Indifferent Behavior

The 1,1 style is characterized by a fundamental unwillingness to become involved in the R2 process of working together. This person has little faith in his or her effort or in the relationships in place, and sees no benefit in taking any actions that would represent a chance, change, or departure from normal routine. This style demonstrates what can happen when people feel little or no commitment to the work they carry out. He or she gives very little in terms of commitment and so receives very little in return in the form of personal fulfillment or reward. The only goal sought is to get through the end of the day, week, month, or career with a minimum amount of change.

Fig. 7-5

1,1 Characteristics of Behaviors
INDIFFERENT (Evade & Elude)

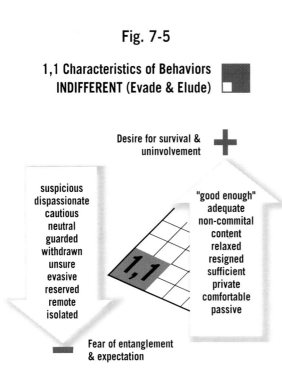

Desire for survival &
uninvolvement

suspicious
dispassionate
cautious
neutral
guarded
withdrawn
unsure
evasive
reserved
remote
isolated

1,1

"good enough"
adequate
non-commital
content
relaxed
resigned
sufficient
private
comfortable
passive

Fear of entanglement
& expectation

Fig. 7-5 provides key words and phrases that help identify 1,1 behavior. They are presented on the motivation scale to show how the behaviors reflect the positive and negative motivations at work.

Window on 1,1

Ray had worked for a large service organization for close to twenty years. As the only person who managed a key research arm of the company, he had survived many successions of ownership and leadership. Over the years he had managed to move up in the organization at a steady pace. He continued to build on his skills and maintain control over his area of expertise in research.

Over a period of about two years, the company went from a family-owned business with a strict hierarchy to an outside owner who flattened the organization structure, giving individuals more opportunity and responsibility. In addition, the company went through a dramatic restructuring that demanded more self-direction and personal accountability from every employee.

During the first year under the new ownership, tensions built in Ray's team between himself and other members for two reasons. The first was that Ray had always maintained unanimity in his area of expertise. Although he related with the team in research planning and strategy, he maintained control over access to vital information in the database. This control was reinforced by the fact that it was housed in an antiquated and user-unfriendly computer that only Ray knew how to use.

The dependence on Ray created problems on both sides of the issue. Ray felt pressured to provide information "on demand" whenever people wanted without a real appreciation for his flexibility or skills. He was often interrupted with urgent demands where he had to drop everything he was doing to write a database query. He felt no one wanted to take the time to learn the cumbersome computer system and did his best to accommodate everyone's needs.

On the other side, team members were frustrated by being dependent and felt Ray was unwilling to share knowledge by cross-training them in using the system. Ray had even joked that the database was his "job security." With increased pressure and responsibilities, it was easier for everyone involved to simply ask Ray for the information. And so the dependence and frustration on both sides continued.

The second area of tension revolved around Ray's apparent resistance to change and reclusive behavior in general. He was seen by team members as someone who was very capable, but who did not take enough initiative to accept new tasks. While other members were taking on multiple roles, often working long hours to compensate for the reorganization, Ray maintained his original duties and hours as if no changes had occurred.

He also didn't spend a lot of time talking to people in his team, spending most of his time in his office. He expected to be kept informed, however, regarding issues, events, or meetings, and reacted defensively when he wasn't told about something. The other members felt the opposite—that they didn't think it was fair for them to be responsible for updating Ray on every issue on top of their other responsibilities: "How many times a day does he walk by without saying a word, but then he expects us to keep him informed on every event." They felt he needed to take responsibility to stay informed and involved with the team.

During a team development meeting, members gave Ray specific examples of instances where they felt he had not carried his share of responsibility. The impact was very enlightening for both Ray and the other team members. Ray's intentions and the perceptions of his team could not have been farther apart. From Ray's point of view, he felt "shoved into a corner" because he was the only person who knew how to use the old computer system. This created in Ray a deep sense of not being a real part of the team—an outsider. As the sole keeper of research data, he also felt pressured to perform. He had been through several downsizings where people lost their jobs. The bottom line was that the culture of the company had caused him to fear that his job was at stake if he made a mistake or stepped outside the boundaries of what he was told to do.

The team development session produced a remarkable transformation between Ray and his teammates. Other team members realized that they may have been at least partly responsible for some of the problems. With these misconceptions on both sides out in the open, Ray began to realize that with the new structure and culture of the team, a lot of his fears were unfounded and he was able to gain strength from an increased sense of membership and personal commitment in the team. Over the next year, he demonstrated more confidence in taking initiative, and other members gave their support more openly. With the encouragement of his teammates, he also spearheaded a drive to convince the new management of the value of transferring old research data into a state-of-the-art system where it was readily available to all users. While he remained the primary keeper of research data, the installation of the new system provided him the luxury of more time to devote to other initiatives that had been in the back of his mind for years. He began to remember how it felt to be creative and energetic in his job and it showed in the morale and effectiveness of the entire team.

Summary

The 1,1 person represents the minimum level of effort that any person can bring to a relationship. He or she wants the benefits of membership in relationships but ultimately feels like an outsider. In order to survive, the 1,1 works hard to maintain the appearance of involvement without really getting involved. He or she comes to work every morning on time, but seeks out one-alone activities. He or she comes to every meeting, but remains quiet or neutral. He or she turns in reports on time, but never takes the risk of offering a new idea or challenging an unsound one. The 1,1 is visible and accounted for, but not willing to make a commitment or accept personal risk.

The 1,1 style diminishes the opportunity for mutual trust and respect to grow in the team; synergy is not even a remote possibility. If one person is 1,1 and others are not, teams often become polarized around the discrepancy of personal contribution which only increases the sense of isolation from all perspectives. If all members are 1,1, then they are really just "sharing space," working independently with little sense of personal stake or commitment. The only real goal is to get to the end of the day, and eventually to retirement.

The 1,1 style often develops from one or a series of incidents that are never confronted or resolved. Once the relationships are established, the behaviors and attitudes persist, often long after the circumstances that fostered them have passed. The bottom line is that the 1,1 person would not be in the team without skills and capabilities. The style results most often from ineffective utilization of those skills.

The Paternalistic Style: (Prescribe & Guide)

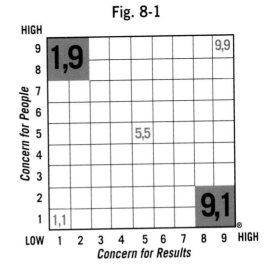

8

Chapter

Overview

The Paternalistic-oriented style results from two individual Grid styles coming together in a way that produces a unique, joined style (see Fig. 8-1). The two styles merge in the same interdependent way that the two concerns do in the other Grid styles. Relationships between the paternalistic-oriented person and co-workers are like those between parent and child, where reward comes from the 1,9 influence to nurture, and punishment comes from the 9,1 influence to dictate behaviors. The resulting style is a person who commands action and results by providing guidance, praise and reward, and subtle punishment.

The paternalist represents one of the most prevalent and powerful leadership styles in successful companies. The style represents a "new and improved" version of the traditional autocratic leader. He or she demonstrates all of the strength, determination, and courage that brings about results, yet also considers people in the process. Paternalists are often viewed as benevolent autocrats—as people who don't just want to control others, but who want them to smile and say, "Thank you!" He or she often has a proven track record of accomplishments and wants to share that expertise by taking care of everyone in what he or she perceives to be a helpful and supportive way. The paternalist comes across as overbearing by imposing help regardless of whether it is wanted or even needed. The trouble is that by doing too much, the paternalist creates dependence in others by limiting their ability to contribute.

Fig. 8-1

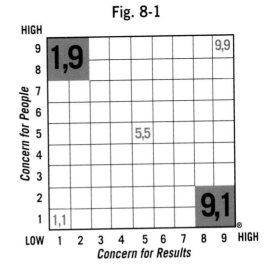

PAT Grid Style: PATERNALISTIC (Prescribe & Guide)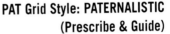

I provide leadership by defining initiatives for myself and others. I offer praise and appreciation for support, and discourage challenges to my thinking.

As a result of the 9,1 influence, the paternalist holds himself or herself up to high standards of performance and expects the same from others. A person who complies with these demands receives rewards in the form of praise, advantage, and benefits, behavior which is more characteristic of the 1,9 style. The "cooperative" team member is still expected to maintain the high standards of performance, but receives more support, encouragement, and overall "help" from the paternalist along the way. A person who does not comply receives more of the 9,1 treatment exemplified by increased scrutiny, a stance that communicates "Prove to me you are worthy of my support," and "This is for your own good" regarding expectations for performance.

Good intentions blind the paternalist to the forcefulness of his or her behaviors. This blindness is further compounded by the fact that people say only what the paternalist wants to hear: "I think that's a great idea, sir!" The paternalist often preempts people with his or her own ideas. This has the effect of deflating whatever enthusiasm the other person may have had regarding his or her own idea, especially when the paternalist is higher up in authority. For those being "helped," it becomes tiresome to have someone taking charge of their lives, making decisions for them, and reaping the rewards of their hard work. They feel like children who have grown up but whose parents refuse to see them as the capable adult individuals they truly are.

The paternalist seeks to create a workplace where he or she is revered and respected as a strong, capable, caring leader. He or she also wants to be seen as a mentor, a guardian, and an "everyman" (a superior person who can mingle with less worthy people in a caring, friendly, and compassionate way). The paternalist encourages people to depend on him or her to think for them: "They need me to take control of this project." "With my help, you can do a great job on this project." A favorite phrase used by a paternalist is, "I think you should … " and a phrase often heard from others is, "Tell me what you think."

The standard of excellence established by the paternalist can be succinctly described as "my way." He or she establishes standards of performance and behavior that mirror his or her own values with an undercurrent of constant judgment which shows disapproval of people who deviate from that image. If the paternalist prefers a special format for proposals, people are expected to praise and copy the format. If he or she makes presentations with a certain formula, then he or she approves when others adopt it. The paternalist may even go so far as to expect people to share the same interests as, or even dress and talk like, him or her. Independence and individuality that challenge the paternalist's preference are resisted with comments such as, "That's an interesting idea, but I think it would be better if you did it my way next time." These kinds of comments can be very subtle but also very powerful by simply using a tone of voice that implies judgment: "So *that's* the way you want to go with this?"

Paternalistic Style at the Team Level

The following examples represent typical paternalistic responses in the workplace.

> The paternalistic response when a team member fails to accomplish his or her share of the workload:

The paternalist expresses disappointment and disapproval. The consequences for disobeying may range from a remark calculated to induce guilt—"I thought I could count on you to handle this"—to overt warning— "We need to talk about your future with this company." The degree of punishment depends on where the person stands with the paternalist. A person already out of favor is judged and punished more harshly. A person on his or her good side is treated with more leniency, perhaps even with encouragement and praise: "I have confidence that you will do what is right."

The paternalistic response to constructive critique from a team member:

Although not expressed overtly, the paternalist is insulted by critique from others. He or she takes negative comments personally and reacts defensively. If the majority of the people involved support the paternalist, he or she makes an example out of the dissenter by imposing some form of punishment. More likely than direct punishment, however, the paternalist will promptly withdraw his or her favor by appearing cooler, not smiling in the usual way, or ignoring the person on social occasions. The paternalist makes sure that the action makes an obvious point to the individual and to others who may want to challenge his or her authority. When the paternalist feels the lesson is learned, he or she resumes the original warm contact. If the negative comment turns out to be obviously well founded, the paternalist may react by blaming others to induce guilt and compassion: "This is what happens when I don't get all of the information I need ahead of time," or "I am overworked and can't be expected to catch every mistake by myself."

Paternalists drain energy from teams by shifting attention away from *what's* right and focusing instead on *who's* right. Realistic standards of excellence are replaced by the paternalist's own point of view. Like the 9,1 team, the paternalistic team is only as effective as the paternalist because he or she controls the R1 resources and R2 relationships. He or she takes control of communication and becomes the focal point for team action as well as for any critique and feedback that take place. This is the same unilateral strength in controlling people as exercised by the 9,1, but paternalism has a distinction that makes it a little more appealing in the short term. Unlike 9,1 individuals, paternalists seem warm, friendly, and caring. Paternalists appeal to people's insecurities by offering concern, encouragement, and support, which makes it much more difficult for teams to confront his or her behavior. After offering so much support with such sincere intentions, no one wants to hurt his or her feelings.

This undercutting of resources leaves team members feeling frustrated and resentful because they are unable to contribute to their full ability. If the paternalist is also the team leader, team members face additional disadvantages because the paternalist can use leverage by pulling rank to get his or her way. Although it holds more appeal than that of the 9,1, this approach is just as controlling. The paternalistic suppression creates barriers to openness and candor in teams. Over time, team members grow tired of condescension and manipulation and see the paternalist as controlling and self-centered. This is a formula for resentment.

The favoritism present in paternalistic teams generates unfair practices that lead to polarization between those in favor and those out of favor. The people out of favor resent being held to higher standards than those in favor; they have to work harder to meet the high standards without the support or rewards enjoyed by those in favor. Those in favor may feel superior, even smug, toward team members out of favor because they know they are afforded more tolerance by the paternalist. Such polarization creates destructive and ineffective teamwork. Members become more concerned with the unfair environment than with working together to achieve sound results.

Standards of excellence for the team are also limited to the values and objectives of the paternalist. If he or she makes poor decisions and mistakes follow, other team members suffer the consequences and may even be blamed to protect the paternalist's ego. The focus of individual commitment shifts away from personal contribution, effectiveness, and feeling a personal stake in the team goal, toward commitment to serving the paternalistic person's agenda.

Because sound alternative ideas are overlooked in favor of the paternalist's preferences, any celebration or praise for accomplishments resulting from the favored approach comes across as shallow, even insincere. Also, the resentment caused by favoritism translates celebrations into "mutual admiration societies" for the paternalist's favorites. Accomplishments by people out of favor are often played down or overlooked completely, reinforcing existing resentments.

The paternalist treats other people more like family members than co-workers, making work relationships too personal. Like a parent, the paternalist wants to tell his or her "children" how to perform, and uses reward and reprimand to see that they "behave." Team members are encouraged to exercise initiative and responsibility—but only within the confines of behavior defined as acceptable by the paternalist. This causes individuals to lose a sense of their own personal intuition and judgment. Eventually, when actions occur which call for exercising judgment, individuals feel helpless and insecure. They have to ask, "What do I do now?" and wait for guidance.

R2 Relationships and the Paternalistic Style

Hierarchy with the paternalist sitting at the top is the foundation for paternalistic relationships. The paternalist sees himself or herself as ultimately responsible for results and views other team members as subordinates whose performance directly reflects on him or her. This leads the paternalist to have an attitude of "If you want something done right, do it yourself." This feeling of exclusive responsibility prevents him or her from letting other people take responsibility for their own actions. An exception is made for those people the paternalist trusts to carry out actions exactly as he or she would (see Fig. 8-2).

The paternalist is most comfortable when taking charge in relationships. For example, if a paternalist is assigned to a task force, he or she takes aggressive steps to initiate a course of action and instruct others. While others carry out the actions, the paternalist feels compelled to monitor progress and establishes himself or herself as the

Fig. 8-2

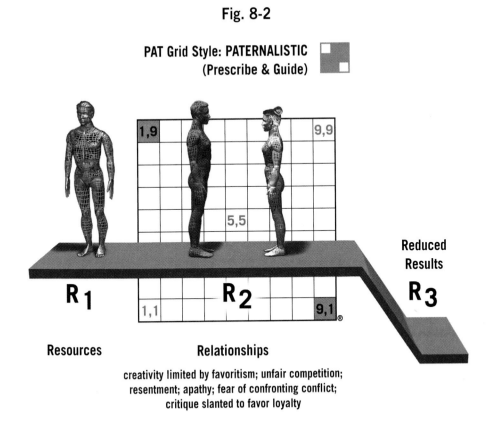

PAT Grid Style: **PATERNALISTIC**
(Prescribe & Guide)

1,9

9,9

5,5

Reduced
Results

R₁

R₂

R₃

1,1

9,1

Resources

Relationships

creativity limited by favoritism; unfair competition;
resentment; apathy; fear of confronting conflict;
critique slanted to favor loyalty

focal point for progress: "Let me know when you finish, and then we can review it together" or "Talk to me before you do anything else." He or she may even hover over people to assure compliance and offers "help" and "guidance" when people get "off track." This effectively smothers any chance for spontaneity outside the expected behaviors.

Paternalism can be difficult to identify in relationships because once established, the control and domination can be subtle, leaving the surface relationship with the appearance of soundness. People working with the paternalist learn what they must do to avoid punishment. After doling out severe punishment a few times, the paternalist can get his or her warning across with a quick look or mild comment that, on the surface, does not seem overbearing or controlling. The paternalist may smile and say in an apparently warm and caring tone, "I was surprised to hear you didn't agree with my proposal. I'm curious about why you didn't make use of the opportunity I gave you." This non-confrontational façade reinforces the paternalist's perception that he or she is a benevolent, compassionate leader.

Another reason why paternalism may remain hidden is that positive reinforcement becomes the driving force for how to proceed, which means everything looks good on the surface; people seem happy and motivated. In this kind of culture, however, people become dependent on the praise and compliments, so merely withholding praise becomes punishment. Once compliance is established, the paternalist rarely has to take harsh action to get results; not giving praise is punishment enough.

If certain people don't adhere to the paternalist's manipulation, he or she gathers the support of loyal followers and takes action to pressure the dissidents for compliance. Depending on the relationship, the action may range from mild to drastic. Giving the person the cold shoulder for a while may be enough in some cases; a simple lecture may work in others. In some situations, outright punishment may be imposed in the form of increased supervision, a disciplinary note in a personnel file, or undermining a competing project. If the paternalist is not confident that he or she can successfully gain loyalty, the person is likely to be transferred or terminated. Such drastic action also provides the benefit of being a dramatic example for others who may have considered challenging the paternalist.

Paternalistic relationships are destructive because of the dependence on the paternalist that develops in co-workers and teammates. Over time, people feel less committed to "doing what's right," and feel forced to do whatever the paternalist wants. They feel defeated and develop an attitude which implies "I know what I have to do to survive around here," or "It doesn't matter if I'm right, it's not worth the fight."

Paternalistic Motivations

Like most of the other styles, the paternalistic approach is based on the assumption that an inherent contradiction exists between concern for people and concern for results. Although the paternalist expresses the high concern for others of the 1,9 style and the high concern for results of the 9,1 style, both of these concerns are distorted by the conditional reward and punishment nature of paternalism. The underlying motivations support this distortion by reflecting a desire for veneration and reverence and a fear of repudiation and betrayal (see Fig. 8-3).

Positive Motivation

The positive motivation for the paternalist is a desire for veneration and reverence. Unlike the 9,1, who simply seeks control and dominance, the paternalist also wants to be seen as a caring and generous person. This positive motivation is fulfilled by establishing veneration as a strong part of the culture; relationships often evolve into a "mutual admiration society" where praise dictates action and reaction.

The paternalist secures ongoing veneration by setting the standard for procedures and operations and offering it to others. People working in a paternalistic culture learn that "sound" (expected and rewarded) behavior means compliance with a smile. Since "mimic me" is the leadership style, others are expected to follow the lead by returning praise and support. People who do not revere the paternalist are viewed as ungrateful, even selfish: "I can't believe he did this, after all I've done to help his career." The paternalist also uses praise and encouragement as a primary motivation strategy: "I've found a solution that I know you're going to love," or "I'm going to give you more responsibility because you have shown me you are capable."

Fig. 8-3

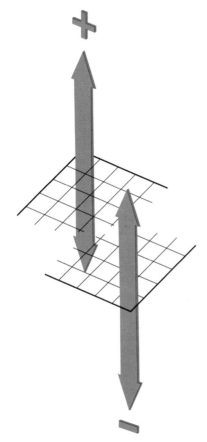

PAT Motivations: PATERNALISTIC
(Prescribe & Guide)

PAT Desire for veneration
& reverence

PAT Fear of repudiation
& betrayal

The paternalist needs to remain the center of attention to maintain the veneration, so people are constantly aware that they must maneuver to avoid upstaging him or her. Because of this, unsound behaviors and actions are often overlooked in a paternalistic culture for fear of retaliation from the paternalist. The prevailing attitude becomes, "I'm not going to make myself a target by delivering bad news." People wait for the paternalist to notice and address any problems rather than risk embarrassing him or her by pointing them out.

The desire for veneration and reverence ultimately makes the paternalist vulnerable by focusing the R3 results on "what *I* think is right." A person trying to undermine the paternalist can do so by appealing to the need for veneration and gaining trust. After trust is established, the paternalist lets his or her guard down. People in favored status are afforded more freedom and opportunity, and can use that freedom to ultimately discredit the paternalist.

Negative Motivation

The negative motivation for the paternalist is a fear of repudiation and betrayal. He or she wants to be seen as a strong, self-determined person, committed to sound relationships that allow colleagues to learn and grow professionally. The paternalist also sees himself or herself as superior, having more experience and better judgment than others. This attitude of superiority allows the paternalist to justify actions that create dependence on him or her: "I know what's best for you," or "You really need to let me show you how to complete this project."

The fulfillment of that fear is avoided by surrounding himself or herself with "yes-people" who say what the paternalist wants to hear: "That's a wonderful idea. I don't know what I would have done without your help." The image he or she maintains of being a selfless and generous leader is threatened when veneration doesn't follow. Using the 1,9 influence, the paternalist also avoids the negative motivation by appealing to people on a personal level. Because he or she expresses caring and concern, others are less likely to subvert suggestions with questions or challenges. This also insulates the paternalist from fault, regardless of how valid the question or challenge may be.

The paternalist reacts to disloyalty by punishing the person perceived to be at fault, sometimes in a dramatic way that sets an example for everyone else. Punishment allows the paternalist to regain control by instilling fear in people who do not accept his or her guidance. Punishment may take many forms. The paternalist may first work to ensure approval and support from others, and then generate criticism against the person "at fault." As a group, the paternalist and his or her supporters put pressure on the dissenter to come around to their way of thinking. The paternalist may also appeal to people's sympathy by expressing self-doubt to regain veneration: "I guess I'm just too generous and trusting," or "Maybe I was wrong entrusting you with all of this responsibility."

Relationship Skills and Paternalistic Behaviors

CRITIQUE

When I give others feedback, I expect them to appreciate it because it is for their own good. I am generous with helpful comments and instruction, but limit critique from others regarding my own effectiveness.

Paternalistic critique is one-way and patronizing, most often in very subtle ways. The paternalist considers it a favor to others to instruct, counsel, and guide them; appreciation is expected in return. Critique is presented for the person's own good, even if the comments are unpleasant. However, others are not allowed to critique the paternalist in this way. People at lower levels of status and authority are considered unworthy of offering an evaluation and their comments are usually dismissed or discounted. This approach limits people to offering the paternalist only two kinds of critique: they can say the paternalist is either good or great.

The paternalist is highly sensitive to critique of any kind and often reacts defensively even to mild comments or suggestions. Even if the critique is sound, the paternalist resists admitting to weakness and often lashes out to discredit or punish accusers. This makes the paternalist a dangerous and destructive force in the team, especially if he or she is the team leader, because people become afraid to confront ineffectiveness.

The guilt-inducing "I told you so" approach is another feature of paternalistic critique that comes from the moralistic advocacy. This feature stems from the "You must…" attitude regarding convictions, where the paternalist offers himself or herself as the benchmark for success. He or she is always quick to point out when mistakes are made, but even more so when mistakes result from not following his or her instructions. When this happens the paternalist takes the opportunity to encourage (or coerce) people to take the instructions to heart next time: "Maybe you'll listen to me next time so you won't make the same mistake twice." The "I told you so" statements also distance the paternalist from having to share responsibility for mistakes.

INITIATIVE

I take strong and decisive action based on what I think is best for everyone involved. I expect others to endorse my efforts, and I express gratitude for support. I discourage attempts to challenge or limit my initiative.

Paternalistic initiative comes across as imposing, even smothering, but often in a subtle way that doesn't instantly offend or turn people off like 9,1 initiative. The paternalist asserts authority and takes charge by enthusiastically offering suggestions: "I have already thought this through and have a plan in mind." When the actions are under way, he or she monitors progress with an ever-present inclination to step in and offer guidance and help. The level of monitoring depends on the degree of trust the paternalist has that the actions will be carried out as specified.

One limitation of this leadership style is the dependence created by the initiative. This dependence leads to a culture that gives the illusion that individuals are able to make decisions, but in reality, they are powerless. Team members are allowed to discuss their opinions and suggest alternatives, but the paternalist has a clear view of how things must be done and rarely allows the course of action to be changed. The paternalist is so subtle, persuasive, and likeable that others are often oblivious to the manipulation until much later. Months may pass before a person with a sounder idea realizes that the paternalist convinced him or her otherwise and suddenly thinks, "He stole my wallet—again!"

Team members sometimes find ways around paternalistic initiative by offering ideas using techniques that allow the paternalist to take credit for and therefore endorse the ideas. This approach is a waste of time and energy, and only works in teams where people don't mind someone else taking credit for their contributions.

The expectation of dependence from one's followers comes into play when something unusual arises while a team member is carrying out the paternalist's specific instructions. The paternalist expects people to let him or her know if anything unusual arises, so "guidance" can be provided; this means production may come to a standstill if the paternalist is unavailable, because no one is willing to take independent initiative (and possibly incur disfavor).

Even if the paternalist makes sound decisions and offers a wealth of experience, the approach has a negative effect. People feel less commitment when their actions are manipulated to reflect the desires and aspirations of someone else. For those who desire strong direction and guidance, like the 5,5, 1,1, or 1,9 styles, paternalism may work, but these people will have little chance to develop and strengthen individual skills. For people who desire more freedom and accountability, like the 9,1 or 9,9 styles (see Chapter 10), the paternalistic initiative only holds them back.

INQUIRY

I seek information from others to reinforce my position. I offer praise and support for inquiry that endorses me, and avoid inquiry that challenges me. I try to influence those with differing opinions to support my views.

The paternalist does not practice enough inquiry to gain a full understanding of the available resources. The high concern for results and people leads the paternalist to actively practice inquiry, but without the objectivity and thoroughness that lead to synergy. The paternalist is so confident in his or her own experience and knowledge that other views are not given as much attention. To make matters worse, people around the paternalist usually respond to inquiry by telling the paternalist what he or she wants to hear instead of what needs to be said. As a result, the quality of the inquiry is only as sound as the R1 resources the paternalist brings to the team, because no other views are really heard.

As with initiative, paternalistic inquiry undermines independence and creativity in others. The objective of paternalistic inquiry is to assure that the person being "helped" clearly understands what he or she should be doing, and is doing it right. Questions are thorough and often patronizing, with an objective of having the person prove that he or she understands what the paternalist wants: "Now, repeat what I just explained, and let's make sure we have a shared understanding," or "Let's go over this one more time."

The paternalist also uses inquiry to maintain a gatekeeper role. If someone has an original idea, it must be "sold" to the paternalist for approval before it can be implemented. The original idea is often diluted because the paternalist often finds a way to take or share responsibility for the idea—otherwise, the paternalist's superior status may be threatened because a colleague looks smarter or more creative.

Paternalistic inquiry is also one-way. He or she does not like being questioned or challenged, but hovers over others to question their performance. Requests for clarification such as, "How do I do this?" or "Would you mind explaining this one more time?" are welcomed because they convey compliance, but questions that challenge the paternalist's thinking are interpreted as threats.

ADVOCACY

I present my convictions with confidence, passion, and authority and encourage others to join me. I vigorously defend my convictions when challenged and stress the importance of loyalty.

Paternalists advocate their point of view quickly and with strong personal conviction. Since he or she feels superior to other team members, the paternalist advocates views and action with confidence and authority. Even though he or she may listen to alternative views, the paternalist sees no real need to explore alternative opinions. Instead, the paternalist feels confident that his or her opinion will provide the needed perspective for everyone involved. The need for veneration makes the paternalist desire praise from others for his or her convictions.

Convictions can take on a moralistic tone reminiscent of parent/child relationships. Convictions are advocated in terms such as, "You should ...," "They need to ...," "We must ..." Team members are expected to jump on board and embrace the paternalist's convictions, preferably with admiration. The paternalist also makes sure that people understand his or her point by adding comments like, "Now, this is important," or "What I'm about to say is critical." The paternalist may also check repeatedly to confirm that the point was heard: "Do you get my point?" or "Am I making myself clear?"

DECISION MAKING

I make decisions based on what I think is best; I offer praise, encouragement, and advantage for people who offer support. I politely listen to alternative views, but persuade others that my decision is best. I am not afraid to tackle controversial decisions in the team and encourage people to give me responsibility.

Paternalistic decision making is unilateral, but he or she goes to great lengths to make it look otherwise. The paternalist seeks out opinions, discusses alternative views, and listens patiently, but his or her mind is already made up. He or she goes through the ritual of selling his or her ideas and gathering enthusiasm and praise, rather than testing ideas for soundness: "Thank you for your ideas, but this is what I think we should do. Don't you agree?" The paternalist also seeks opinions only from people likely to offer support. Individuals likely to test the soundness of a decision are portrayed as negative, and their input is avoided or discredited. This approach makes the paternalist feel good about getting everyone involved, when in fact people are merely being asked to endorse his or her decision.

The paternalist takes pride in making resolute and conclusive decisions; he or she sees this decisiveness as selfless and helpful: "I have a lot of experience to offer, and I only want what's best for everyone involved." Making decisions for everyone else also keeps the paternalist from worrying about being upstaged or supplanted, because outcomes are determined in advance. As long as people can be kept happy with rewards and praise, the paternalist can maintain control over decisions.

CONFLICT RESOLUTION

I take responsibility for diminishing disagreement in my relationships. I consider conflict as a sign of weakness. I appeal to people's loyalty by offering advantages or withdrawing approval to ensure cooperation and continued support. I defend myself vigorously when challenged.

The paternalist manages conflict by establishing himself or herself as an authority figure and by using reward and punishment to control behavior. The paternalist offers

himself or herself as the ideal model and sets out to close the gap between where people are and where they "should be." Praise, advantage, and reward are used to gain commitment, and team members soon learn that anything other than full cooperation is not
acceptable. This leads to a culture where people offer the paternalist lip service—
approval and endorsement—whether they mean it or not. This gives the paternalist a
false sense of confidence regarding his or her effectiveness. The paternalist's ego
expands even more, because no one wants to be the person to disagree or cause conflict
(see Fig. 8-4).

When conflict does arise, the paternalist works hard to reestablish his or her authority and esteemed image as a sound leader. Since the paternalist hates conflict that casts
him or her in a bad light, the initial attempts to address problems are subtle. Praise and
support are quietly withdrawn and mild comments of disapproval are offered. This is
often surprisingly effective because paternalistic cultures include a heightened awareness of the paternalist's moods: "Stay out of his way today, he's in a bad mood," or "He's
really in a good mood about sales today. You should ask him to approve your proposal
now."

If subtle disapproval is not effective, the paternalist feels forced to take a more
direct approach. This may include overt comments to the offending person or an indirect comment expressing disapproval in a general meeting. This is unpleasant and difficult for the paternalist because he or she wants people to be happy. He or she is likely

Fig. 8-4

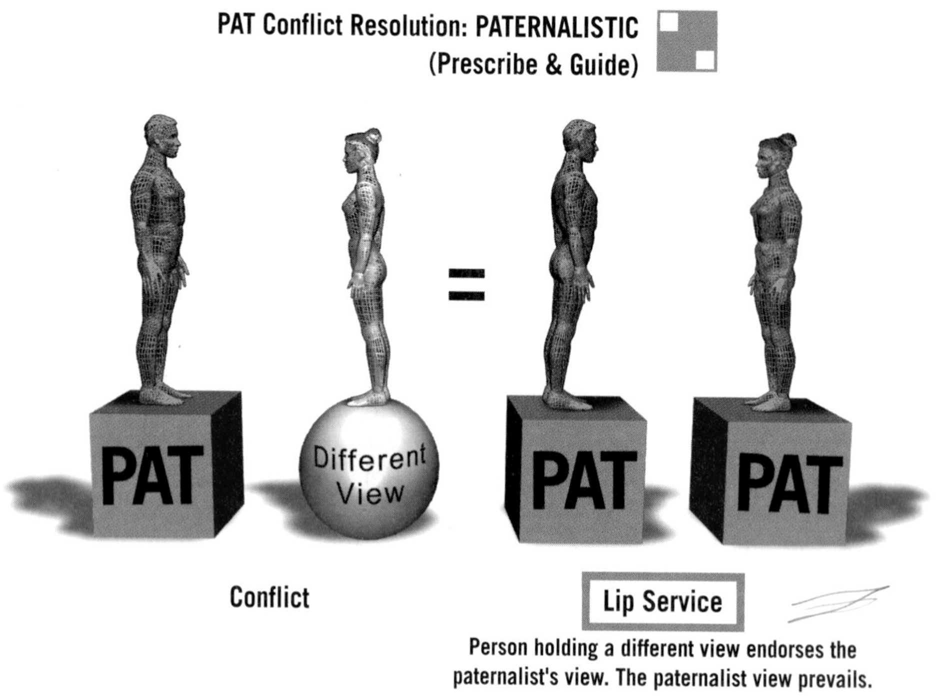

PAT Conflict Resolution: PATERNALISTIC
(Prescribe & Guide)

PAT   Different View   =   PAT   PAT

Conflict   Lip Service

Person holding a different view endorses the
paternalist's view. The paternalist view prevails.

Fig. 8-5

**PAT Conflict Resolution: PATERNALISTIC
(Prescribe & Guide)**

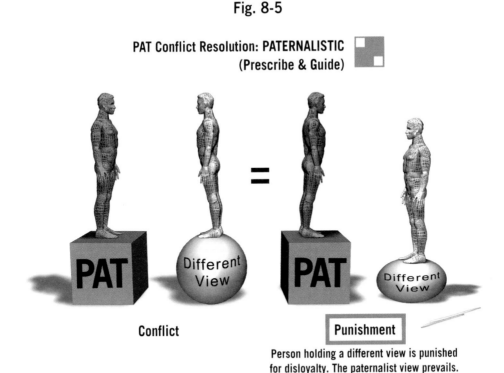

Conflict

Punishment

Person holding a different view is punished
for disloyalty. The paternalist view prevails.

to express sadness and regret for the "horrible problem," which is meant to stimulate people to express sympathy and take action to ease the paternalist's suffering.

If the conflict persists, the paternalist takes harsh action to punish those responsible. Punishment usually includes ostracizing them so they can no longer enjoy the privileges of being a part of the paternalist's entourage (see Fig. 8-5). When conflict escalates to the point where the paternalist publicly imposes punishment, it is not likely that the condemned person will easily be able to regain his or her previous stature; the paternalist risks losing control over his or her remaining followers if such mercy is allowed. If the person is given another chance, the paternalist makes it clear that he or she will have to work hard to get back into good graces.

RESILIENCE

I strive for success and rally people to join my efforts. I initiate celebrations to reinforce support when we succeed. When I suffer setbacks, I express disappointment and withdraw. When confronted with failure, I rely on people close to me for support.

Like other paternalistic behaviors, resilience is also contingent on having support and admiration from others. The paternalist wants to be admired as a strong and capable leader and so with support and veneration, he or she can be fierce and fearless in overcoming adversity. He or she truly feels obligated to loyal followers and will go to any lengths necessary to come through for them. This may include taking on additional work, working long and arduous hours, and making personal sacrifices. The weakness with paternalistic resilience is the need to maintain control and receive recognition for those efforts. This leads to a lack of objectivity when evaluating problems and obstacles. The paternalist is so determined to see his or her approach succeed that opportunities for creative alternatives and synergy are missed.

Paternalist resilience falters when support and admiration are lacking because this is where the confidence to forge ahead originates. Without strong support, the paternalist is vulnerable and less capable of bouncing back. Behind the apparent confidence is an insecure person who expects too much of himself or herself and of others. He or she must maintain an image of superiority, and thus sets high and often unrealistic standards. This means always making sound decisions, exceeding expectations, pleasing everyone, coming through on promises—basically being flawless.

Paternalism lacks one of the most valuable characteristics of successful resilience: humility. Admitting to weakness and failure means dealing with others as equals. This does not come easily to the paternalist.

Recognizing Paternalistic Behavior

Paternalistic behaviors in the workplace are often overlooked because his or her overwhelming intention is to help people. The paternalist is often so nice about dominating others that people are reluctant to retaliate for fear of making themselves look selfish or ungrateful. The fundamental approach to maintaining control over people and results is offering praise, advice, guidance, and help in general, which are noble qualities that people are often reluctant to criticize. The distinctive characteristic of this assistance which makes it paternalistic is that the "help"

Fig. 8-6

PAT Characteristics of Behaviors
PATERNALISTIC (Prescribe & Guide)

Desire for veneration & reverence

judgmental
biased
self-righteous
moralistic
guilt-inducing
lecturing
disapproving
admonishing
micro-managing
condescending
patronizing

1,9

expert
proud
confident
mentor
controlling
detailed
zealous
protective
enthusiastic
nurturing
insistent

9,1

Fear of repudiation & betrayal

is given in a way that prevents others from learning for themselves, taking independent initiative, and exploring individual creativity.

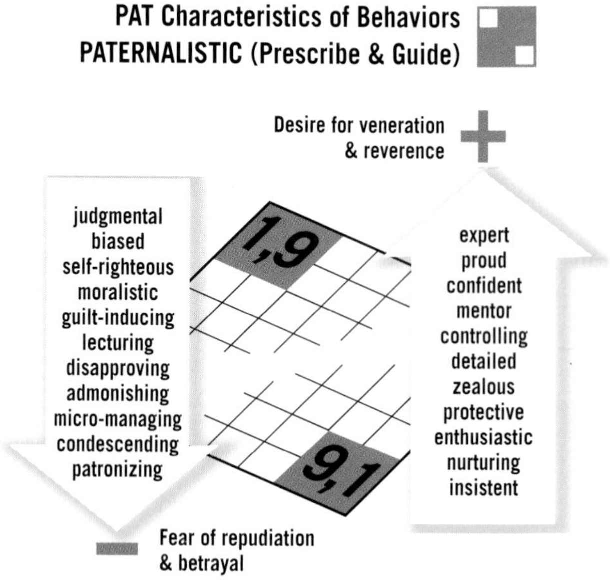

Fig. 8-6 provides key words and phrases that help identify paternalistic behavior in the workplace. They are presented on the motivation scale to show how these behaviors reflect the positive and negative motivations.

Window on Paternalism

The following story illustrates the subtlety and power of the paternalist. While the issue in this story is not a large one from a corporate point of view, it illustrates the ease and effortlessness with which the paternalist maintains control and keeps people happy at the same time.

George was president and owner of a small oil and gas exploration company. He had started the company with three partners five years earlier. They had an impressive record of steady growth in a high-risk industry. Today they employ 38 people and have generated revenues of $14.2 million and profits of $1.7 million in the last fiscal year.

George's secretary, Helen, had been with him from the start and had expanded her skills extensively to become his executive assistant and a valuable part of the company's successful operation.

Helen was given the opportunity to drive a company vehicle, which was very exciting for her since her own car was aging and frequently in the shop for costly repairs. She and George discussed the criteria at length and decided that a small station wagon would work for her and the company and she was given some price guidelines to begin her search. "You know," George mentioned, "the new colors they have for cars now are wonderful. Something in teal would go great with our corporate logo."

A few days later Helen came back quite excited with her choice. The decision was made to go with her choice and as she left the room, George casually asked what color she had chosen. "Plum," she replied.

George paused in reflection and said, "Plum," turning it into more of a question or concern.

Helen of course noticed George's hesitation and subtle lack of endorsement for the color and asked, "Don't you like plum?"

George said, "No, no, plum is fine."

Helen's response was typical of an employee's reaction to a paternalist. She said, "You know it doesn't make any difference to me. I didn't think of the corporate colors, but now that you mention it ... sure, teal's a great color." George nodded and smiled.

George was sitting at his desk 15 minutes later thinking of the interaction and how he had yet again subtly and effectively gotten what he wanted without anyone objecting. This was exactly the kind of thing his 16-year-old daughter had told him a month earlier that she resented most about him.

His daughter's comment had initially annoyed him greatly but the more he thought about it, the more he saw this pattern of behavior occurring in all his relationships. He got up from his desk, went straight to Helen, and said, "Get the plum."

Summary

Paternalists are often very capable and talented overachievers to the point of being "martyrs." They expect too much of themselves, and have trouble accepting help because they dislike revealing weaknesses. Paternalists tend to see issues in terms of loyalty: "You're either with me or against me." As a result, they feel either completely in control or completely subjugated. They are proud and superior to others or they are helpless and dependent. This prevents the paternalist from experiencing the true mutual trust, respect, and synergy that come from sound relationships.

The paternalist wants to be the best for himself or herself and everyone else. This is, of course, an impossible standard for anyone to maintain, and so paternalists constantly walk a tightrope between the poles of total success and total failure. In a shifting worldwide workplace environment where team accomplishment is stronger than the sum of its members, the paternalist is destined to suffer disappointment. Without the ability to come down to the level of others to truly share resources, the paternalist places too much distance between himself or herself and other team members to experience the benefits of sound teamwork and synergy.

The Opportunistic Style: (Exploit & Manipulate)

9

Chapter

Overview

The opportunist-oriented style can use any other style found on the Grid. The opportunist approaches every situation with the underlying attitude of "What's in it for me?" and then takes on whatever style is most likely to result in private advantage. The person operating from an opportunist orientation stands out from every other Grid style because the expressed levels of concern shift as needed to create a convincing façade (see Fig. 9-1). The inconsistency in the approach used makes the style difficult to identify in the short term. Depending on the perceived advantage, the opportunist may come across as strong and capable of leading others, vulnerable and needing guidance, or politically oriented. The style chosen depends on the people and situation faced in conjunction with the potential gain perceived.

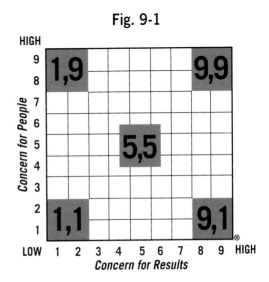

Fig. 9-1

OPP Grid Style: OPPORTUNISTIC (Exploit & Manipulate)

I persuade others to support results that offer me private benefit. If they also benefit, that's even better in gaining support. I rely on whatever approach is needed to secure an advantage.

The opportunist approaches teamwork like a game that he or she must win. The key to successful opportunism is the ability to persuade people to support selfish objectives without revealing the underlying motives. The opportunist doesn't want to bother with traditional ways of building trust and respect—the traditional approach is too slow and the rewards uncertain. He or she prefers to "cut to the chase" and secure this trust and reap the results as quickly as possible. To accomplish this, the opportunist appeals to people personally and professionally. Once he or she has capitalized on the trust, the opportunist feels little obligation to continue the relationship unless there is potential future gain; he or she has "won" and can move on without the encumbrance of long-term commitments.

The method of appeal may take the form of any Grid style. The opportunist may take the 9,1 or paternalistic approach of appearing confident and capable, so that people feel encouraged to follow and be supportive. Another approach is to appear innocent and submissive in a 1,1, 1,9 or 5,5 way. This prompts people with higher levels of concern for results to take the opportunist under his or her wing. This "submissive" approach could be valuable for gaining information from a paternalist. In order to gain another loyal follower, a paternalist might eventually come to see the opportunist as a confidante. The 9,1 person is easily seduced by an opportunist who appears to work twice as hard as everyone else with little concern for making friends. In every case, once the selfish objectives are reached, the opportunist feels no further loyalty or obligation.

The opportunist approaches every team activity as a "deal." He or she takes action only when something is expected in return—there is no such thing as a selfless act. The opportunist may make this fact clear up front, to establish obligation: "I'll do this for you, but you owe me." Or, nothing may be said until later, when he or she needs something from that person: "I did that for you, and now I need something." More often the reminder of obligation is subtle, such as, "Remember when I helped you out last week? I could really use your help now." If someone asks the opportunist for help, he or she weighs the request against what that person has done in the past: "You helped me last week, so I owe you."

Opportunistic Style at the Team Level

The following examples represent typical opportunistic responses in the workplace.

The opportunist response when a team member fails to accomplish his or her share of the workload:

The opportunist will examine the situation looking for potential advantage. Will he or she look effective in comparison to another's poor performance? If so, the opportunist seeks to gain this advantage by consoling the under-achieving person: "They are really expecting too much from you, Tony." At the same time, he or she is telling Tony's supervisor, "It's too bad we can't count on him, but can I help?"

The opportunistic response to constructive critique from a team member:

The reaction depends on whether or not the opportunist wants to be in good favor with the person making the critique. If support is needed from the person, the opportunist expresses remorse and makes an attempt to improve. If the opportunist needs no support, he or she may acknowledge the comments and agree to change, but makes little effort afterward.

Opportunists prefer one-to-one relationships to team relationships because team settings more readily reveal inconsistencies in behavior. The classic example of an opportunist is the door-to-door salesman who says anything and everything to make a sale and then disappears. Once an opportunist has been exposed as selfish in a team setting, people are on guard, and he or she is less able to continue deceiving them. At this point, the opportunist typically moves on to another department or company altogether, to avoid the scrutiny and reduced payoff.

Only the most devious and persuasive opportunists can survive in an intact team for an extended amount of time, because members perceive the inconsistency and refuse to play along. In order to survive, the opportunist is forced to tone down the selfish actions and behave in a more consistent and sincere manner. He or she is more comfortable in teams where turnover is high because the same people are never dealt with for an extended period of time.

Successful opportunists must be subtle and convincing in team relationships. The only chance to succeed is to deal with people on a one-on-one basis whenever possible and then to maintain a consistent style in team settings. The opportunist gains support at the one-to-one level by making each person feel special or privileged: "I'm going to let you in on a secret, but please don't tell anyone else right now." "I don't want to let him know about this because it may upset him right now." This approach allows the opportunist to maintain distinct and compartmentalized relationships and to minimize the likelihood that disparity in behavior will be revealed.

The opportunist appeals to each member according to what he or she wants. For example, an opportunist may deal with a paternalistic team leader by taking on a 1,9 style, offering praise and veneration: "I really admire your strength. I wish I could be more like you." This veneration encourages the paternalist to extend approval and relax restrictions. With individual team members, however, the opportunist may appear more 9,1 in order to gain compliance. In a group setting, the opportunist must be careful to maintain consistency within each one-to-one relationship.

In most cases, the approach taken in a team setting is to appear neutral and save personal lobbying for subsequent individual meetings. The opportunist does not want to jeopardize individual relationships by contradicting something said or done in a group setting. For instance, if the paternalist sees the opportunist dealing with team-mates in a 9,1 way, he or she is less likely to believe that the opportunist is loyal. If the 1,9 person sees the opportunist take swift 9,1 action, he or she is less likely to open up in a trusting way.

Strategic neutrality also gives the opportunist the advantage of quickly changing his or her mind when one side loses strength to another. This approach initially allows the opportunist to switch allegiance without incident. But over time it can also appear evasive and team members are left feeling frustrated by an apparent lack of commitment and convictions: "Why doesn't she just come out and say what she means?" "I get so tired of listening to him dance around a topic without stating a position."

The opportunist can also be destructive in team settings because he or she is often over-competitive. Regardless of whether the competition is for a small weekly goal or a huge annual project, the opportunist sets out to win at any cost. He or she may even play dirty, undermining other teammates' efforts, or try to polarize members against one another to gain personal advantage. This kind of destructive competition drains valuable resources as people become more concerned with protecting themselves and lose sight of goals and objectives.

R2 Relationships and the Opportunistic Style

Since the opportunist's primary objective is to exploit opportunities and people for personal benefit, he or she does not generate the mutual trust and respect needed for long-lasting, sound relationships. The opportunist views relationships as a means to an end and so does not participate in them in any genuine sense. Interactions are superficial and often sporadic—just enough to get what he or she needs. This is the "fair-weather" friend who maintains a relationship when something is needed, but does not go out of the way to maintain close contact after getting what he or she wants. Relationships and teamwork are perceived as unappealing but necessary to get ahead.

Fig. 9-2

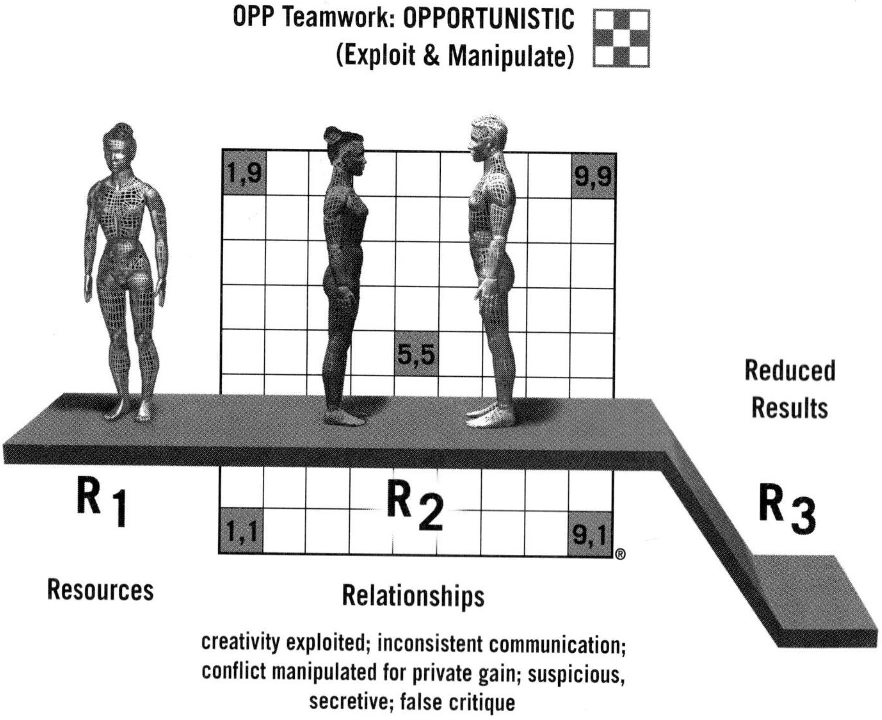

OPP Teamwork: OPPORTUNISTIC
(Exploit & Manipulate)

R₁ — Resources
R₂ — Relationships
R₃ — Reduced Results

1,9   9,9
5,5
1,1   9,1

creativity exploited; inconsistent communication;
conflict manipulated for private gain; suspicious,
secretive; false critique

The opportunist takes pride in being smarter and more cunning than anyone else in the team; participating in relationships is part of the "game," and no real value is seen in genuinely sharing resources for mutual benefit and growth (see Fig. 9-2). This attitude of superiority makes it easier for the opportunist to continue exploiting people for personal gain—it's easier to double-cross someone when you feel disdain for him or her: "If he wasn't even smart enough to see what was going on, he deserved to lose that sale. How gullible can a person be?"

The opportunist is also ineffective in relationships because he or she resists making commitments. "I want to keep my options open" is one way to describe the opportunistic, noncommittal attitude. This comes across as vacillating on polarized issues instead of taking a clear stand. He or she avoids completely burning bridges because "You never know when you might need that bridge again." Since the opportunist never wants to be cornered by having made or supported a bad decision, or by having made an alliance with a person who suffers defeat, he or she often appears cagey in team settings. This attitude prevents strong relationships from forming because people do not feel that they can count on the opportunist to carry through with team objectives.

Opportunistic Motivations

The opportunist sees no true connection between the concern for people and concern for results. No commitment is felt for either concern, but he or she goes through the motions needed to achieve private success. The underlying motivations reflect a desire for advantage and gain, and a fear of entrapment and ridicule (see Fig. 9-3).

Positive Motivation

The positive motivation for the opportunist is a desire for advantage and gain. He or she constantly pursues relationships and opportunities according to the perceived advantage. Every meeting, discussion, proposal, or suggestion is geared toward advancing him or her closer to winning. This does not mean that the opportunist goes out of the way to hurt people or undermine company objectives, but others and their objectives are secondary to the opportunist's personal gain. If, by sheer coincidence, the opportunist causes personal advantage for others, then he or she benefits even further by not appearing as obviously selfish.

The opportunist fulfills the motivation of advantage and gain by skillfully playing a "relationship game." He or she works hard to make a compelling impression. This means getting to know people at a personal level, expressing interest, and ultimately gaining trust and confidence. This may be accomplished by lending a helping hand at a crucial time of need, taking the blame for a mistake, or working twice as hard as others. Make no mistake, however; he or she expects something in return for every gesture or favor.

Another way to nurture the positive motivation is by maintaining a professional advantage over people. Information is key to maintaining an edge, and the opportunist often holds valuable resources in the form of knowledge, skills, and experience. The opportunist wants to be in a position where people depend on him or her for information. This is accomplished by staying informed about the latest technology, competitor advances, current events, and inside company information.

Fig. 9-3

Negative Motivation

OPP Motivations: OPPORTUNISTIC
(Exploit & Manipulate)

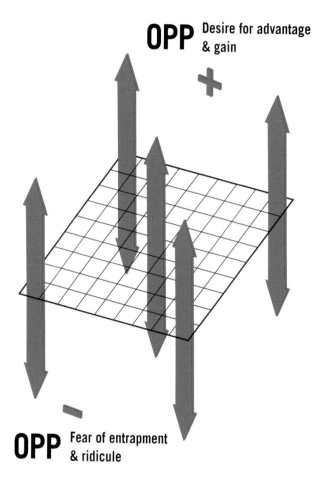

OPP Desire for advantage & gain

+

OPP Fear of entrapment & ridicule

The negative motivation for the opportunist is a fear of entrapment and ridicule. The only way the opportunist can succeed in the game is by fooling people into believing that his or her motives are sincere. Once exposed, the opportunist will be ostracized and lose any chance for advantage and gain; not only do people now realize they have been used but they will likely increase scrutiny and even exact revenge. A bonus achieved by the opportunist may be taken away; a promotion that seemed a sure thing instead becomes a demotion or termination; a source of critical inside information goes silent because all eyes are now on the opportunist. This forces the impatient opportunist to start over from ground zero to establish trust and gain advantage "the hard way," through sincere mutual effort. More often, however, after an opportunist has been exposed, he or she will just move on to another position and initiate the same process with different victims.

The opportunist lives in an all-or-nothing world where a thin line divides total success and total failure. The opportunist wants to avoid exposure and ridicule, but tempts fate by taking actions that may backfire at any moment. This shifts the negative motivation into a driving, adrenaline-pumping type of energy that makes the opportunist willing—perhaps eager—to take risks, even dangerous ones, in order to increase the odds. The more confident and successful the opportunist, the bolder the steps taken to tempt fate.

The negative motivation has three distinct impacts. It forces the opportunist to

- diligently work to maneuver on a course of personal advantage,

- continuously convince people that his or her intentions are sincere, and

- constantly balance the façade presented to others against the opportunist's true underlying goals.

He or she juggles relationships to assure continued support while constantly keeping track of "Which approach do I use with him?" and "Now, what was it I promised to her?"

When the strategy fails and the opportunist's worst fears come true, he or she will often leave rather than face the consequences. Because the opportunist maintains an attitude of superiority, he or she is unable to bear abject criticism and ridicule; once the trouble explodes, the humiliated opportunist usually makes a quick exit.

Relationship Skills and Opportunistic Behaviors

CRITIQUE

I participate in critique as a way to constantly gauge the level of support for my personal goals. I encourage others to confide in me, but often avoid revealing my own evaluations in an effort to keep my options open.

The opportunist uses critique to reinforce existing support and generate new support. Since the opportunist keeps his or her finger on the pulse of where people stand regarding current issues, the company culture, and history, he or she works from a point of advantage. This information is used to initiate critique so that the discussions show him or her in the best possible light. Thus, the opportunist initiates critique and solicits feedback only when the expected outcome is favorable. Weaknesses and problems, when addressed at all, are played down or presented in ways that relieve the opportunist of responsibility. If a bad decision is made, the opportunist draws attention to circumstances beyond his or her control. If the opportunist's team falls far behind on a project, the critique is manipulated so that other team members look responsible.

Critique is also useful to draw attention to a rival's weaknesses in a way that leaves the opportunist looking innocent. This is a way for the opportunist to build himself or herself up by tearing down someone else. For example, he or she may initiate critique in a meeting to draw attention to a mistake without presenting the entire picture. Another approach would be for the opportunist to abuse his or her authority by presenting a biased or incomplete picture of events in a formal critique setting to make someone else look bad. If the person being critiqued by the opportunist attempts to present an alternative view, he or she is cut off or accused of being "unreceptive" or "defensive." Since the opportunist holds the cards, the person being accused has little chance to recover his or her reputation unless the opportunist is exposed.

A great deal of opportunistic critique takes place through underground channels of communication. The opportunist is well informed and so again works from a point of advantage because he or she knows when and how to do damage. He or she knows when and where to make subtle remarks that are sure to be picked up and passed on.

Before long, the comments turn into rumors which grow and spread, while the source is long forgotten.

INITIATIVE

I exercise strong initiative when the result benefits me personally, regardless of the overall impact. I assure support by whatever means necessary, which may include bullying, cajoling, bargaining, encouraging, or ingratiating myself. When I have no personal stake in the outcome, I show no preference. If conflict arises, I search for a covert way to continue my efforts.

Opportunistic initiative is proactive, but manipulative. The attitude reflected in the opportunist's actions is to be first in line for suggestions and to find a way to make things happen to his or her advantage. This attitude may be evidenced in many subtle ways. If others involved are less proactive and seek direction, the opportunist takes an assertive approach. The opportunist may or may not need team member support. If support is needed, the opportunist appeals to the 1,9 individual's concern for people by pointing out all of the expected benefits: "This project is just what we need to reinstall pride in this company. I promise you that people will walk in this door with a smile every day." With 5,5 individuals, the opportunist appeals to their sense of status-consciousness: "This project will bring us in line with every one of our competitors without causing the painful disruption we don't want. We are already behind the times, and we risk falling ever farther if we don't move forward."

If the people involved are more proactive and determined, the opportunist takes an indirect approach. With a paternalist, the opportunist may appeal by planting the idea in a subtle way so that the paternalist later comes up with the same idea "on his or her own." All the while, the opportunist is appealing to the paternalist's need for veneration: "I would really appreciate your advice on this idea I've got. I think I'm probably off base, but I know you can help me put my thoughts in perspective." With a 9,1 individual, the opportunist appeals to the high concern for results: "This project will make it harder for people to take advantage of the company by slacking off between projects. We can increase productivity by 25 percent immediately, and by even more after it's established." This kind of statement is music to 9,1 ears!

Whatever approach is used, the opportunist remains proactive in seeing that actions taken promote his or her intended path. If support begins to wane, the opportunist quickly moves in to reinforce enthusiasm and progress in whatever way is needed—but only if the goal continues to promise private advantage.

The opportunist may also first assess where others stand before making a move. This creates more time to take in information and to prepare both a counterposition and a more persuasive proposal if needed. The opportunist may also use subtle comments and suggestions to generate fear and doubt or to build confidence for another position.

If the opportunist has low stakes in the initiative, he or she shows less enthusiasm. In these situations, the opportunist uses several approaches to take advantage of this time off from pursuing personal goals. He or she may use the opportunity to ensure future support by extending help to others. Another approach may be to take advantage of the low stakes and slack off in a 1,1 way.

INQUIRY

I inquire to obtain information from others in a calculated way by asking questions that establish trust and confidence. With this information, I tailor my approach to gain advantage for my personal goals. I overcome different opinions by shifting my inquiry to be more acceptable.

The opportunist needs to know what is going on all of the time for two fundamental reasons: he or she wants to be the most informed person regarding company actions, technology, etc., and also wants to be in touch with people's perceptions. These two forms of information provide the point of advantage that the opportunist wants to maintain. Professional information regarding technology, competition, and trends allows the opportunist to stay one step ahead of most people and to be more prepared to win. This need for information creates a strong utilization of inquiry skills on many levels.

The opportunist establishes strong lines of communication within the company. He or she uses inquiry skills, bargains, favors—whatever is necessary—to find out information about past, present, and future company strategy. The kind of information desired is usually outside of formal channels and is obtained through personal, even devious, methods. For example, the opportunist makes friends with the vice president's assistant to find out who is favored for a promotion. He or she establishes contacts in the human resources department to find out who is coming and going. The opportunist stays ahead of the game by being more prepared and better informed.

The opportunist has a special talent for getting people to divulge information. He or she knows how to express concern and asks questions in ways that make people open up and offer information, sometimes even when they shouldn't. This ability to acquire information is part of the persuasive appeal that is common among successful opportunists. Such a person can observe behavior and actions and then ask the right questions to find out how to move forward.

Any information gathered is constantly tested for validity. The opportunist does not want to risk exposure and ridicule, and so ultimately trusts no one; he or she takes the information at its apparent face value, but then does thorough verification and cross checking. This gives the opportunist the advantage of spotting and dealing with contradictions immediately, preferably before any damage is done to his or her personal goal.

ADVOCACY

I express convictions in a persuasive way when the result supports my personal goals. When little or no personal stake is involved, I endorse ideas that may provide personal advantage in the future.

The opportunist uses the information gathered from thorough inquiry to create a buffer between the convictions he or she actually holds and the "convictions" that must be expressed in order to achieve personal advantage. The real objective of private benefit cannot be revealed, so the opportunist uses the information to "create" convictions to express. Circumstances are evaluated in advance, with an understanding of the history, different perspectives, and options available. The opportunist utilizes whatever form of advocacy is most likely to result in personal gain. Although he or she may go through the motions of clarifying points with people and asking more questions, the opportunist is already advocating from a position of strategy.

Like other relationship skills, with opportunism, advocacy is simply another facet of the game. The opportunist views advocacy as important for lobbying support and eliminating opposition. Part of the process includes locating proponents and adversaries; once identified, these people are "worked" directly and indirectly to ensure success. Those extending support are played up to with favors and other benefits that ensure continued support. Adversaries are undermined, usually in subtle ways, so that the selfish motives will not be discovered. The opportunist may, for example, start rumors to damage the person's credibility and raise doubt. All of these behind-the-scenes activities allow the opportunist to advocate from an advantageous position when the issue finally comes up for formal consideration.

How the convictions are expressed depends on the people and personal stakes involved. If the stakes are low and those involved have no real influence, the opportunist expresses convictions in ways that garner support. He or she considers these situations low-risk and valuable for establishing credibility. When the opportunist lacks sufficient information, however, he or she withholds declarations of convictions as long as possible. When the individuals involved are more informed and higher-ranking than the opportunist, the fear of exposure keeps the opportunist from declaring convictions. Instead, he or she prefers to take a solicitous approach of listening, asking questions, and offering support.

DECISION MAKING

I subtly lobby for decisions that benefit me personally, regardless of the overall results. I encourage others to confide in me and listen sympathetically so that I know the best approach needed to gain support. I avoid taking responsibility in the team for controversial decisions unless the personal benefit to me outweighs the potential of alienating others.

The opportunist approaches decision making like a puppet master. This is where all of the preparation and maneuvering pays off. When decisions come up for team consideration, the opportunist leads the discussions to reveal the strengths and weaknesses that benefit him or her personally. The key to the success of this approach is that the opportunist comes away looking innocent and "objective."

Whenever possible, he or she takes control and maneuvers discussions so that supportive points are elaborated and contradictory points are played down. This maneuvering may take on any form, depending on the situation. If supportive points are raised, the opportunist says, "That's a good point. Let's elaborate on that more." If a contradictory point is raised, the opportunist guides attention in another direction: "You may have a point, but I think the other perspective has more validity, and here's why." If attention cannot be shifted away from the contradictory side, the opportunist may attempt to delay the decision. This delay provides more time to generate support before a final decision is made.

The opportunist feels that one-alone decisions are much easier and require much less lobbying for support, especially if the opportunist is in a position of authority and doesn't have to answer to anyone. He or she makes decisions that benefit him or her personally but presents them with an explanation or spin to play down that aspect: "I made the decision to personally take the trip to Hawaii instead of sending you, because I want to deal with some of the problems myself." Unless the opportunist is very talented in covering his or her tracks, people see through these kinds of unilateral and self-serving decisions. Favors and benefits may be offered to others in compensation, but a blatant opportunist sitting in the highest seat of authority may not even care what others think—because he or she doesn't have to answer to anyone.

As with other opportunistic objectives, the goal of decision making is to advance results that have personal benefit. If others benefit from these goals, then the opportunist is more than happy to have them jump on board; if others do not benefit, the opportunist has to work harder to cover his or her tracks to look sincere, but that, too, is just part of the game.

CONFLICT RESOLUTION

If I have something to gain, I manipulate conflict to further my personal ambitions without exposing my intentions. My tactics range from subtly encouraging disagreement, actually resolving conflict, taking sides to gain support, to offering sympathy. If I have no personal stake in the result, I take little interest in resolving conflict.

The opportunist avoids conflict because it creates situations where it is difficult to remain flexible. Conflict causes people to demand a statement of convictions and can easily lead to polarized points of view. If caught unprepared, the opportunist could damage his or her own chances of coming out ahead. The opportunist prefers the one-on-one persuasive approach as opposed to confronting conflict openly in a group setting. The one-on-one approach provides a better chance of widespread support because the opportunist can appear to be on both sides of the conflict. The opportunist resists being forced to state a position or committing to a specific point of view in an open setting.

Conflict is avoided by maintaining a safe distance. When the chips are down, the opportunist is usually the first to run, rather than face the consequences. This evasive approach may take many forms. If the opportunist is in a position of authority, he or she may halt discussion or distract attention from potentially damaging issues: "Let's move on and we'll deal with this later." When the opportunist is a person of lower ranking, he or she takes an evasive approach to escape responsibility: "I don't know what happened. I was just doing my job." This allows him or her to salvage support from both sides by playing innocent. Another approach is to support the view that is most likely to look good to others. If a co-worker is involved in a conflict with a superior, the opportunist may try hard to make a good impression on the superior: "I heard about some of the problems you have been having with Tom. Let me tell you about some other problems I've heard about him."

The opportunist may try a completely different way to create distance from the conflict. He or she may find the risk too high and prefer to reverse the tables altogether by taking the "martyr" role of stepping aside and letting someone else win. The opportunist is, in effect, giving a victory to someone else in order to look better in the long run. This approach also has the ironic advantage of making the other person appear selfish, while the opportunist looks like the victim: "I just couldn't bear to take an action that would hurt so many people. I know I was wrong, but at least I can sleep at night."

Still another approach to conflict resolution is to circumvent it by encouraging reciprocity. The opportunist wants to prevent a polarized impasse as much as possible, and so encourages each side to work something out. The alternative encouraged is, of course, the one that benefits the opportunist, but that is less apparent than his or her efforts to reach a resolution: "I only want what's best for everyone involved." "You have a good point, but let's look at another alternative." The objective of the negotiation is to reduce tension and provide ample room for the opportunist's position to emerge as the

Fig. 9-4

OPP Conflict Resolution: OPPORTUNISTIC
(Exploit & Manipulate)

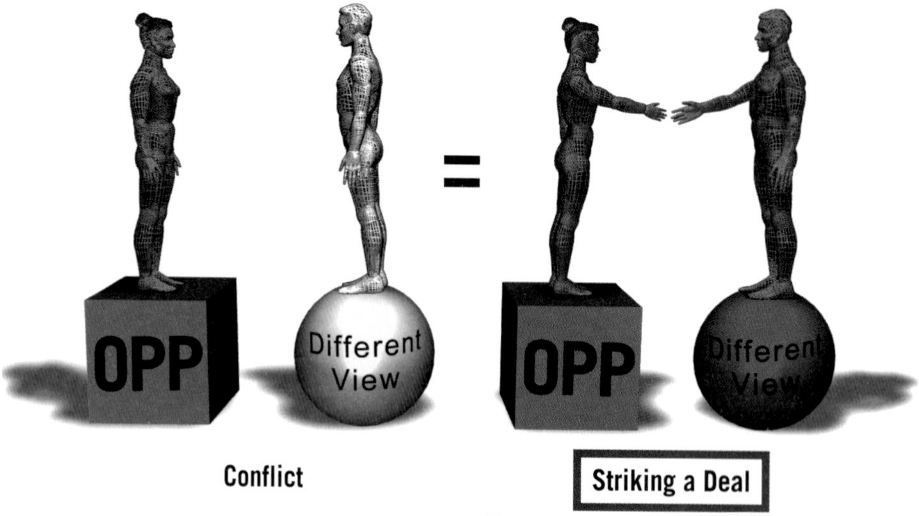

Conflict   Striking a Deal

The opportunist strikes a deal to win favor
through obligation. The opportunistic view prevails.

favorite. This approach is similar to the 5,5 search for compromise, but unlike 5,5, the opportunist is only concerned with maintaining widespread support and ultimately winning. Status and fitting in politically is not important per se, only as a means to an end. A bold and aggressive alternative may just as easily be advocated as a compromise position if it poses the strongest outcome for the opportunist.

Another opportunistic approach to conflict resolution involves striking a deal with an opponent (see Fig. 9-4). Because of his or her thorough inquiry skills, the opportunist knows what people want, fear, and need, and he or she does not hesitate to use that information when backed into a corner. This is the time to remind people of their debts. Such bargaining may be subtle or overt, and it is often the last approach used because it brings the opportunist much closer to exposure. The opportunist may voice a direct threat: "Get me out of this, or I'll reveal what happened on that last deal," or it may be subtle: "I was thinking about that deal I helped you with last month, and I could really use your help now. I would hate to have to see all that business come out." Whatever the method, the opportunist takes whatever risk is necessary to get himself or herself out of a tight spot.

RESILIENCE

I focus my energies on my own success. I do this by constantly walking a fine line between serving my own needs and gaining and maintaining the trust of others. Failure is part of the game; I usually deal with it by covering up, shifting the responsibility, or moving on rather than facing the negative personal exposure.

The opportunist is highly resilient to setbacks, as long as private advantage is still possible and he or she can find a way to continue playing the game. From the opportunist's perspective, the possibility of failure and setbacks makes things interesting by challenging the odds. The opportunist's extensive preparation creates an arrogance regarding setbacks, giving the opportunist an "I can do anything" attitude. When working with people, he or she takes pride in meeting every challenge and beating the odds, especially if it means increasing the end-result personal benefits. He or she may even seek out risk to make the game more exciting.

The level of confidence in taking risks is only present when the opportunist is very secure regarding relationships and the expected results. After the façade presented to others is established, he or she feels comfortable and confident enough to raise the stakes without being caught. If the goal of getting a boss's job becomes too easy, the opportunist may try for a higher position. If the goal is to damage the credibility of a colleague, the opportunist may go even further and try to get the colleague fired.

When the opportunist faces total exposure from which no escape is possible, he or she has no resilience. The last thing the opportunist wants to do is face the people he or she has betrayed and endure their resentment and bitterness. The only alternative to this kind of exposure is to leave the team to avoid ridicule and try to salvage whatever benefit is possible. For example, he or she may convince a company to sign a lucrative exit package that establishes financial security while discretely securing another job.

Another example is a person who secretly uses company resources like existing clients to establish employment somewhere else. Once the opportunist faces exposure, no loyalty is felt toward the people or company. He or she takes whatever is needed to move on and never looks back.

Being so informed and thorough, however, the opportunist is often in tune with company activities and finds a way to escape without having to face the consequences. He or she may anticipate the exposure and set someone else up for the fall. If he or she is unable to avoid confrontation, the opportunist offers any excuse to lessen personal culpability. This may include blaming people (especially people who are not there) or making false accusations. The least likely possibility is that the opportunist will face up to and take responsibility for his or her actions.

Recognizing Opportunistic Behavior

Opportunistic behaviors can be difficult to recognize on the surface because they include any Grid style. The distinction comes across in two distinct ways. First, the opportunist deals with others in superficial terms. Relationships are maintained only when he or she wants something now or in the future. A team member may be suffering through numerous problems, personal or otherwise, but the opportunist rarely offers support unless he or she needs something in return. A simplified example is, "I am so sorry to hear you lost the key person on your project last month, and by the way, I need a favor ... "

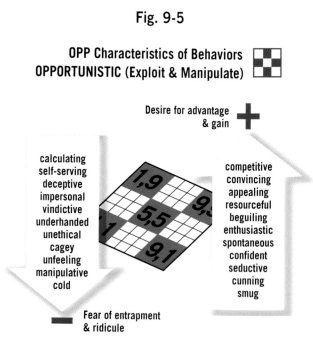

Fig. 9-5

OPP Characteristics of Behaviors
OPPORTUNISTIC (Exploit & Manipulate)

Desire for advantage & gain

calculating
self-serving
deceptive
impersonal
vindictive
underhanded
unethical
cagey
unfeeling
manipulative
cold

competitive
convincing
appealing
resourceful
beguiling
enthusiastic
spontaneous
confident
seductive
cunning
smug

Fear of entrapment & ridicule

Opportunistic behavior can also be distinguished by inconsistent efforts to establish relationships. The opportunist gets as close to a person as needed to get what he or she wants, but is not interested in maintaining the kind of lasting relationships that are based on mutual trust and respect. The superficial nature of the behavior often comes across as an inconsistency. For example, the opportunist may express a high interest in a project while he or she is involved, but not acknowledge or keep up with progress beyond. This insincere aspect of opportunistic behavior may take longer to reveal because the relationship may be mutually beneficial for as long as he or she is a member of the team or as long as the supervisor in question holds authority (and the possibility for a promotion) in his or her hands.

Fig. 9-5 provides key words and phrases that help identify opportunistic behavior. They are presented on the motivation scale to show how the behaviors reflect the positive and negative motivations at work.

Window on Opportunism

Philip was a new member of a marketing division team for a sports equipment company. He was brought in as a high-profile representative for the team, having competed successfully as an athlete. Philip also had a degree in kinesiology, and after spending a few years in sports training, had decided to pursue a career in business.

He was the youngest team member and was determined to make the same kind of splash early in this career as he had as an athlete. Philip spent his first six months pouring himself into the job. He found out everything he possibly could about the latest trends in the industry and made a personal commitment to come up with an innovation that no one else had thought of. He thought this would allow him to jump quickly up a few rungs on the corporate ladder. He didn't want to deliberately hurt his team members, but, after all, they would benefit from any innovations he developed and they would "owe" him. He felt their scrutiny, but he was determined to prove himself. He knew that at least two senior people in the company had been passed over for his job, and that some people were skeptical about his ability to perform. He had even overheard someone in the break room one day making the comment, "Sure, he's great for our image, but we don't need a figurehead. We need someone who knows the business." He had always worked best alone and under pressure and he was invigorated by this challenge.

He worked hard and proved to be an indomitable force in the team. This would be valuable later on when the team members would have to accept him as their boss. And he was certain he could make that happen. He prepared for meetings weeks in advance, rehearsed his portion of presentations over and over again, and reviewed every industry periodical he could get his hands on. He did not want to be caught off guard. His philosophy was "Always look ready for your boss's job." In addition to working hard within the team, he worked alone for months on a new idea and organized a surprise presentation at a key department meeting where they would begin planning a strategy for next year's marketing focus.

None of his teammates had a clue about his presentation. However, his supervisors were impressed with his presentation and research, and his plan was incorporated into the marketing goals for the next year. His team's response, however, was reserved. He felt that they only "tolerated" him and were jealous of his accomplishing so much in so little time.

At a team development meeting, his team members confronted him with their impressions: "Every team decision is a competition with you." "You constantly jump in and cut us off before we can offer a suggestion because you've read some article, or talked to someone at another company." "You worked alone for six months on an elaborate plan and didn't include any of us. You made us all look unprepared." Each comment was followed up with specific examples.

The comments went on and on. At first, Philip was amazed at the team's perception of him, but then he remembered he had heard the same types of comments from his siblings and even his wife. This realization really hit him hard. The kind of training that had encouraged him to "win at all costs" was making him lousy at relationships. "I wanted trust and respect, but was going about it all wrong. Instead of working to build relationships from the ground up, I was trying to rush the process and circumvent the very people I needed to cultivate."

Philip immediately began working to shift his focus to a collaborative approach that included involving team members more in his own development. He asked for their advice and asked questions when he wasn't sure about an idea instead of depending on covert inquiry. The respect he craved came with time and the relationships he developed were much more rewarding than any he had ever experienced. By the time his idea was fully developed into a marketing strategy the following year, it was stronger and more complete because of the critique and input from his teammates. And everyone, not just Philip, was committed to seeing it succeed.

Summary

The opportunist never experiences the benefits of sound teamwork. He or she works from a distorted perspective and believes that the only way to succeed and gain personal reward is at the expense of others. Teamwork, in the sense of sharing responsibilities and resources, is viewed ultimately as a compromise to success; the opportunist never gets close enough to people to understand how sharing responsibilities can lead to new, innovative perspectives. The tension of maintaining a façade never subsides, because he or she cannot share true feelings and spread the responsibility for success to others.

Because of the combination of increased resentment from team members and an inability to understand the benefits of teamwork, the opportunist works at more of a disadvantage than any other style. Even though the opportunist may appear untrustworthy, team members who extend trust and support have a better chance of making an opportunist more team-oriented. The opportunist has great resources to bring to a team because of his or her talent for inquiry and investigation, but is usually too competitive to trust or respect others. If he or she has the opportunity to experience team synergy, it is possible that change will follow.

In theory, people may see business as a dog-eat-dog world where everyone has to do whatever it takes to get by. In reality, however, no one wants to work with an opportunist. People want to trust their co-workers, because there is enough to worry about with competitors, customers, and other "outside" antagonists. No one wants to have to worry about a team member undermining him or her for a promotion. Trust is seen as a fundamental value and a requirement for sound teamwork. Opportunism undermines trust.

Because of this untrustworthiness, opportunism is often seen as the least redeemable style. People are slower to help an opportunist change than they are with any other Grid style, because they have often "been taken" by him or her before. The opportunist has to work harder to prove his or her sincerity because, in some prior situation, he or she has gained and then betrayed the very trust that is now desired.

The 9,9 Style: Sound (Contribute & Commit)

Overview

The 9,9-oriented style is located on the top right corner of the Grid figure and integrates a high concern for people with a high concern for results. The difference between the person operating from a 9,9 orientation and the other six Grid styles is that the 9,9 person sees no contradiction in demonstrating a high concern for both people and results (see Fig. 10-1). He or she feels no need to restrain, control, or diminish the concerns for people or results in relationships. The consequence is a freedom to test the limits of success with enthusiasm and confidence. The 9,9 attitude leads to more effective work relationships based on *what's right* rather than *who's* right.

The full integration of concern for people and results is in contrast to the levels of control evident in each other style. The 9,1 person feels that a high concern for results reduces the expression of a high concern for people. The 1,9 person feels the reverse —that a high concern for people is more important than results. The 5,5 feels that a high concern for either is too risky, and prefers to remain at a middle level to maintain the status quo. The 1,1 sees any high concern as unrealistic and too demanding. The paternalist expresses a high concern for results and for people, but is unable to relinquish control and allow others to make their own contribution. The opportunist sees a contradiction in working with others in the first place and so uses people and organizations to further selfish goals.

Fig. 10-1

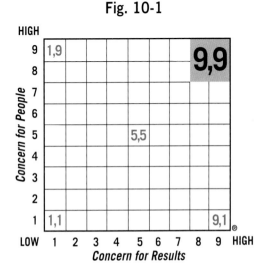

9,9 Grid Style: SOUND (Contribute & Commit)

I initiate team action in a way that invites involvement and commitment. I explore all facts and alternative views to reach a shared understanding of the best solution.

127

The 9,9 style is firmly entrenched in logical reasoning and common sense business thinking: If you have a problem, get it out into the open and work through it. This person is truly objective, and is not afraid to tackle tough issues openly and honestly. This approach brings strength and focus to team resources and potential R3 results, but can also lead to dramatic resistance in a culture unfamiliar with the style. Although effective, the 9,9 style can come across as forceful and blunt in a team or company where the culture dictates playing politics, smoothing over conflict, or always deferring to one or more people in authority regardless of how sound or unsound their actions might be. Over time, however, 9,9 actions demonstrated in a team overcome any fears that prevent people from embracing the style.

9,9 Sound at the Team Level

The following examples represent typical 9,9 responses in the workplace.

The 9,9 response when a team member fails to accomplish his or her share of the workload:

The 9,9 person challenges the teammate based on facts. He or she is not afraid to confront a teammate and to be firm if necessary. The 9,9 person discusses the workload to develop a shared understanding of what is expected and to reach agreement on how to improve. If the teammate has a repeated history of not sharing the workload, the 9,9 clearly outlines the consequences for not meeting the steps for improvement.

The 9,9 response to constructive critique from a team member:

The 9,9 willingly accepts the comments and asks questions to explore whether the points made are valid. If they are, the 9,9 does not hesitate to change his or her thinking to reflect the new ideas. If the ideas are not sound, the 9,9 person provides the critiquer with sound rationale in an effort to reach a shared understanding.

When it comes to describing sound teamwork, many people assume the following conditions must apply:

- Teamwork occurs only when members are assembled in a face-to-face setting like a task force, committee, or meeting.
- Successful teamwork cannot occur at the one-alone initiative level.
- Effective teamwork only results when all members involved reach agreement.

All three assumptions are incorrect. The 9,9 team approach is often misunderstood, as people picture teams that spend all of their time holding meetings and discussing decisions. In fact, 9,9 teamwork reduces the number of meetings as well as the duration of those that are held. Effective results come when people are kept informed and up to date on the information that will enable them to carry out their responsibilities to the fullest. It is this emphasis on clear, concise communication—inquiry, advocacy, and critique—that enables members of the 9,9 team to dispense with politics, favoritism, or hidden agendas and to offer ideas and suggestions openly.

In a lean and fast-paced office environment or where employees are linked remotely by computers, face-to-face meetings are less practical. But when 9,9 principles are in place, neither the physical location of employees or pace of work are barriers to making sound decisions and achieving high-end results. The high level of communication in the 9,9 team keeps team members informed in a way that enables them to make sound, one-alone decisions when it becomes necessary. Team members know what is going on in the team because they are constantly taking advantage of all resources available. 9,9 teamwork is no accident. It comes as a result of a concerted and determined effort by everyone involved.

Effective meetings result by keeping people informed, addressing problems that arise, and involving only those who need to be involved. Successful 9,9 teams may hold formal meetings very infrequently. In some teams, solo action may be the dominant characteristic, with each person working alone, while team-wide meetings occur only for updating purposes. Another task may require that two members work together; at other times several, but not all, team members will work together on a problem. In each case, only those who have the knowledge, skill, or expertise to contribute to the outcome (R3 results) are involved.

9,9 teams are characterized by enthusiasm, confidence, and commitment. They can sometimes be seen by outsiders as "cult-like" because of the openness and trust that is unfamiliar in many work settings. This increased commitment develops in three distinct ways:

- increased and better quality involvement among members;

- discussion of ideas in depth without fear of recrimination; and

- exploration of creative possibilities often withheld in other teams.

These are the kinds of conversations that lead to truly thinking "outside the box." Steve Jobs, co-founder and current CEO of Apple computers, had the first vision of a "personal computer on every desktop" in the 1970s. More recently, he envisioned an affordable computer (the iMAC) that could be taken out of a box and plugged into the wall with virtually no setup requirements. But this kind of thinking doesn't bear fruit unless people feel confident enough in their relationships to initiate in-depth and creative discussions.

In the 9,9 team, even when their ideas are not embraced, people feel they have been given the chance to offer opinions that have been "heard." As a result, when a 9,9 leader makes a tough decision, others are more likely to support it even if they don't agree with the solution. With barriers to communication gone, individuals feel safe and confident to express even far reaching ideas without fear of embarrassment or other negative consequences. This high-involvement approach leads to a deeper commitment to objectives and an increased sense of personal stake. If one member's creative idea is incorporated into a strategy, he or she feels more commitment to seeing the strategy succeed. People always feel a higher sense of commitment to something they helped create.

People feel more enthusiastic and committed in the 9,9 team because they are more informed. Information is not hidden or edited to protect people or personal agendas. The high involvement of the 9,9 style includes sharing information in an open and candid way so that every possible alternative can be explored. This means addressing problems openly and honestly and providing constructive critique and support to teammates to help them improve. When people are more informed, possible problems dissipate and many others never appear. When people have all the facts, there is less chance that circumstances will get blown out of proportion by rumor and speculation. There is also less chance for misunderstanding and resentment to go unchecked because of the commitment to confront and resolve differences.

The 9,9 high-involvement attitude fosters confidence within teams. Mutual trust and respect increases as members feel free to express their feelings and opinions, take risks, and explore creative solutions together. Because the contributions are evaluated on merit rather than personal popularity or power, the fears present in other styles are replaced by a willingness to be vulnerable and a sincere desire among teammates to help each other. If one member's idea leads to problems, the entire team shares the responsibility for supporting the idea and works together to improve.

Despite this increased sense of team membership and support, the 9,9 approach does not take away from a person's sense of individual contribution. The increased support within teams means that individual members are more likely to take chances in exploring creative ideas without fear of ridicule. Since contributions are judged on merit, people also feel more pride when an individual suggestion leads to success. The result is a constant "raising of the bar," where healthy competition challenges people to continually learn and increase their effectiveness.

R2 Relationships and the 9,9 Sound Style

By eliminating the perceived contradiction between the concern for people and the concern for results, the 9,9 approach automatically increases available resources. All of the energies spent in other Grid styles to diminish the concern for people or results can now be spent enhancing them.

The high level of openness and candor reduces stress in all relationships because members feel free to express themselves. People confide in each other and build a foundation of support; members help each other overcome obstacles and achieve personal and team goals. These relationships also provide increased resilience to problems and setbacks because teams resources have been optimized. This does not mean that politics, resentments, fears, and unhealthy competition disappear; they can always arise as a part of any group activity. The difference is that the likelihood is reduced that these kinds of problems will advance to the point of impasse because the discussions are focused on remaining objective and following logic and facts. When openness and candor characterize the work setting, behaviors are addressed and resolved quickly so peo-

Fig. 10-2

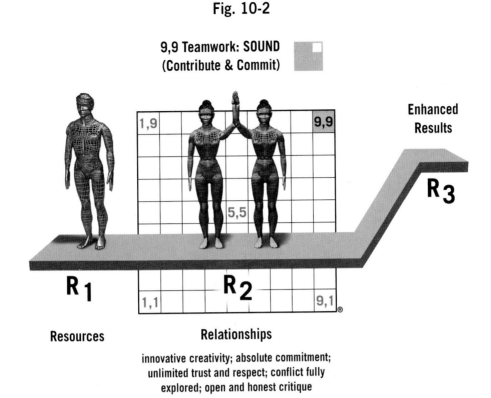

**9,9 Teamwork: SOUND
(Contribute & Commit)**

Enhanced
Results

R₃

1,9

9,9

5,5

R₁

R₂

1,1

9,1

Resources

Relationships

innovative creativity; absolute commitment;
unlimited trust and respect; conflict fully
explored; open and honest critique

ple can move on. The openness and candor gives team members a better chance to address problems early and more effectively instead of withholding, covering up, or smoothing over information until it "blows up" and causes unnecessary damage and setbacks (see Fig. 10-2).

9,9 Sound Teamwork and Synergy

Relationships based on mutual trust, respect, and candor contribute to synergy. Synergy is difficult to achieve without a work environment where people can express convictions openly and feel free to challenge ideas. When a truly open environment exists, information previously unknown, hidden, or repressed becomes available for objective consideration. Synergy results when this information leads to newly emerging ideas and possibilities greater than what would be expected from each individual.

9,9 Sound Motivations

The 9,9 approach is based on the assumption that no contradiction exists between the concern for people and the concern for results, and so the soundest approach is to express a high concern for both (see Fig. 10-3). Although the style helps to eliminate

Fig. 10-3

**9,9 Motivations: SOUND
(Contribute & Commit)**

9,9 Desire for contribution
& commitment

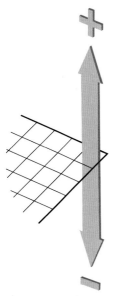

9,9 Fear of selfishness &
missed opportunity

the unhealthy use of fear as a motivator, the 9,9 person still experiences the basic human motivations of fear and desire. These motivations include a positive desire for contribution and commitment and a fear of selfishness and missed opportunity.

Positive Motivation

The 9,9 person is motivated by a positive desire to make a contribution with a sense of commitment at the personal, team, and organization level. He or she wants to feel that the efforts make a difference and have a positive influence. The 9,9 individual works with enthusiasm, determination, and respect for co-workers. If the 9,9 person sees human resources with untapped potential, he or she works with teammates to build those resources. Individuals can expand their skills and gain experience—valuable to the individual as well as the team—under 9,9 leadership. When the 9,9 person feels that desired outcomes are worth the risk and sacrifice, he or she sets an example by declaring personal commitment.

This positive motivation also reflects the *what's* right (as opposed to *who's* right) attitude that is the foundation of 9,9 actions. The 9,9 wants to make a contribution, but not at the expense of people or results; personal or team accomplishment that works against company goals is not attractive because this conflicts with *what's* right. The same goes for company goals that work against personal or team goals. The 9,9 person is not afraid to point out contradictions in a constructive way, and to then work for mutual resolution.

The *what's right* motivation—to make a contribution and demonstrate commitment—leaves the 9,9 person and his or her team with the feeling that "I did my best." This makes it easier to accept both positive and negative consequences without regrets.

Negative Motivation

The negative motivation for the 9,9 is a fear of selfishness and missed opportunity. He or she fears developing a biased attitude and losing the ability to remain objective. If this happens, the 9,9 person loses the capacity to pursue relationships and goals on a *what's right* basis. Subsequent selfish behavior ultimately prevents the 9,9 from being able to make a sound contribution. The 9,9 person knows that in order to achieve sound goals, all available resources are needed. If people perceive the 9,9 as selfish, mutual trust and respect is damaged and he or she loses access to these resources. The "lost resources" are the missed opportunities for everyone involved.

The 9,9 avoids these fears by communicating with people in an open and honest way, taking proactive steps to stay in touch with team actions. This means maintaining an awareness of team morale, progress, and problems so they can be addressed and changes can be made quickly. If, for example, a team member completes an advanced degree, new skill training, or simply completes some other relevant learning, the 9,9 person seeks to incorporate those new resources into the team. This proactive attitude makes it obvious that he or she wants to make the soundest contribution possible so that everyone benefits.

Relationship Skills and 9,9 Sound Behaviors

CRITIQUE

I promote thorough critique that explores all concerns and alternatives. I keep critique objective, especially when the circumstances are emotional or difficult. I welcome critique and explore comments to assure continued progress and learning.

The most striking characteristic of the 9,9 style is the openness and candor present in relationships. This characteristic is most obvious in the 9,9 approach to critique and feedback. 9,9 critique includes a continuous examination of effectiveness in team actions by incorporating pre-, periodic, concurrent, and post-critique. This continuous approach leads to faster and more effective problem solving, because problems are either anticipated and eliminated ahead of time, or are caught and resolved quickly as they occur. The increased awareness in the team enhances the chance that problems are caught early before extensive damage occurs.

People usually think of critique as something that occurs only when an activity is finished, where it is often a celebration of success. And many teams never bother to examine how and why they achieved success. Instead, the critique results in praise and celebration meant to boost morale and build confidence without analyzing the effectiveness of the effort or making plans for further improvement. This kind of celebration can lead to complacency, one of the most damaging side effects of success; people become so confident in their successes that they begin to feel they have reached the pinnacle of accomplishment. As time passes, overconfidence leads to loose standards and lowered expectations. Corporate history is full of examples of companies experiencing great successes only to be followed by prolonged periods of retrenchment and rebuilding.

The 9,9 team enjoys success and celebrates accomplishments, but also analyzes them in the context of expectations and possible outcomes. Just because a team increases sales by 20 percent doesn't mean they should not set a goal of 40 percent. If the success was far beyond expectations, perhaps the original goals and objectives were too low. The team can enjoy the celebration but still continue to pursue new efforts with a high level of determination and commitment.

Another common view of critique is to use it in a 9,1 or paternalistic way as a convenient excuse to vent criticism and impose blame. In this case, "critique" sessions are authority-based "attack sessions" where people are punished for noncompliance. For many people who have experienced this kind of criticism, the mere mention of the word "critique" sends chills up their spine. This is an abuse of critique and usually reflects someone's need to place blame, often onto someone of lower rank. 9,9 personal critique is void of this abuse or malice. The intention is to build, not to tear down. 9,9 people are also committed to receiving objective and personal critique in addition to fulfilling an obligation to provide it for others.

The 9,9 approach to both constructive and negative critique is twofold.

1. **The 9,9 person offers observations in the spirit of mutual trust and respect.** This makes comments easier to give and receive because both parties know the ultimate objective is to search for ways to improve. This supportive approach will also help a team member recover from a setback by not feeling isolated or rejected. The team attitude is, "We're all in this together." This is not to say that the 9,9 person doesn't get angry or doesn't express anger. The difference is that when anger is expressed, it is more constructive and focused on improvement. Instead of saying "I can't stand being in the same room with you right now!" the 9,9 person says, "I am so angry right now that I can't talk about this. It will be more productive if we meet later this morning."

2. **9,9 critique involves *how* the comments are given.** In any critique, the most useful comments focus on the behaviors experienced and the impact those behaviors have on team progress. This represents a shift away from judgmental criticism and instead focuses on objective and useful evaluation of effectiveness. For example, it's much more constructive to say, "When your report didn't come in on time, I could not meet my deadline," than to say, "You really let me down when you didn't turn in that report." The first approach provides a specific example that helps the person understand how his or her behavior affected the team, and helps everyone understand what needs to be done; the second comment reflects and evokes an emotional reaction and does not present any concrete impact or solution to the problem. There is no way to proceed from the second example except retaliation and anger.

One of the most interesting side effects of 9,9 critique is that people gain so much from the experience that they actually begin *seeking* critique from others. If the critique helps a person understand the impact of actions and changes behaviors to be more effective, the natural response is to come back for more. As a result, the person originally least likely to ask for critique may one day tap his teammate on the shoulder and say, "I've got this idea and I'd really like to know what you think."

INITIATIVE

I take the lead in initiating actions that encourage participation and commitment from others. I actively seek resources needed to achieve quality results. I welcome suggestions that increase team effectiveness. I confront conflict for resolution so initiatives under way do not suffer.

The 9,9 person takes proactive initiative based on an objective review of the R1 resources. Unlike 9,1 initiative, 9,9 initiative is based on a high concern for both people and results. The 9,9 person feels no need to play politics, soothe feelings, or take control, but does take actions in respect and consideration of others. This approach encourages team members to spontaneously explore resources and begin planning a course of action. He or she is highly informed about what the team is capable of achieving and understands how an action will affect each individual on a personal level. If the action means more work for less pay, the 9,9 person recognizes and addresses this impact. If an action means lay-offs, this is addressed up front.

The 9,9 "can do" attitude encourages others to get involved because the focus is on an objective evaluation of facts. The 9,9 person immediately explores the *best way* to proceed and the enthusiasm is often contagious. Spontaneous enthusiasm does not mean jumping in too fast or ignoring obstacles and fears, but stepping back and evaluating actions within the larger framework of available resources, solutions, and strategy. Where 1,9, 5,5, or 1,1 initiative is delayed by fear of the unknown, 9,9 initiative moves ahead to actively find information and develop a strategy. Where 9,1 initiative is focused on results to the exclusion of people, the 9,9 person addresses fears up front to incorporate them in the strategy. This objective approach provides the benefit of a sounder, more realistic perspective of a proposed action's feasibility based on facts, data, and logic.

The 9,9 person's approach to initiative is strengthened by candor. He or she is not afraid to address the facts when it comes to taking action. If actions are going to be successful, obstacles must be confronted and resolved up front; if this means confronting a teammate about poor participation, the 9,9 person does so: "Bill, your participation is critical, but you have not followed through on your reports for the last two weeks. Are you confident you can meet these deadlines?" If more resources, such as additional equipment or labor, are needed to carry out an action, the 9,9 isn't afraid to make a request: "We have a clear plan of action, but let me explain why we need some additional equipment to make it work."

9,9 initiative continues beyond the planning stages of a project. The 9,9 person continually prioritizes and evaluates the feasibility and progress of a plan and recommends adjustments as needed. Whereas many team members tend to want to go off and simply do their work, the 9,9 establishes criteria and encourages progress checks. When actions are completed, the 9,9 individual also initiates an evaluation of how effectively the team achieved its goals and makes any adjustments necessary for future efforts.

I search for and seek to verify information. I invite and listen to ideas and attitudes different from my own. I continually test the soundness of my own thinking by comparing it with the thoughts of others.

While other Grid styles often work to hide, suppress, or dominate information, the 9,9 wants to get everything out in the open for impartial consideration. This quality makes candor the defining characteristic of 9,9 inquiry. The 9,9 person wants to evaluate resources as accurately as possible. This cannot be done without getting a complete picture. The 9,9 wants the best results possible and so is not afraid to dig deep and ask questions. If a team member's skills are questionable, the 9,9 individual is not afraid to explore this issue up front: "I appreciate your initiative, but I'm not sure your research skills are strong enough. You came in late on the last project and had several mistakes. How would you feel about pairing up with someone more experienced?"

If someone is having problems with a project, the 9,9 addresses the problems through direct inquiry by stating facts and providing specific examples. The following examples illustrate the difference between 9,9 inquiry and the other six Grid styles by showing how different people react when a teammate misstates a key objective during a presentation.

- **9,1 Inquiry:** "You obviously weren't prepared this morning. What is wrong with you, anyway? You made the whole team look bad."

- **1,9 Inquiry:** "You did such a great job with the presentation this morning. I really enjoyed it."

- **5,5 Inquiry:** "You might have been able to do a better job, but I've seen worse presentations."

- **1,1 Inquiry:** "I saw your presentation."

- **Paternalistic Inquiry:** "I would have been happy to help you with your presentation, if you had only asked. You really let us down."

- **Opportunistic Inquiry:** "Listen, I thought we had an agreement that you could pull this off. You made me look bad up there."

- **9,9 Inquiry:** "I noticed you had trouble with the financial part of the presentation. Can we try to figure out what happened?"

9,9 inquiry is empathetic, but also direct, specific, and focused on resolving the problem.

The 9,9 person's questions encourage participation by being open-ended. Compare the difference between closed-ended and open-ended inquiry:

- **Closed-ended paternalism:** "I really think this is what we need to do. Don't you agree?"

- **Closed-ended 9,1:** "This is what we're going to do. Do you understand?"

- **Open-ended 9,9:** "I really want your opinion. Can you give me some critique on this idea?"

Closed-ended inquiry leaves room only for yes or no answers. Open-ended inquiry invites participation without imposing a point of view. This is particularly important if the inquirer ranks higher in the organization than the person being asked. People have a natural tendency to defer to those in authority regardless of whether or not they agree. Even subtle statements like "This is what I think. What do you think?" may encourage others to simply go along with what the team leader thinks.

Open-ended questioning only works when the inquirer has not already made up his or her mind before asking. A paternalist or 9,1 person may use open-ended questions to "test" people's understanding and then attack the person when he or she doesn't agree. This kind of abuse of inquiry is manipulative, damages trust, and creates an atmosphere where team members are unwilling to express ideas and opinions. The reaction by team members is, quite reasonably, "Why did you ask me if you had already made up your mind?"

ADVOCACY

I advocate my position with strong convictions and encourage others to do the same. If differences arise, I am willing to change my mind if a sounder solution is presented.

Candor also characterizes 9,9 advocacy. The 9,9 approach is to present ideas and feelings clearly and confidently, but also with an open mind. The high concern for people *and* results makes the 9,9 person not only advocate strongly for achieving the best results, but it also makes the 9,9 able to advocate without offending or creating defensiveness. Strong (even aggressive) initiative is not meant to cut others off or prevent them from challenging propositions. The 9,9 attitude is simply that no idea exists that cannot be improved—no matter how deeply a concept is believed, if evidence proves otherwise, then the convictions (not the person) are incorrect.

Many approaches to advocacy reflect a win/lose attitude. A person's point of view is either adopted by the team (win), or rejected by the team (lose). The 9,9 approach replaces the win/lose mentality with a win/win approach—the *what's* right vs. the *who's* right attitude in action. The 9,9 person wants to prove that convictions are sound, based on solid rationale and facts. He or she gains a clearer understanding of his or her own convictions by expressing and clarifying them with others. These discussions test the soundness of ideas. If the discussions reinforce the 9,9 person's convictions, he or she can continue with greater strength and the support of team members. If a better idea emerges, the 9,9 person does not hesitate to change his or her convictions to reflect the sounder idea. If members disagree even though his or her reasoning is sound, the 9,9 person can move forward with the confidence that the best possible effort was offered.

DECISION MAKING

I place a high value on reaching sound decisions that best serve the team's shared objectives. I explore and compare opinions against rigorous standards and work for understanding and agreement. I do not avoid making difficult decisions.

9,9 decisions are based on an open exchange of relevant ideas, opinions, and facts. As a result, decisions are based on mutual understanding and agreement regarding the best course of action. This approach creates the best opportunity for success because there is a greater chance that reservations and potential problems have been considered ahead of time.

The key to 9,9 effectiveness in decision making is in the high quality of involvement. The 9,9 concept of quality involvement means that people are free to explore and present alternatives, challenge ideas, and air disagreements. The quality of suggestions is weighed against the facts and evaluated for soundness. This approach leads to a final decision emerging almost as a natural consequence of candid discussion. In contrast, 1,9, 5,5, paternalistic, and opportunistic decision making includes a high level of involvement, but the quality is low. In the 5,5 team, decisions reflect an attempt to avoid risk and justify actions based on what is considered acceptable. In the 1,9 team, co-workers are involved in the decision, but are too focused on the social impact of the decision and rarely challenge ideas. Paternalistic decisions are dominated by a need to venerate the paternalist. Opportunistic decisions are dominated by manipulation that leads to private benefit. 1,1 decisions reflect short-term focus with a desire to simply move on.

The high quality of 9,9 involvement also increases commitment to the decisions made. As mentioned earlier, people support what they help create. Even if full agreement is not possible, team members are informed of all facts, opinions, and actions. They share a sense of commitment because each person has had the opportunity to offer opinions, suggestions, doubts, and reservations. This commitment also strengthens the team because even if only one person voiced the original idea, everyone shares the responsibility for supporting and implementing it.

The number of people involved as well as the determination of who, specifically, will be involved in a decision depends on who *needs* to be involved. If a person has something to contribute in the form of experience, skill, or responsibility, then he or she participates. The resource pool may include team members as well as outsiders. In many ways, decisions are less complicated in a 9,9 team because the identity and status of individuals matter less than the quality of their contributions. If the team member with the least experience makes the best suggestion, that suggestion is embraced based on its merits. If the leader or member with the most experience offers a poor suggestion, the suggestion is rejected based on its lack of merit. This approach may mean that, for some decisions, the entire team is involved. For other decisions, it may be appropriate for only one or two members to take responsibility for reaching a decision.

Another reason 9,9 decision making is less complicated is because of the high levels of mutual trust and respect present. Members trust each other to make sound decisions and do not feel the need to participate in the decision-making process unless they have resources to offer. Without trust, team members feel a need to involve themselves in the process to maintain control (9,1), to help people make the right decision (paternalism), to help maintain peace and harmony (1,9), to assure decisions maintain the status quo (5,5), or to assure decisions benefit them personally (opportunism). The 1,1 person does not get involved in decisions unless forced to do so. With these fears and barriers removed, teams are able to make honest and swift decisions regardless of who is physically involved in the actual decision-making process.

CONFLICT RESOLUTION

I explore disagreements and conflict openly in order to surface underlying causes that are barriers to effectiveness. I encourage team members to work through differences in a constructive way to ensure effective resolution.

The 9,9 person approaches conflict from a fundamentally different perspective than any of the other six Grid styles. Each of the other styles seeks to avoid or suppress conflict, based on the following assumptions:

- **9,1:** Conflict causes disruptions and emotional expressions that obstruct results.
- **1,9:** Conflict prevents people from enjoying working together.
- **5,5:** Conflict creates the risk of polarization of views and makes the status quo harder to maintain.
- **1,1:** Conflict is too demanding and makes it harder to remain neutral.
- **Paternalistic:** Conflict is sometimes necessary, but only under controlled conditions involving clear authority.
- **Opportunistic:** Conflict makes it difficult to remain flexible by forcing polarization of views and a statement of convictions.

The 9,9 person, in contrast, sees conflict as an inevitable component of progress and as a powerful source of energy and creativity. Few people relish the thought of confronting conflict, but the 9,9 sees it as vital for progress. The 9,9 reaction to conflict is to explore it objectively in order to reveal underlying problems. The attitude is that suppressing conflict does more damage to teams and often causes a snowball effect that leads to more disruptive obstacles later. When people air disagreements, fears, and reservations, they are more likely to overcome problems and move forward.

Conflict is beneficial in teams where candor, mutual trust, and respect exist because it focuses resources and convictions. For example, this approach makes it easier to confront discrepancies in decisions about who works on a project. The person with the most experience, for example, may not be the best person to lead a project. A person who is thought to not have the necessary resources may surprise everyone on the team by demonstrating a strong ability and advocacy. This person is given the opportunity to try in a 9,9 team rather than simply deferring to the person with more experience. When people believe in something strongly enough to advocate for it, they have the kind of passion it takes to tackle obstacles and challenge each other rather than settle for less in order to maintain harmony.

The *what's right* approach is crucial to productive conflict resolution. People develop the courage to advocate their ideas, take risks, and challenge each other when they feel confident that the consequences are truly based on considerations of what is right for the team and all individuals involved. Proactive, constructive conflict resolution suffers when pitted against avoidance tactics like smoothing over, seeking compromise, or dictatorial action. People lose confidence that their convictions are treated with objectivity and fairness and are left wondering why they went through the trouble of getting involved at all. When the conflict resolution remains direct, objective, and based on facts, people are not hesitant to state their convictions.

Many of the other styles avoid conflict because the emotional aspects of conflict make people uncomfortable. If strong advocacy includes anger in the form of physical gestures, crying, or shouting, many people rightly want to run for cover rather than face that emotion. Different people have different thresholds for the level of emotion they can tolerate. Tears may make one person uncomfortable, while shouting offends another. Avoiding these kinds of emotions, however, can make the conflict worse by leaving people dissatisfied. People want to be heard and need an open forum to articulate convictions, especially when they are suffering.

Fig. 10-4

9,9 Conflict Resolution: SOUND
(Contribute & Commit)

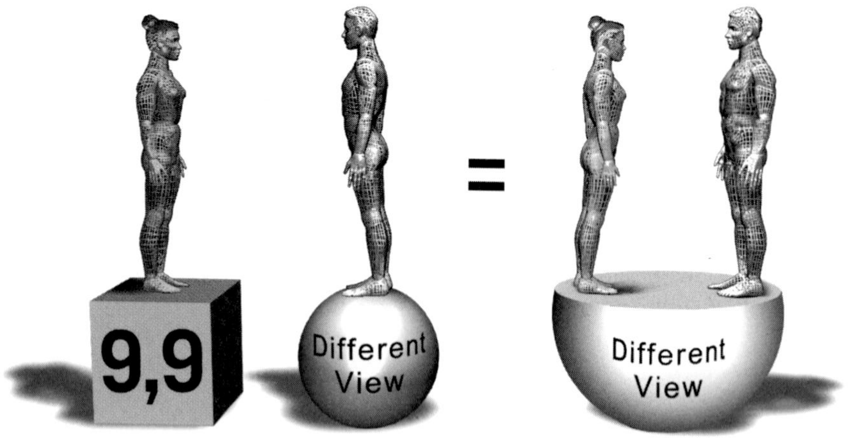

9,9

Different View = **Different View**

Conflict

Different View Prevails

The different view prevails through sound analysis of facts, data, and logic.

Fig. 10-5

9,9 Conflict Resolution: SOUND
(Contribute & Commit)

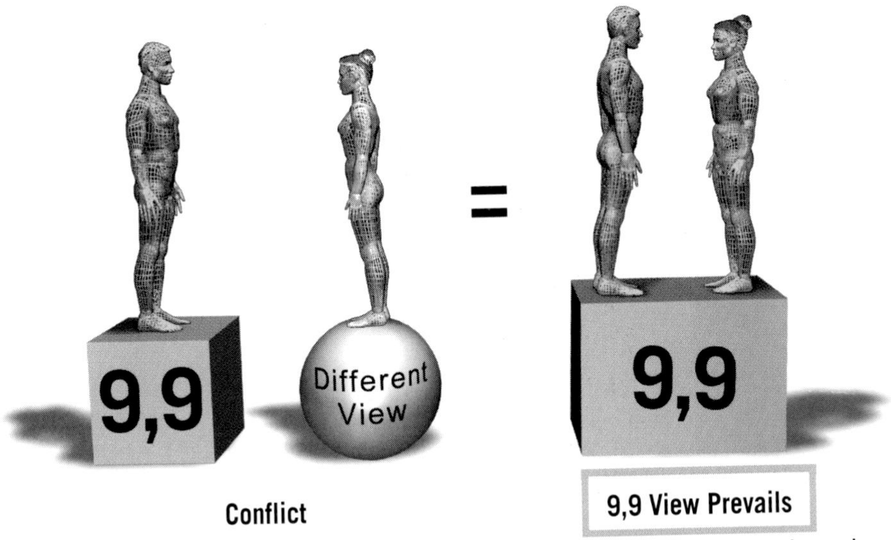

9,9

Different View

=

9,9

Conflict

9,9 View Prevails

The 9,9 view prevails through sound
analysis of facts, data, and logic.

The 9,9 approach to the emotional aspect of conflict is to allow people to express themselves while keeping the issues focused on facts and reason. This may be done by getting one or more members involved as objective observers. Having an objective perspective is crucial if the people directly involved have lost the ability to remain impartial. Resolution is accomplished by focusing discussions on facts and backing them up with rationale and specific examples whenever possible. This keeps the discussions centered on resolution and helps prevent anger from turning to rage or sadness turning into resentment. Often the best time to confront conflict in this way is when emotions are high so the specific examples can be captured and focused and people can find relief in expressing themselves. This also helps to harness the convictions for productive ends. If the situation is so emotional that the people involved cannot be objective and focus on resolution, there may be no choice but to temporarily delay action.

When the *what's right* approach to conflict resolution is embraced by a team, members work out their disagreements by concentrating on facts, data, and reason. When a solution is reached, it reflects a shared understanding of the best options. There are three possible results to 9,9 conflict resolution. The first, shown in Fig. 10-4, occurs when two team members hold different views regarding how to proceed. Through discussions, the 9,9 member discovers new evidence, possibly supplied by the other person that makes his or her ideas less feasible. The conclusion reached, then, is that the other idea is the best approach. The 9,9 team member changes his or her mind out of a genuine belief that the other view is the better idea.

The second possible outcome, shown in Fig. 10-5, reflects the reverse. Through discussions, the team member with a different view discovers new evidence that changes his or her mind. The conclusion reached is that the 9,9 team member has presented the best approach. The conclusion is based on a convincing argument that causes a genuine shift in perception. In the 9,9 team, when a person changes his or her mind, this shift is not based on authority, politics, compliance, or manipulation, but on the conviction that the alternative view is sounder.

Examining these outcomes leads to another distinctive characteristic of 9,9 conflict resolution. Many styles view conflict as a win/lose situation between people where one person beats out another in a battle. The 9,9 perspective puts the *ideas* up against each other rather than pitting *people* against each other. When everyone involved wants *what's right,* the person whose idea is contradicted, negated, or revised is not angry or resentful. The attitude expressed is, "My original ideas were limited; I believe your ideas reflect a better course of action." There is no sense of loss in this change of mind, because everyone involved benefits from the better idea.

Fig. 10-6

**9,9 Conflict Resolution: SOUND
(Contribute & Commit)**

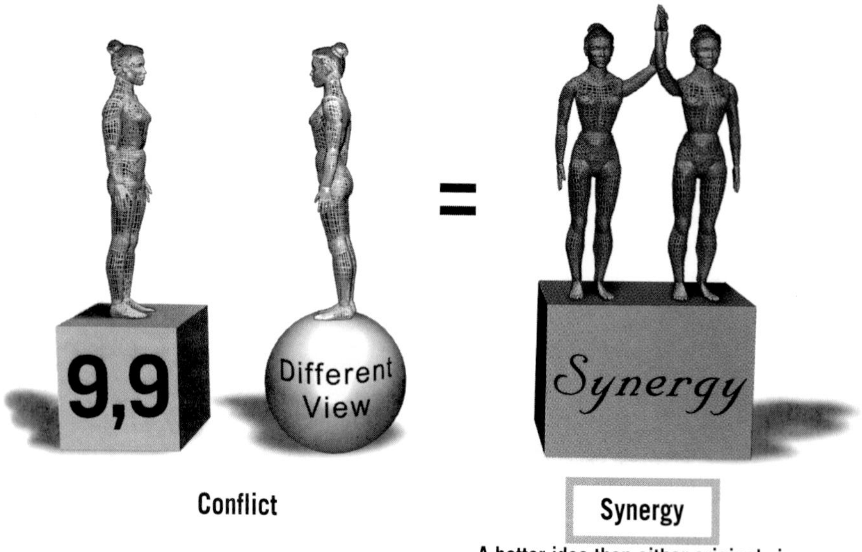

Conflict   =   Synergy

A better idea than either original view
emerges as a result of sound teamwork.

The third possible outcome with 9,9 conflict resolution is synergy (see Fig. 10-6). Two members meet to compare and contrast their views and a new idea that is better than either original idea emerges. Although aspects of the two original ideas may be incorporated, the new idea is unique and more inclusive rather than a compromise or mixed 5,5 solution. Synergy is the ultimate accomplishment of any team and is only possible when teams confront conflict for resolution rather than trying to suppress or smooth it.

Conflict can be the most destructive force a team can experience, because it has the potential to bring progress to a standstill. As mentioned earlier, people become angry, resentful, and mistrustful when their convictions are smoothed over, dismissed, or manipulated in some way. These kinds of manipulative experiences lead people to withhold or misrepresent information, become skeptical and suspicious of each other, or even make efforts to undermine others in destructive ways. This is why attempts to avoid conflict often produce more problems in the long run. Conflict never just *goes away;* it just *goes underground* only to resurface later. More damaging, however, is that unresolved conflict robs the team of the energy, commitment, and passion needed to produce excellence.

RESILIENCE

Success and failure are equally valuable learning experiences. I avoid letting success lead to complacency by reevaluating my current standards. I confront failure in order to gain understanding and bounce back.

The 9,9 person demonstrates strong resilience. He or she has the advantage of ongoing support from teammates and has the satisfaction of knowing that resources were optimized and every effort was made to succeed. Given this confidence, the 9,9 views setbacks and failures as valuable learning experiences. And each of these learning experiences provides new information to incorporate into future efforts.

This attitude does not make the 9,9 person immune to disappointment, frustration, or regret in the face of setbacks. The difference lies in how the 9,9 person handles these feelings. Many people react to a setback by wanting to put it behind them and move on; this may include focusing on the positive efforts made or benefits enjoyed, and overlooking the problems as a 1,9 person might. A 9,1 or a paternalist may distance himself or herself from the controversy by blaming others. The 5,5 person might seek comfort in sharing losses with others without really examining the experience for future learning. The 1,1 person might simply move on and elude responsibility. The opportunist might try to manipulate the situation to maximize personal gain.

The 9,9 person, however, does not want to move on until an understanding is gained from the experience. He or she wants to discuss how obstacles emerged and why efforts to overcome them failed. This discussion is not intended to assess blame or "rub in" a sense of loss, but to prevent a recurrence of problems. Once this awareness is achieved, lessons learned are immediately incorporated into team actions so learning is not lost.

Recognizing 9,9 Sound Behavior

9,9 behaviors are characterized by openness and objectivity rather than being influenced by politics and fears. The 9,9 person is often referred to as a person who "tells it like it is."

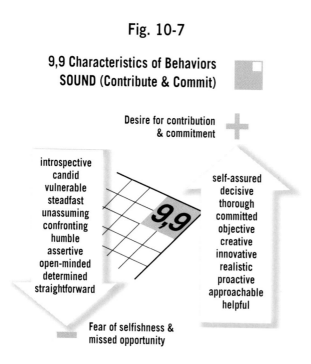

Fig. 10-7

9,9 Characteristics of Behaviors
SOUND (Contribute & Commit)

Desire for contribution
& commitment

introspective
candid
vulnerable
steadfast
unassuming
confronting
humble
assertive
open-minded
determined
straightforward

9,9

self-assured
decisive
thorough
committed
objective
creative
innovative
realistic
proactive
approachable
helpful

Fear of selfishness &
missed opportunity

Fig. 10-7 provides key words and phrases that help identify 9,9 behavior. They are presented on the motivation scale to show how the behaviors reflect the positive and negative motivations at work.

Window on 9,9

Harley owns a small retail clothing chain for petite-sized women that includes four stores and 100 employees. He started out with a partner 12 years ago, leasing a small corner in a larger clothing store. Until recently, Harley had been concerned mainly with the financial aspects of the business and most of the leadership decisions had been left up to his partner. A year ago, he bought his partner out and took a hands-on approach in the leadership of the company.

Since most of his previous expertise had been in finance and accounting, he relied heavily on the experience and knowledge of his four store managers to make this work. One piece of advice his partner had given him before she left was, "Remember, running a business is more than numbers. They are smart people. Listen to them, and hear what they're saying before you make decisions. Numbers are black and white," she said. "If an amount is wrong, it's wrong—that's it. If the numbers are down—they're down, plain and simple. But sometimes that's not the whole story." Harley found that accounting rules were a cinch compared to making the sometimes fuzzy or "gray" leadership decisions now required of him. The parting advice his partner had given him proved invaluable.

A weekly meeting of Harley and his store managers had reached the "new business" part of the agenda. "Does anyone have anything they want to talk about?" Harley asked. No one spoke. "Okay," he continued, "everything is perfect, right? At least that's what I'm hearing, people."

"All right, all right, I'm game. I'll take the bait." Alfredo, one of the store managers spoke up. "Tarah, one of my salespeople, mentioned something to me a while back. I've been giving it some thought and at first I was going to let it slide, but the longer I think about it, the bigger it gets."

"What?" Harley asked.

Alfredo continued, "We pride ourselves on having the widest selection of the most stylish clothes for petite women in the state. I dare say that's probably true, but Tarah's pointed out an area where we've really dropped the ball. She said a lot of potential customers aren't just short, they're short and heavy, too. They're disappointed even though they love our clothes and the reasonable prices."

Alfredo continued to relate the rest of Tarah's story, concluding with a statement that startled Harley—that Tarah never buys her own clothes at their stores, even with her employee discount. "Our sizes just don't come large enough. There's a whole market of women out there who leave our stores empty-handed."

Harley frowned and looked around at the other store managers. "Anybody else seen this happening?"

They all nodded. One manager said, "Yes, I've seen it, but I haven't really given it much thought—you know, the whole dynamics of the problem. But what can we do about it? How can we capture that market without taking a huge financial hit?"

"Maybe we don't," answered Harley quizzically.

"You mean, we're just going to pretend like this isn't happening and let it go?" asked Alfredo.

Harley was deep in thought. The wheels were already spinning in his head. "No, I don't mean we let it go. I mean, that maybe we decide to start carrying larger sizes. Maybe that costs us an arm and a leg at first. Maybe this results in increased business that balances out in the short term and increases profits in the long term."

"That's a lot of 'maybes'," Alfredo said. "How do we know ahead of time what will happen?"

"Begin at the beginning," Harley answered. "First we need to establish whether or not this is happening on as large a scale as we think. And if it is, do we want to do anything about it. And if we do, what do we do? Anybody have suggestions?"

"Well, it seems to me," Alfredo began, "that if we want to know the size of the problem, we start at the customer level—right in the stores—establish a way to determine the scale of the problem. Frankly, I'm stumped on that one."

Harley and the managers put their heads together and began brainstorming. After exploring every avenue they could think of, they decided that consulting a marketing and research firm about market demographics and trends would be a good starting point. But more than that, they decided to let the store employees be the first line in assessing the situation by getting their input on the scale of the problem along with suggestions for solutions.

"But what about the rest of the plan?" asked one of the managers.

"The rest of the plan," Harley answered, "is to wait until we get these results before detailing the rest of the plan. First, we compile this information and make a decision to pursue this idea or not. Once that decision is made, we start looking at ways to implement it and the financial feasibility. There's no sense in wasting a lot of time looking at numbers on something that we're not sure we even want to do. Just like there's no sense in ignoring this situation just because we 'think' it might not be fiscally possible." He paused. "Am I making any sense here?"

Everyone smiled and nodded—a few chuckles here and there. "Yes," Alfredo answered, "it makes sense. We want to decide whether to go swimming or not before we rush out and buy a new suit?"

"Couldn't have put it better myself," Harley said. "You summed up the situation in a nutshell. Okay, is everyone clear on the first step of this?" The managers all agreed they knew what they needed to do but some had questions about how to proceed.

"Well," Harley began, "I'm leaving that up to you. Each of you has a personal schedule and certain shifts to be manned in the stores. How you do this will be strictly up to you. You are in the best position to figure this out. What we need to do now is set a date for our meeting to analyze the information you collect."

Here is an example of 9,9 in action. The management team has discovered a possible new market for the business from an idea suggested by a store salesclerk not even present in the meeting. In a vast majority of situations, this idea might never have been heard at all. And rather than look at *who* made the suggestion, the team judged the *merit of the suggestion itself.* There is obviously a high degree of mutual trust and respect between Harley and his store managers and between the store managers and their employees.

The store managers and Harley himself are active listeners who not only give others an opportunity to speak, but they also *hear* what is being said. Rather than a "ready-*fire*-aim" approach, they are engaging in careful pre-critique of the situation by first determining whether the idea is worth pursuing on a grander scale. For this, they will "begin at the beginning," where the problem is being felt—with their customers' needs and desires. Whatever they do from that point will be guided by this determination.

Harley has taken his former partner's advice to heart. He asks, he listens, and then he acts, leaving the details up to those most equipped to handle them.

Summary

The 9,9 approach goes hand in hand with teamwork because it is the only style that sees no need to dominate, accommodate, compromise, evade, prescribe, or exploit teamwork actions. This unfettered attitude brings a refreshing and contagious strength to teams, and provides a strong upper hand in achieving results.

The key to 9,9 strength lies in four fundamental characteristics:

1. The 9,9 person is highly informed. His or her attitude promotes a free-flowing exchange of information. The 9,9 person actively seeks information and generates awareness so that people involved remain in a constant state of readiness.

2. The 9,9 person encourages openness and candor. He or she sets an example by expressing convictions in an open and honest way, based on facts and reason. The 9,9 is not afraid to admit personal weakness or failure, and welcomes sounder ideas from others involved. This spirit of openness generates a conta-

gious effect in teams as others are also encouraged to join in. And certainly openness and candor are critical ingredients to resolving conflict.

3. 9,9 actions are based on *what's right,* not *who's right.* This fundamental attitude eliminates the need to play politics, protect or control people, or fear involvement. By shifting the focus of team actions away from the people as individuals and onto the soundness of ideas, the personal pressure on people is alleviated. The ideas offered are evaluated based on merit and feasibility. The fear of looking inferior is replaced by a willingness to explore creative, even wild, ideas for possible advantage. This approach makes it much easier for teams to work together for the best possible outcomes rather than jockeying for recognition and personal contribution. Personal contributions are still recognized and rewarding to individuals, but now within the context of team achievement.

4. The 9,9 person promotes involvement of people affected by the decision. This consensus, once established, provides the commitment needed for sound effective implementation.

Like any other Grid style approach, the 9,9 style can still create problems in teams. The rewards from 9,9 teamwork do not come without hard work. In fact, the approach does not work at all until team members develop mutual trust and respect; without trust, members do not share information, and true candor cannot develop. No team can expect simply to come in one day and "be" 9,9—years of bad habits and unpleasant experiences make this impossible, and the road to awareness is often rough. Candor leads to critique which, to the uninitiated, can sometimes seem like criticism or even punishment. The attitudes driving unsound behavior are based on deeply held (and often hidden) values that are highly resistant to change. The 9,1 person, for example, does not see himself or herself as controlling; if asked, he or she sees personal actions as sound and even expresses a deep sense of pride in the high concern for results.

Due to the increased freedom and accountability, the 9,9 style is much more demanding, but it is also more rewarding for everyone involved. The 9,9 person maintains proactive efforts to stay informed instead of waiting for people to give him or her information. Proving a point using reason and rationale and submitting it for evaluation can be an uncomfortable experience. Many people accustomed to an authority-compliance structure don't like having to provide reason and rationale for actions.

The increased level of effort causes problems in teams where one or two members may not be carrying their weight. Many teams are used to one or more members doing most of the work while other members do less without worrying about disciplinary action. The authority figure responsible for assessing discipline is often remote and not likely to step in and take action. However, this is not the case in a 9,9 team: the pressure to participate comes not from a distant authority figure, but from peers working side by side every day. The increased team involvement and pressure make it harder for people to remain uninvolved. The candor and enthusiasm present in other members places increased pressure on everyone to get involved.

9,9 behavior often stands out and usually gains respect in the workplace because people are attracted to the confidence and leadership demonstrated. This does not mean that the 9,9 person is infallible or never makes mistakes. The 9,9 is just as vulnerable to fears and other negative influences, but he or she has more dynamic skills that help in overcoming problems.

Despite a sometimes rough transition to a 9,9 approach, there is no looking back once team members commit to it and begin to experience the increased rewards and sense of personal bonding derived from working together and achieving a great success. The fear of the unknown may make change appear risky and dangerous, but that is only because mutual trust and respect and other rewards have not yet been experienced and so cannot be easily understood. The effect of seeing synergy in other teams often motivates people to explore how to achieve it themselves.

The Power of Vision

11

Chapter

This nation should commit itself to achieving the goal, before the decade is out, of landing a man on the moon and returning him safely to earth.

—JOHN F. KENNEDY, 1961

John F. Kennedy created a vision in 1961 that galvanized the space program and created the inspiration necessary to harness a nation's resources. The boldness of this vision at the time is hard to fully appreciate now, decades later. It was a simple picture that everyone understood, and it inspired an entire generation to feel they were a part of the space program. The astronauts were heroes known around the world who made school-age children want to grow up to be like them.

Grid theory and skills represent a sound pathway for getting from R1 resources to R3 results, but theory and skills alone cannot define the *destination.* The unifying and motivating power of having a clear destination is why having a vivid and inspiring vision is vital. From the perspective of an individual or major corporation, having a clear vision of the future and possessing the values and skills represent two essential ingredients for achieving success.

What is a Vision Statement?

But what, in practical terms, is a vision, and how do personal visions relate to corporate visions? Richard C. Whiteley describes vision in *The Customer Driven Company* as: "A vivid picture of an ambitious, desirable future state that is connected to the customer and better in some important way than the current state."[1]

Perhaps the reason why the idea of vision is so misunderstood is because it is truly a much simpler concept than most people realize. If a person wants to go somewhere he or she needs to have a picture in mind of where that is before beginning. That image becomes the driving force that motivates people to keep going, despite all of the obstacles that may be in the way. Similarly, if teams want to accomplish something everyone needs to see and understand what that is before beginning. The clearer and more per-

---

1 Richard C. Whiteley, *The Customer Driven Company* (Reading, MA: Addison-Wesley Publishing Company, 1991), p. 26.

sonally relevant the vision statement the more it "speaks" to every individual involved and the better the chance that people can step up to the challenge with commitment.

The vision statement does something else to increase motivation. Having a clear vision statement makes the consequences of *not* achieving the vision unacceptable. People become inspired to overcome obstacles and strive to win. Fear also motivates progress by forcing people into action. For example, the Kennedy space program was also greatly motivated by the cold war and a fear of the Soviet Union getting to the moon first. In business, a bold vision statement by a company establishes a challenge for competitors to keep up.

How Companies Use Vision

Companies that declare and commit to a clear and meaningful vision provide a focal point for people to join forces. Effective vision statements share four fundamental characteristics.

- Developed by respected leaders who understand the company values and purpose.

- Shared and supported by teams and individuals at all levels.

- Comprehensive and specific so that everyone clearly understands how he or she fits in.

- Positive and inspiring so that the vision attracts and motivates people.

Collins and Porras define vision in *Built to Last* as the key ingredient for success in the 18 companies that, despite dramatic leadership, industry, and product changes, maintained a clear vision and reaped success for more than 50 years. "Visionary companies faced setbacks, and made mistakes, yet they display a remarkable resiliency and ability to bounce back from adversity."[2]

And these companies were not *just* successful, but enjoyed *remarkable* success over their comparison companies. As an example, one dollar invested in a visionary company in 1926 was valued at $6,356 as of 1994 when the first edition of the book was published, versus a 1994 value of $955 for the comparison companies listed. All 36 companies enjoyed success, but the visionary companies demonstrated phenomenal achievement and resilience.

Collins and Porras define vision by examining the comprehensive vision strategy of each company. The strategy includes three main parts. First is the company's core ideology (values and purpose). The core ideology is a set of basic precepts that plant a fixed stake in the ground: "This is who we are; this is what we stand for; this is what we are all about."[3] This ideology is a vital shaping force that remains constant while everything else about the company, including products, leaders, and industries, can and does change. This is why Walt Disney's core ideology of "bringing happiness to the world" remains constant while its products have changed dramatically over the years

---

[2] James C. Collins and Jerry I. Porras, *Built to Last: Successful Habits of Visionary Companies* (New York: HarperCollins Publishers, 1997), p. 4.

[3] Collins and Porras, *Built to Last,* p. 221.

from cartoons to theme parks, movie studios, and cruise lines. Some visionary companies ranged in the focus of their core ideologies. Some focused on customers or employees, while others focused on products, services, risk taking, or innovation. Collins and Porras found in the 18 companies that there is no right or wrong core ideology and vision. The power comes simply from *having* them.

Table 11-1

Merck, 1930-Present	
Core Ideology:	Corporate social responsibility Unequivocal excellence in all aspects of the company
Core Values:	Honesty and integrity Profit, but profit from work that benefits humanity
Purpose:	To preserve and improve human life
Envisioned Future BHAG:	To transform this company from a chemical manufacturer into one of the preeminent drug-making companies in the world, with a research capability that rivals any major university
Vivid Description:	With the tools we have supplied, science will be advanced, knowledge increased, and human life win ever a greater freedom from disease . . .

Source: James C. Collins and James I. Porras, *Built to Last: Successful Habits of Visionary Companies* (New York: HarperCollins Publishers, 1997), pp. 236-237.

The second part of the strategy envisioned a future defined by a 10-30 year Big Hairy Audacious Goal, or BHAG. A BHAG describes a specific goal to achieve within a stated time frame. Imagine what Boeing employees felt like in 1952 when they announced their BHAG. They bet the company on building the first commercial jet airliner. Consider the odds against them. Up to that point, their primary customer was the military, and all their experience was with military aircraft. Propeller planes were expected to continue dominating the commercial market and there was little interest in a commercial jet. Also, the prototype would cost 25 percent of the company's entire net worth. Despite all this, Boeing bet the company and established itself as *the* major player in the commercial airline industry with the 707, and by 1965, the 747.

The final part of the complete vision statement is a vibrant, engaging, and specific description of what it will be like to achieve the BHAG. An example of a complete vision statement from *Built to Last* for Merck is shown in Table 11-1.

Vision and Bottom-Line Results

Merck's core values and vision have defined its actions over the years. For example, after World War II, Merck provided Japan with streptomycin to wipe out tuberculosis. It later developed and gave away Mectizan, a drug to cure river blindness, a disease that infected more than a million people in third-world countries. Merck's actions supported core values and purpose despite short-term financial losses because it believed these actions would pay off in the long run—and they did. As of 1990 Merck was the largest American pharmaceutical company in Japan. George Merck II explained the paradox of profits versus the core values of goodwill in 1950:

> We try to remember that medicine is for the patient. We try never to forget that medicine is for the people. It is not for the profits. The profits follow, and if we have remembered that, they have never failed to appear. The better we have embraced it, the larger they have been. [4]

Johnson and Johnson accomplished similar results after the 1982 Tylenol crisis. Five people were killed when someone put cyanide in Tylenol capsules. Based on its vision, Johnson and Johnson and its subsidiary, McNeil Pharmaceuticals, mobilized to recall the contaminated lot, and later, all Tylenol capsules from the market. Two more capsules were discovered because of the recall. The company acted without hesitation to recall the pills when they could easily have left the matter to police. Johnson and Johnson took action based on its company vision "We believe our first responsibility is to doctors, nurses, and patients, to mothers and all others who use our products and services." This clear and compelling vision allowed the company to mobilize within hours with swift and deliberate action. It followed the crisis by incorporating tamper-resistant packaging which has become a standard in the industry. By 1985 the company had recovered almost all of its 35 percent analgesic market share.

The most challenging aspect of vision statements is that they confront people to go beyond strategic and tactical planning and think in visionary terms. "The BHAG should not be a sure bet—perhaps only 50 to 70 percent probability of success—but the organization must believe 'we can do it anyway.'"[5] Even though the journey is risky, dangerous, and unknown, the fear is motivating and the potential gain far exceeds the alternative of staying on the current or expected path. This great sense of possibility is what motivates people to join with commitment, even passion.

The BHAG also provides the motivation by challenging norms and people to change. If it is to work, the BHAG must be constantly repeated and reinforced and not forgotten in a manual somewhere. The goal must inspire so that people are always talking about it, referencing it, restating it. At the individual level, "secure five new super accounts by the end of the year," can easily be translated into specific work goals for an individual or team. Others begin hearing about the dream, and are challenged to join the effort. An energizing and clear vision statement is something people never get tired of using in their informal conversations in the hall or during their formal presentations and year-end meetings. And every time people talk about the vision, they are reinforcing a commitment to achieving it.

---

[4] Collins and Porras, *Built to Last,* p. 48.
[5] Collins and Porras, *Built to Last,* p. 232.

Stating a vision is an act of defiance in many ways by staking a claim on a bold achievement. Articulating the vision generates fears of being seen as boasting or arrogant, even generating resentment from others for such a bold statement of intention. The thought of staking such a claim brings out a fear of obstacles, barriers, and other "what ifs." The Boeing model is a classic example of a BHAG. Another is Henry Ford who had a vision to "democratize the automobile." In 1907 he saw beyond the horse and carriage and said,

> ... it will be so low in price that no man making a good salary will be unable to own one ... everybody will be able to afford one and everyone will have one. The horse will have disappeared from our highways, the automobile will be taken for granted.[6]

Why Buy-in is Critical

Visionary companies also share across the board buy-in from employees. The core values and visions are not just words posted on the wall or in a policy manual somewhere, but are alive and embraced by every person. Any person from the entry-level worker to the senior executive in a visionary company can probably describe the core values and vision. A legendary example of how a vision can inspire people throughout an organization was a statement by a janitor working for the Apollo man-on-the-moon project. When asked one day what he was doing, he leaned on his broom and said, "I'm helping us go to the moon." With few exceptions, the vision is understood, relevant, and a source of pride for every person because it is embedded in the culture. Leaders create the buy-in by not simply carrying the message to the company, but by demonstrating commitment in their actions. Art Wegner, president of Pratt and Whitney, a jet engine manufacturer, summarized sound leadership based on his experience in the U.S. Navy and later in his corporate career.

> You [are] put in a situation where you had to get the job done through others' efforts. That's where a lot of people come unstuck in big business. They may be very smart, but one smart person is not as effective as ten or a hundred people all going in the same direction.[7]

Ford Motor Company used vision to lead dramatic change in the 1980s. It stated the vision "Quality is Job 1" and then backed it up by breaking down barriers to quality in the organization structure. Ford reorganized the entire design process for the Ford Taurus to open communication between internal customers in market research, design, engineering, and manufacturing. As a result, welders on the assembly floor challenged

---

[6] Collins and Porras, *Built to Last,* p. 87.

[7] Whiteley, *The Customer Driven Company,* p. 178.

engineering designs by asking questions like: "Why do we have to use three different welding guns on the body assembly line, all suspended from the ceiling and getting in our way?" In response, engineers designed a single gun which saved assembly time and equipment costs, and reduced the potential for mistakes. Ford made 700 similar changes suggested by people on the line that simplified the assembly process and improved quality. Each of these changes saved up to $700,000. The Ford Taurus was also the most successful American car in the 1980s. Without a unified vision reflected throughout the operating structure of the company, the welder might have said, "Look what those genius engineers have thrown at us now," and continued about his work, uninspired. The vision created the driving force to change the culture by challenging existing norms.

The organization with an ever-present vision often creates cult-like cultures, not in a negative sense, but in a sense of unified and mutually supportive behaviors and norms. This can be seen in companies like Walt Disney where employees enthusiastically refer to each other as "cast members." Customers are "guests," and a job is a "part." Proctor and Gamble creates buy-in and loyalty through progressive pay and benefit programs that further bind people to the company. For example, in 1887, P&G was one of the first companies to introduce a profit-sharing plan, followed by a stock ownership plan, and a comprehensive sickness-disability-retirement-life insurance plan. These specific strategies align the vision with a corporate culture of company dedication and commitment. P&G's strategy secured the best and brightest people and built commitment in them to pursue the company's vision.

A sound vision statement is an idea that not only inspires employees but also captures the interest of customers and suppliers and is often the envy of the competitors. These are the companies that defy the status quo by doing what others thought impossible. Sam Walton did it when he changed the retail industry with the WalMart Store, and Bernie Marcus and Arthur Blank followed suit with the Home Depot stores. These are the organizations that stand above their competitors as targets for others to match or exceed. An inspirational vision encourages all of the various divisions and departments of a company to write their own vision statements attuned to the overall corporate vision. This tends to occur naturally and not because of direction from above, but because people are inspired to find their own place in the effort.

Individual and Team Vision

Vision statements work in the same way at the individual and team level. Personal or team improvement steps that build a foundation for the vision include actions that help make the vision possible. When the vision is vivid and inspiring, people look for ways to make their own contribution. Once the vision statement is clear, individuals and teams can begin defining specific goals that will make the vision happen. The welder at Ford looks for ways to improve quality on the assembly line. The engineer at Tylenol designs tamper-resistant packaging that improves safety for the entire industry. The Disney "cast member" reinforces the culture of wholesomeness by keeping his uniform and grounds spotless.

Whether an individual, a team, or an entire organization, a key component to making any vision work is to keep it alive. This is accomplished by leaders who define, write down, talk about, and live the vision so that buy-in and commitment follow. In 1979, Motorola CEO Robert Galvan made a company commitment to improving quality and customer service. Then he demonstrated his own commitment by visiting customers every month. This is the *CEO* taking time to personally visit people at any level—not just top managers—who are using his products. Galvan's actions made a strong impression. Paul Noakes, a general manager at the time, said,

> I was embarrassed—there were times he knew more about my business than I did. And so I realized there's a great learning process in visiting customers. I started doing the same thing. And now all officers do the same thing, go out once a month and spend a day with customers.[8]

Making the vision tangible is often the scariest step, especially if the vision represents a bold departure from current conditions. All of the negative fears come forward, saying, "What makes me think I could ever do this? What will people think of me if I fail?" These fears are real but also tremendously motivating when an entire team or company shares the commitment. For an individual or team, co-workers provide support and creative ideas to strengthen the vision. Chances are likely that a vision and effort will inspire envy and the support of people in the best position to help. Every subsequent conversation has the potential for new perspectives, creative ideas, opportunities, and ultimately, synergy, which would never occur if the vision remained ill defined.

Finally, having a vision provides a motivational gap for people to stretch themselves to span. Once defined, the statement motivates people to move ahead because current and possible conditions stand out in comparison to each other in bold relief. In fact, a truly inspiring vision clarifies how painful it would be to *not* succeed. The more people invest in stating a vision, the more commitment grows to see it through or face the consequences. In the Merck example, vision made the company fear the consequences of *not* wiping out tuberculosis in Japan, or *not* curing river blindness in third-world countries when it had the resources to do it. In the Kennedy example, no American could bear the thought of another country's flag on the moon first. In the Ford example, the line worker could not stand by and watch poor quality pass across his assembly line.

Using Grid as a Pathway

The possibility of implementing Grid values and skills on a lasting basis is limited in a company with no clear vision or values. Grid values and skills create an environment where change can occur and people can unify efforts around a vision, but there

---

[8] Whiteley, *The Customer Driven Company*, p. 203.

has to be a vision in place. Grid values and skills strengthen commitment to company vision by promoting relationship skills that encourage the values of openness, candor, mutual trust, respect, and synergy. Grid values provide a solid foundation on which people can stand securely while they are reaching and stretching to achieve their vision. Our message is not that Grid is the *only* value system that can bring about change—far from it. Research has proven, however, that successful companies with vision all have one common thread: they share strong convictions around specific values that guide their actions. At the individual level, leadership in its most succinct definition is about vision and values. Providing the foundation of values gives people the power to identify, articulate, and ultimately achieve vision.

The Dynamics of Group Behavior

12

Chapter

It's not the biggest, the brightest or the best that will survive, but those who adapt the quickest.

—CHARLES DARWIN

This book has demonstrated how, at the individual level, attitudes, values, and beliefs drive behavior and decisions to produce R3 results. Chapters 4–10 focus on how individual attitudes, values, and beliefs influence the way a person relates to others. If, for example, an individual has a set of attitudes, values, and beliefs characterized as largely 1,9, he or she would behave, make decisions, and achieve R3 results consistent with that style. Conversely, if an individual is interested in achieving 9,9 results on a permanent basis, then changes must first occur in existing attitudes, values, and beliefs.

This chapter enlarges the scope to encompass how individual attitudes, values, beliefs, and feelings influence group behavior and results.

Group Dynamics

The same influence on results present at the individual level occurs at the group level. The difference is that now the attitudes, values, and beliefs are expressed in group norms and standards, and are represented by the *Power Zone* located in the second column of Table 12-1.

The area of group dynamics is where change efforts either succeed by building support and commitment or fail by building resistance. The *Power Zone* becomes the principle arena of activity and focus for any change initiative whether at the individual, group, or organization level. It is here that norms develop through three basic laws of human behavior: convergence, cohesion, and conformity. In the same way that comprehending the law of gravity helps to understand the behavior of objects, comprehending the basic laws of group dynamics helps in understanding the power of their influence on R3 results. This chapter examines each of these laws and how they create and maintain norms with the silent, invisible, but powerful force to regulate the behavior, decisions, and ultimately the R3 results achieved in work groups. Understanding how groups develop and reinforce existing norms provides a leader with the critical insight and the necessary tools required to implement change.

Table 12-1

The Path of Influence in Groups

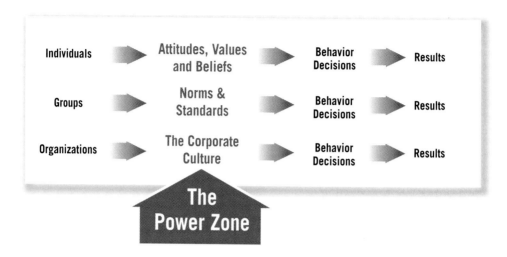

Group Norms

A norm is any uniform attitude or action that two or more people share by virtue of group membership. People think of values and attitudes as private, personal, and unique, but research shows that most personal attitudes arise from group norms.[1] As a result, team attitudes determine the quality of individual work effort more than most people realize. The norms of a group are reflected in its traditions, precedents, habits, rites, rules, rituals, regulations, policies, operating procedures, customs, taboos, and past practices. These norms and standards begin forming through the process known as convergence (see Fig. 12-1).

Convergence: Convergence initiates norms spontaneously by shifting individual attitudes or patterns of behavior toward a uniform group pattern that every member shares. Few social pressures are more important for understanding change than the human tendency to converge around a common idea in a group setting. For example, a team has five members, each of whom starts out a planning meeting with an opinion regarding how much productivity is "enough." One person thinks fifteen "units" per day is adequate, another recommends only five, while other members suggest thirteen, nine, and eight. As people work together and exchange ideas, the opinions expressed lead to a shift in attitudes around a more uniform norm. This begins with the two extreme positions shifting from fifteen to thirteen and from five to seven. Over time, the overall norms of the team converge to embrace ten units as the benchmark for enough productivity.

---

[1] Robert R. Blake and Jane S. Mouton, *Productivity: The Human Side* (New York: AMACOM, 1981).

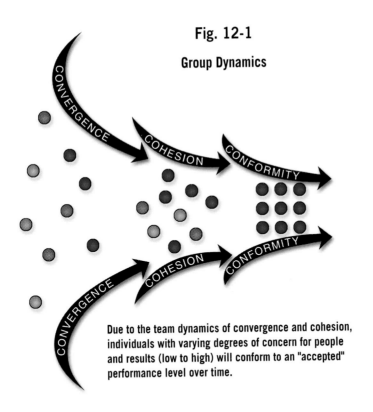

Fig. 12-1

Group Dynamics

Due to the team dynamics of convergence and cohesion, individuals with varying degrees of concern for people and results (low to high) will conform to an "accepted" performance level over time.

Cohesion: Cohesion, another group dynamic, is the phenomenon of people in groups congregating around common interests and values. Cohesion is one of the most significant forces for social organization. People are naturally drawn to others who share a common experience that allows them to bypass the formalities that they follow with outsiders. Examples of cohesion surface in every aspect of life as people tend to gravitate toward and give preference to others who share a common interest or experience. This preference may follow the lines of race, religion, politics, socioeconomic status, education, etc. In organization life, other dimensions apply, such as years of service, position, level of training, or common experience.

Cohesion accelerates the development of norms because it represents an emotional bond people feel with one another. When cohesion is high, people relate with a higher sense of trust and confidence in each other and commitment to the group—people embrace the norms with pride because the shared experience feels comfortable and right. Cohesion is demonstrated in comments like, "We've done it before and I know we can get through this."

Conformity: Conformity is the phenomenon that leads group members to maintain an established group norm. Conformity enforces the norm by creating pressure, often subtly, to "fall in line" with the group in reinforcing the norm. Conformity happens every time a co-worker says, "I know it's a little unusual, but we don't use a formal agenda for these meetings," or "You're coming across too strong in meetings. We like to keep these meetings relaxed and spontaneous." The message, whether given by a gesture, comment, or outright directive, is "You need to change your behavior to fit in." The price of non-conformity is ostracism.

The Power of Norms and Standards

In order to illustrate the subtle and powerful influence of norms, the following scenario tracks the conformity of a new employee toward a norm.

> At John's previous employer, division vice presidents spent a great deal of time preparing for weekly staff meetings. Executives expected each of them to take detailed notes and be prepared for the possibility of making an unscheduled presentation. John continued this practice at his new job because he was proud of his level of readiness, and he wasn't going to be embarrassed at his new job by being caught off guard. He soon learned, however, that meetings in the new company had a completely different feel. They rarely lasted more than 30 minutes, and the chair of the meeting prepared the agenda according to current priorities. After a few meetings where he came in with a stack of notes and files, his co-workers began making comments about his overpreparation. "Hey, if you're looking for more work to do, we'll give you some of ours," and "What are you trying to do, make us look bad?" After that, John's preparations began tapering off until finally he came to the meetings with nothing but a blank pad of paper and his coffee.

Most organizations underestimate the power of group norms on individual behavior or believe they can overcome the norms through rational explanation, incentives, force, or authority. Once the dynamics are understood, the key question for every organization is "Are we conforming to norms and standards that help us or hinder us?" In the same way that individuals can become aware of individual behavior and its impact on others (Chapters 4–10), teams and entire organizations can become aware of their norms and standards and the impact on results.

The Impact of Norms and Standards: Organization-wide Conformity

Conformity itself is neither good nor bad but is a group dynamic that simply "happens." Like other natural laws, group dynamics operate 24 hours a day, rain or shine, profit or loss.

Organization members conform to requirements placed on them by colleagues and superiors. This readiness to conform permits regularity, order, and predictability. Adherence to group norms provides a basis for any organized effort. Self-regulated conformity brings a sense of identification, membership, and high morale.

Barriers to effectiveness are created by conformity because of convergence around ineffective, unsound, or outdated norms and standards. Many norms, once established, are never questioned again. A norm may be effective initially but later become obsolete, yet groups carry on simply because it is familiar and commonplace. For example, a car manufacturer may state a norm: "It has been routine for us to change models every five years," and explain it by saying, "That's often enough," or "Technological innovations can be collected and introduced more economically every few years." However, competitors who change models every year or two can capture an increased market share (profit) by being more responsive to the consumer.

When team norms are based on unsound values and attitudes, they act as a significant barrier to change. At its worst, conformity to entrenched traditions, precedents, and past practices (corporate politics) may become so great that the capacity to change is lost, creating "dinosaurs" in the business world. The constant interplay of destructive corporate politics becomes the norm for team interaction. People may even become aware of this dynamic but will dismiss or minimize it with comments like, "I hate having to do this but what else can we do?"

When teams gain an awareness of these dynamics, meaningful change becomes possible. Once the dynamic of conformity is understood, people start to resist accepting norms at face value, and instead compare them against standards of excellence. Excuses like, "We've always done it that way," "It's a good idea but I think it will upset too many people," or even, "The boss thinks we should do it that way," are overlooked as people begin to ask, "What's the *best* way?"

Changing Norms and Standards

Group leaders play a preeminent role in shaping norms. By being aware of group dynamics and understanding how they work, a leader can use these naturally occurring forces to support change efforts in a systematic way. This is where individual Grid styles have tremendous influence.

A chaos of conflicting, reluctant, and confused responses develops every time a change is introduced. This chaos provides the leader with a critical opportunity to influence change because within the confusion lies valuable energy and emotion. Another source of energy lies in the human dynamics of convergence, cohesion, and conformity, and will naturally create order out of chaos by shifting opinions around a uniform group norm. At this pivotal point, when the group is beginning to form new norms, a leader's style can influence how the group converges. For example:

- **9,1 Leadership:** Members are forced to converge around highly demanding norms that provide short-term results, regardless of conflict or problems that may arise.

- **1,9 Leadership:** Members converge around norms that are popular, safe, and pleasant, regardless of the resulting effectiveness.

- **5,5 Leadership:** The group converges around norms that balance an acceptable level of results with an acceptable level of concern for people. History and compromise are held out as viable bases for agreement.

- **1,1 Leadership:** Members simply let convergence happen with a minimum degree of effort by following whatever norms emerge.

- **Paternalistic Leadership**: Members are rewarded for converging around norms of the paternalist's choice. They comply out of loyalty and fear of being out of favor.

- **Opportunistic Leadership:** Members carefully endorse norms according to how much they stand to benefit personally, regardless of how effective or ineffective the norms may be.

- **9,9 Leadership:** Members constantly challenge norms by comparing them to shared standards of excellence. There are no "sacred cows."

It is essential for leaders to be aware that these three valuable sources of energy—convergence, cohesion, and conformity—exist during periods of change and to learn how to harness them productively. Once the norm is established, the group works to maintain the norms created by reinforcing them and pressuring others to follow. The following example illustrates how 9,9 leadership can introduce change and lead the transition from a norm that inhibits progress to a norm that supports progress.

After a long-standing history of increasing labor difficulties, and in the aftermath of a very painful strike, the concerned president of a company contemplated his options. "Having had the strike, I knew that things were never going to be the same again. The biggest challenge was to change things and make them better." He knew the settlement wasn't the end of the open warfare. "It was only a cease fire, not an armistice," the union leader would later concur.

The stakes were high. Old norms and standards of behavior had put employees in the middle of an escalating battle over their loyalty to the company for four decades. It had clearly become a lose/lose situation. Relying on Grid training and experience, it was time to change the norms and standards of behavior in management's relationship with the union. Openness, honesty, and candor needed to replace mistrust and confrontation.

Change began at the top. When senior level discussions began, the rules (new norms and standards) were simple: "Everyone gets heard. Nothing gets ridiculed. We all listen." What followed set aside tradition and past practices. It even broke a taboo, setting the tone for the rest of the organization: the union leader was a surprise guest at the annual manager's convention. Management staff, divided into teams, presented their views to both the president of the company and the president of the union on what the barriers were to a better relationship with the union.

The stage was set to successfully shift the norms and standards for this key business relationship. And it worked. The company is now growing again. A new contract has been negotiated which offered a buy-out, substantial wage savings to the organization, and the assurance that only half of the locations would be affected by a strike at once. The union has grown due to voluntary recognition in previously non-union locations and new locations made possible by the new contract. Grievances (and their related costs) are down 80 percent because of a new focus by managers and shop stewards alike on *what's right* instead of *who's right.*

Norms and standards can easily manage behavior. However, through awareness, the process can reverse; people can manage norms and standards and, by doing so, harness the power to change. Companies that succeed in staying on the cutting edge of competition all have one thing in common: they question everything and constantly challenge norms so that complacency never sets in. Unless they are challenged, norms can become outmoded, ineffective, and deeply entrenched in the culture. When this occurs, companies perpetuate unsound practices because "That's the way we do it around here."

Leading Change

13

Chapter

Lech Walesa told Congress that there is a declining world market for words. He's right. The only thing the world believes anymore is behavior, because we all see it instantaneously. None of us may preach anymore. We must behave.

—Max DuPree, Chairman, Herman Miller

The process of change in the modern workplace requires leadership rather than authority, and freedom rather than control. Leadership is not about *making* the right decision anymore, but about *making sure the right decision is made.* The only way to lead in today's flattened organization structures is to create a sense of ownership at every level of the organization. The most successful efforts to improve organizations are led by example with vision, values, and change originating at the top. These values are then reinforced through actions that lead to support at the individual and group levels. Change led in this manner is embraced throughout the organization with a strong culture of commitment. Individuals participate with enthusiasm and enjoy greater job satisfaction, stronger commitment, increased effectiveness, and competitive advantage.

Achieving lasting and effective change requires three fundamental and courageous tasks of a leader.

- Address fear in the workplace
- Build a foundation for change
- Lead by example

Addressing Fear in the Workplace

Franklin D. Roosevelt believed, "The only thing we have to fear is fear itself." His wife, Eleanor Roosevelt, described fear as "the most debilitating and soul-destroying emotion known to man." Unprecedented levels of fear exist in workplaces today with the impact of information technology and the flattening of organization structures. The autocratic approach of the past where people demonstrated loyalty and worked for a company for life is now replaced by a Darwinian organization where people are challenged to constantly change in order to survive.

Understanding the Fear of Change

People usually favor and even encourage change when it involves someone else. Change is also welcomed when it involves enhancing proven or widely supported skills. For example, people are less likely to object to computer and software upgrades to increase efficiency in existing procedures than they would be to an entire set of different procedures.

Fear emerges when the change in question affects people on a personal level. Change becomes threatening when it involves the personal habits, traditions, and relationships that are proven and familiar to a person. Fear is even more intense when the change addresses or questions an individual's personal values and attitudes in the workplace. From the very beginning, personal change challenges both the individual's identity and relationship to the group or organization. Fear is a natural response.

People associate change with a loss of personal control. Most individuals believe that change is something that happens *to* them, not something they *choose*. The result is that people perceive change as a threat to their independence or autonomy. This dynamic is completely reversed when a person chooses a course of change; then the same fear invigorates and motivates the person to pursue the change with courage. Everyone has experienced the futility of trying to change another person when it is not the individual's chosen course of action. Many times suggestions in performance appraisals have been ignored or reasoned away—"Oh, I don't have time,"—only to be fully acted on when the individual decides the changes are personally desired. How many of us have tried in vain to help a friend or family member who has been advised, for health reasons, to quit smoking, lose weight, or stop excessive drinking only to see the changes happen with conviction when the person decides *for himself or herself* that this change was desired.

Another source of fear stems from a lack of information and understanding when candor is not forthcoming. Without all the information, people's fears can lead them to think in terms of a worst case scenario instead of looking for solutions. This kind of thinking causes people to withdraw and hold back instead of thinking creatively to maximize resources. Even when someone recognizes that change is necessary and *wants* to change, that doesn't mean he or she knows *how* to change. This is especially true when the person has no involvement or shared commitment with others to help see the change through.

Fear—The Grid Perspective

Positive and negative motivations are presented in detail in each Grid style chapter. These provide a useful starting point for understanding how individual desires and fears can appear in the workplace.

Table 13-1

Positive Motivations (desire for . . .)	GRID STYLE	Negative Motivations (fear of . . .)
control & domination	9,1 CONTROLLING Direct & Dominate	failure & helplessness
agreement & approval	1,9 ACCOMMODATING Yield & Comply	rejection & abandonment
continuity & belonging	5,5 STATUS QUO Balance & Compromise	embarrassment & humiliation
survival & uninvolvement	1,1 INDIFFERENT Evade & Elude	entanglement & expectation
veneration & reverence	PATERNALISM Prescribe & Guide	repudiation & betrayal
advantage & gain	OPPORTUNISM Exploit & Manipulate	entrapment & ridicule
contribution & commitment	9,9 SOUND Contribute & Commit	selfishness & missed opportunity

When an individual is threatened by change, fears and desires surface quickly. The survival mechanisms of control (force, charm, persuasion, manipulation, politics, or withholding) are grasped quickly in an effort to restore confidence and order. This is the point where fear of change is demonstrated as resistance to change through individual behavior and group norms.

Them-ism—A By-product of Fear

Individual fears and resistance in the workplace cause people to pull back and begin to disown problems even when they may hold the solutions in their hands. This leads to an amazingly common yet ineffective norm in which team members sit by and watch problems develop and escalate without doing anything to stop them. This phenomenon is referred to as *them-ism,* and stands for all of the excuses people use to abdicate responsibility for problems that they could, in fact, contribute to resolving. Instead, they rationalize the lack of action by fear of retaliation, or blaming such factors as poor regulations, poor procedures, poor planning, history, a supervisor, other team members, or not enough time. Each response is an excuse to avoid the risk of trying something new or wading into the unknown arena of change. Instead, these team members turn a blind eye to ineffectiveness with an attitude of, "That's not my problem," or "I can't make any difference."

Addressing Individual Fears

The first and most important step in addressing fear and the barriers it creates is to understand, accept, and acknowledge fear so it can be recognized and considered in any change effort. But recognition alone is not enough. Effective leaders make time at the beginning of any change project to allow participants an open forum to share their doubts, frustrations, and fears and genuinely listen to and consider points of view offered. This generates a meaningful and insightful opportunity to discuss the change, and often leads to the level of commitment required for effective implementation.

The simple act of being able to express an opinion to people in authority can dramatically increase personal commitment to change because people feel their views have been considered. Then, even when contrary decisions are made, people are more likely to cooperate because they trust and respect each other and have a better understanding of why the change is happening. Once change initiatives are in progress, teams can include regular critiques during all operational meetings to give team members an ongoing opportunity to address personal difficulties and concerns. During these critiques, thorough inquiry by the team is essential to ensure all issues are discussed and appropriate actions are taken.

Understanding Fear at the Team Level

At the team level, fears can become greatly strengthened and in some cases impenetrable. Fear demonstrated by a leader may be further strengthened when team members embrace the same fear. "If my supervisor is unwilling to challenge these decisions, what chance do I have?"

Team dynamics can also make fear contagious. Individuals may have all the knowledge necessary, all the reasons for change explained, and all the resources needed to move ahead, but the fear of stepping outside team norms keeps them at an impasse.

When fear strikes at the team level, members withdraw into a comfort zone (norm) that is safe, even if they know it's ineffective. These are the teams which are eliminated because companies see them as hopeless. Sometimes, leaders are replaced by outsiders in hopes of "shaking up" the status quo. This often makes matters worse, introducing more uncertainty and exacerbating individual fears.

One reason fears generally remain hidden in teams is because there is a shared, often unspoken norm that discourages open discussion regarding personal fears, particularly among men. Admitting to fear is seen as professional weakness. Most men are socialized toward being confident, strong, and fearless. Anything less than emotional control is unacceptable, sometimes devastating. In turn, many women are socialized to maintain a tough appearance if they want to succeed in the business world. As a result, they may suppress fears because they don't want to be seen as weak or helpless.

Difficulties in expressing fear grow the higher up individuals progress in an organization. At the executive level of major corporations, chronic complaints include, "No one tells it to me straight," "I can't get my people to be candid with me," and "I need to hear the bad news … I can celebrate good news later." This is the dynamic illustrated in the children's fable about the emperor who thought he had new clothes but was really naked. Only a young, innocent child without guile or a sense of fear would tell him the truth.

As in the following example, successful leaders of change search for candor and ways to surface internal dialogues, both their own and those of others.

> During a merger workshop, six months of frustration and lack of progress were remedied when the chairman of the smaller company candidly revealed what both sides suspected but had never said. At the end of one long session he said, "What we're afraid of is getting swallowed up by you guys. We're known for research and innovation. That's what got us here. You are the production wizards and once we hand over a design concept to you, we get lost in the dust." This was the key piece in the stalemate. Months of polite but unproductive formal discussion supported by lengthy reports and studies that gently pointed out differences in operations, procedures, and corporate cultures suddenly ended. The two sides now knew what the real issue was and could immediately get to work on the real problem.

Building a Foundation for Change

Although fear cannot be eliminated, it can be managed by building a foundation that enables people to work through the various stages of change in an objective, systematic, and coordinated way. People learn ways to minimize adverse affects by accepting, learning from, and managing fear.

Step One: A Shared Model—Common Language and Skills

The first step in building a foundation is to bring the fear of change into manageable perspective by developing skills of openness, candor, and objectivity. The Leadership Grid theory provides an effective way to establish candor by defining a range of styles and behaviors. These profiles give people a way to have objective discussions about personal behaviors rather than using personal opinion, history, or precedent as the departure point. This allows people to be objective in exploring *what's right.* The theory allows people to begin with a clean slate and establish candor by saying "I don't agree with that idea," instead of having to say, "I don't agree with *you.*" Once the discussions establish a clear model of soundest behavior, people are confident to confront individual differences because they are not *criticizing* a person, but comparing the person's behavior to behavior everyone agrees is soundest. As a result, people feel confident in saying, "I don't agree with your unilateral decision making because we decided consensus decision making is the soundest approach."

The simple act of using a model to discuss and compare the personal values and attitudes that people hold reduces fear and resistance by creating a strong foundation of shared assumptions. Many teams work together for years and never question the fundamental issues that have a direct impact on the quality of their effort:

- What is the most effective way to track progress and communicate?

- What is the best way for us to take initiative?

- How should we be practicing inquiry?

- How strong are our convictions regarding the new goals we have set for the upcoming year?

- How should we make the best possible decisions?

- What is the best way for us to resolve conflict?

- How can we be more resilient in the face of failure?

Using a model for discussions helps put individual and team behaviors in perspective. The range of styles and descriptions of behaviors explored in the Grid theory allow people to use their own judgment to reach agreement on sound behaviors and then evaluate their own behavior in comparison. This approach is self-convincing because people evaluate the evidence and reach their own conclusions about the best way to make decisions, resolve conflict, take initiative, etc. Like any personal change effort, genuine and lasting change only occurs when people are *convinced* current behaviors are unsound and want to change to more effective ones. For example, a leader may have used a controlling or compromise approach for years and sees himself or herself as successful. Simply *telling* this leader that controlling decisions has a negative impact on others, or that encouraging compromise reduces the possibility for synergy, is not likely to be convincing. If a model provides objective evidence by comparison with other styles, however, the leader will become convinced on his or her own that the behavior is unsound, and will then desire the change.

Comparing Against the Model: Once these discussions around the model have occurred and shared assumptions are in place, change becomes a surmountable obstacle. If Joseph believes that results are the single most important objective to achieve, team members can discuss and explore if and why they agree or disagree. Then the next time Joseph loses his temper because production numbers are down, team members understand why and can help. However, without a model to use as criteria for progress, evaluations can easily come across as subjective corporate directives, personal preferences, or even revenge.

The model also allows people to create their own standards of excellence in relationships. For example, members can make a commitment to develop a list of criteria for their team to take initiative, or to incorporate concurrent critique into day-to-day activities. Teams can use the model to develop their own criteria for sound conflict resolution, ensuring that all necessary resources, opinions, and viable possibilities have been explored. Once developed, these team standards become a baseline for challenging unsound behavior and norms in objective and measurable terms. They also become a source of pride and commitment among team members to help one another do their best.

At the organization level, the Grid framework acts as a catalyst for gaining commitment to widespread change. As shared values begin to spread, individual change leads to new team norms, and ultimately changes the entire organization culture.

Objective comparison against this new, shared model offers a starting point for individual change. People begin to see themselves from the perspective of how others experience their behavior. Since most people want to be more effective, they will naturally feel a deeper sense of commitment to changing personal behavior. The commitment is deeper and more personal than it would be if change were simply advised or imposed.

Step Two: Building Relationships and New Team Norms

The second step in building a foundation for change is to develop strong relationships and create new team norms that can endure change. Strong relationships allow teams to begin following through on change strategies with strong commitment and resilience. For this to happen, members must feel free to participate in critique without recrimination—a vital dynamic of managing fear.

Often fears in the workplace are based on false assumptions, misunderstandings, or conditions that no longer exist. As openness and candor emerge in developing teams, these unfounded fears subside. Being able to challenge up, challenge across, and challenge down becomes an essential part of corporate excellence. *What's* right, not *who's* right, becomes a new corporate norm and standard. Teams shift from an attitude of, "That can't be done," or "I could never do that," to an attitude of, "We're in this together and we're committed to making it work."

Factors as simple as openness, honesty, and candor are fundamental in the development of trust and mutual respect. This climate of trust and respect also accelerates the change process. Increased commitment to team achievement follows mutual trust and respect, along with an increased sense of personal contribution. Synergy also becomes possible as inhibitions and fears no longer keep people from exploring new ideas and taking calculated risks that represent the unproven and unknown. Resources that were once hidden or repressed emerge in creative and innovative ways.

With sound R2 relationships in place, teams and companies can begin tackling change in strategic terms. Instead of resistance, people bring strength, creativity, commitment, and resilience out in the open. With all of the fears discussed and a clear, shared model of effective leadership established, teams can focus 100 percent of their effort on developing the R1 resources to achieve the best possible R3 results.

By addressing personal values, attitudes, and the group dynamics in place, companies can attain the level of buy-in needed to build deep commitment to change. Companies that fail to recognize natural human dynamics before they begin change initiatives are destined to carry on in the same manner as before, despite all the words, slogans, meetings, and memos.

The key to obtaining commitment is to recognize that people embrace what they help create. This means that the process of shaping an effort involves the people responsible for carrying out the change. Amazingly enough, most change initiatives today are comprised of well-meaning communication efforts with legitimate explanations and underlying rationale but accompanied by totally unrealistic time frames which are proposed to employees as directives after the fact. This approach invites resistance to change in people by encouraging the attitude, "What do they know about actually making this work? No one consulted me, but I'm expected to make this happen!"

The pressures of change are tremendous and most managers and leaders react to this by expecting too much too soon and increasing the pressure with threats or ultimatums. This approach polarizes issues and can easily bring progress to a screeching halt. People are creative and can find many ways to make it look like they are accepting the new changes when in reality they are not. Instead, they continue to reinforce the norms of resistance in place. During periods of global change, corporations that fail to understand this resistance to change can face extinction. The world has countless examples of organizations, companies, and governments that no longer exist because they did not or could not overcome an inherent human resistance to change.

The Power to Change: The Grid Approach to Organization Development

The Grid approach to change involves a four-step organization development process that builds a culture of mutual trust, respect and candor. The process begins with individual development and then moves to intact teams, then group to group relationships, and finally, to organization-wide strategic planning. The objective of Grid Organization Development is to first build a foundation of standards of excellence at the individual level with strong supporting skills, and to develop candor in the workplace so people can use the skills effectively. This allows a company's culture to change into one of personal accountability and commitment to excellence. The underlying assumption is that tackling attitudes, values, and norms up front builds a strategically strong culture from the inside out so that organizations can maximize resources. When individuals and teams have the skills to confront unsound behavior, norms, and culture issues, those issues will no longer block organization-wide strategic progress.

Individual Development

Development begins at the individual level by building increased awareness and skills. The Leadership Grid Seminar demonstrates how individual behaviors have a direct impact on team results. Participants work in teams to clarify convictions around what behaviors are sound and unsound. The activities examine personal values and attitudes and help people understand how individual decision making and conflict resolution, for example, can help or hurt results.

The seminar helps people consider personal behaviors in objective terms with the same strategic focus that they would consider accounting or engineering principles. This objective view is essential for challenging unsound individual values, norms, and behaviors. The theory provides a way for people to have the critical discussions surrounding poor leadership and unsound norms in strategic terms. This creates awareness at the *Power Zone* level of values and attitudes, where change happens.

By the end of the seminar, participants are armed with clear and shared convictions regarding soundest behaviors as well as how existing behaviors differ from the soundest. They also leave with an understanding of how their behavior impacts others, and have specific strategies in place for changing behaviors with the support of co-workers back on the job.

Intact Team Development

Building Spectacular Teams is the second phase of development and transfers the individual learning and skills to intact teams back on the job. With individual awareness and critique skills in place, intact teams can tackle strategic issues with candor and objectivity. The seminar activities unlock the team's potential by establishing standards of excellence. This is accomplished by defining soundest team norms and comparing them with existing norms, clarifying team roles and responsibilities, discussing the consequences of personal behavior, and developing improvement strategies for each member. As a final step, teams define an action plan to put the skills to use in a strategic project that includes planning, implementation, and measurement.

Intergroup Development

The third phase is Building Spectacular Partnerships, a seminar in which work groups resolve team to team conflict and build strong relationships based on mutual trust, respect, and candor. Work groups like management and union, subsidiaries, purchasers/suppliers, divisions and departments, or project teams and individuals develop shared understanding of the cross-functional roles and develop standards of excellence for working together. The seminar breaks down barriers and unhealthy competition between groups that share resources. Building Spectacular Partnerships is a proven means of forging resilient, healthy, and productive relationships.

Strategic Plan Development

The final stage of development includes Grid Ideal Strategic Modeling in which companies take full advantage of the common language, standards of excellence, and skills in place to undertake organization-wide strategic planning. The seminar provides specific steps for leaders to define organization-wide vision and strategies in ways that maximize buy-in and commitment at all levels.

Unlike other training approaches, Grid organization development is self-convincing and experiential, shifting the responsibility for learning, practice, and change into the hands of seminar participants. Participants take responsibility for learning, practicing, and measuring the results of new skills. This increases involvement and responsibility at every level and creates strong commitment and mutual support for change efforts. By addressing values, people are motivated to change because they believe in and are committed to continuous improvement. Change efforts are strengthened through critique skills that involve co-workers in every stage to verify soundness and progress.

Leading by Example

Actions taken at the top level of an organization affect every level and every relationship. Leaders set the tone for a change effort through their own actions.

Whenever management or leadership at any level attempts to create change of any magnitude, the first question that should be answered is, "Are we (in management) facing up to the real barriers preventing change from occurring, or are we ignoring and perpetuating them?" Only in this way can leaders actually appreciate the complexity and extent of personal challenge inherent in the change process. This provides insight and awareness into what they are asking of others in the organization and prepares the leader for the job ahead. By experiencing firsthand the intellectual and emotional challenge of questioning their most basic assumptions, leaders set an example right from the outset.

Management's willingness to articulate its contribution to the problem becomes an example of openness, honesty, and candor. In short, management must be willing to "walk the walk." It is difficult to conceive of any successful change initiative occurring without a significant shift in attitude and perception in those at the top. Human energy is what ignites and inspires every corporate achievement. Human energy is a powerful, motivating, and unifying force when this inspiration flows naturally through the entire organization from the top.

Despite this fact, many companies still see the barriers to change as existing only at levels further down into the organization. Strategies on paper are nothing more than a statement of good intentions left to someone else (them) to implement. *Striving* for corporate soundness becomes *driving* for corporate soundness. No matter how well intended, driving people creates resistance and fear. People feel taken advantage of, exploited, or left out. Pressuring for change by forcing people to reject current norms only ensures that they will find ways to resist, overtly or covertly. Exerting pressure to improve operational results without understanding and resolving the human conditions that cause limitations will, at best, only address the symptoms. Although short-term benefit may result, the real problems will go underground and resurface later, often with more severe negative consequences.

In contrast, an effort to manage change in a way that addresses fear, provides a sound model, builds relationships and effective team norms, and leads by example will eliminate most problems early in the process, maximize resources, and make strategic issues easier to handle when they do arise. This type of change effort is effective, invigorating, and contagious.

Suggested Reading

Built to Last: Successful Habits of Visionary Companies. James C. Collins and Jerry I. Porras (HarperCollins Publishers, 1997).

Change by Design. Robert R. Blake, Jane S. Mouton, and Anne Adams McCanse (Addison-Wesley Publishing Company, 1989).

Dialogue: Rediscover the Transforming Power of Conversation. Linda Ellinor and Glenna Gerard (New York: John Wiley & Sons, Inc., 1998).

Good to Great. Jim Collins (New York: Harper Business, 2001).

Intellectual Capitol: The Wealth of Organizations. Thomas A. Stewart (Doubleday, 1997).

Leadership Dilemmas—Grid Solutions. Robert R. Blake and Ann Adams McCanse (Gulf Publishing Company, 1991).

Making Experience Work: The Grid Approach to Critique. Robert R. Blake and Jane S. Mouton (McGraw-Hill Book Company, 1978).

Productivity: The Human Side. Robert R. Blake and Jane S. Mouton (New York, AMA-COM, 1981).

Reinventing HR. Margaret Butteriss (John Wiley & Son Ltd., 1998)

Spectacular Teamwork: How to Develop the Leadership Skills for Team Success. Robert R. Blake, Jane S. Mouton, and Robert L. Allen (John Wiley & Sons, Inc. Publishers, 1987)

The Customer Driven Company. Richard C. Whiteley (Addison-Wesley Publishing Company, 1991).

The New Managerial Grid. Robert R. Blake and Jane S. Mouton (Gulf Publishing Company, 1978).

Working with Emotional Intelligence. Daniel Goleman (Bantam Books, 1998).

Index*

A

Advocacy
    1,1 relationship skill *87*
    1,9 relationship skill *59*
    5,5 relationship skill *75*
    9,1 relationship skill *44*
    as a relationship skill *31*
    clarifying skills *24*
    opportunistic relationship skill *119*
    paternalistic relationship skill *104*

B

backup style. See Grid Style, consistency
BHAG *151*
Blake, Robert R. *vi, vii*
    and Jane Mouton *vii, 158, 175*
Boeing *151, 153*
Boston Ballet Company *34*
Butteriss, Margaret *175*

C

cohesion. See group behavior
Collins and Porras *3, 13, 150, 151, 152, 153, 175*
concern for people *15,* **15.** See also Leadership Grid
concern for results **14,** *15.* See also Leadership Grid
Conflict resolution
    1,1 relationship skill *89,* **90**
    1,9 relationship skill *60,* **61**
    5,5 relationship skill *77,* **77**
    9,1 relationship skill *46,* **46,47**
    9,9 relationship skill *139,* **140, 141, 142**
    as a relationship skill *34*
    assumptions regarding *139*
    clarifying skills *24*
    constructive use of *35, 139*
    expressing emotions *141*
    opportunistic relationship skill *121,* **122**
    paternalistic relationship skill *105,* **106, 107**
    synergistic resolution *143*
    unresolved *11*
conformity. See group behavior
conformity in organization life *160*
convergence. See group behavior
convergence and leadership style *161*
    in 1,1 leadership *162*
    in 1,9 leadership *161*
    in 5,5 leadership *161*
    in 9,1 leadership *161*
    in 9,9 leadership *162*
    in opportunistic leadership *162*
    in paternalistic leadership *162*
Critique
    1,1 relationship skill *85*
    1,1 response to *82*
    1,9 relationship skill *56*
    1,9 response to *52*
    5,5 relationship skill *71*
    5,5 response to *67*
    9,1 relationship skill *42*
    9,1 response to *38*
    9,9 approach to *134*
    9,9 relationship skill *133*
    9,9 response to *128*
    addressing individual fears *167*
    as a relationship skill *24*
    building relationships *170*
    clarifying skills *23*
    concurrent critique *25*
    criteria as foundation *27*
    effective behavior critique *28*
    in advocacy *31*
    in dominant Grid styles *19*
    in effective listening *31*
    in resilience *35*

---

* bold type indicates an illustration

J-K

L